A BICENTENNIAL EDITION

Thomas Jefferson: Revolutionary Philosopher

A SELECTION OF WRITINGS

Edited by

JOHN S. PANCAKE Professor of History
University of Alabama
University, Alabama

with

N. SHARON SUMMERS Research Editor
University of Alabama
University, Alabama

BARRON'S EDUCATIONAL SERIES, INC. WOODBURY, NEW YORK

All inquiries should be addressed to:
Barron's Educational Series, Inc.
113 Crossways Park Drive
Woodbury, New York 11797

Library of Congress Catalog Card No. 75-43501

International Standard Book No. 0-8120-0657-7

Library of Congress Cataloging in Publication Data

Library of Congress Cataloging in Publication Data
Jefferson, Thomas, Pres. U. S., 1743-1826.
    Thomas Jefferson, revolutionary philosopher.

    Bibliography: p.
    SUMMARY: Documents representing Jefferson's views on a wide
variety of subjects.
    1. United States—History—Revolution, 1775-1783—
Collected works.   2. United States—History—1783-1815
—Collected works.   [1. United States—History—
Revolution, 1775-1783.   2. United States—History—
1783-1815]   I. Title.
E302.J59   973.4'092'4   75-43501
ISBN 0-8120-0657-7

CONTENTS ★

PREFACE ★

Thomas Jefferson has always had a strong attraction for students of American history. The reasons are obvious. His Declaration of Independence is the nation's birth certificate. He was not only one of the greatest of the Founding Fathers but he was in public life for forty years, serving in the whole range of public offices—legislator, governor, diplomat, and president. Yet his public life was only one facet of this man who was also a scientist, architect, philosopher, inventor, and (the title he preferred) farmer.

His attraction also lies in the fact that he left us so much of himself in his voluminous writings. Only in the middle of the twentieth century have scholars undertaken the formidable task of collecting all of his writings. When Professor Julian Boyd and his associates at Princeton complete their work there will be more than fifty volumes of *The Papers of Thomas Jefferson*. Of these, eighteen thousand items alone are personal letters. So students whose curiosity is aroused by the Sage of Monticello will find an almost inexhaustible source of first-hand material for their study.

We hope that this volume will serve as a useful introduction to this remarkable man and that it will convey something of the range and depth of his mind and spirit. In the eighteenth century the word "philosopher" meant someone who attempted to master all fields of knowledge, and it was in this sense that we made the selections which are included here. We also mean to convey the idea that Jefferson was a revolutionary beyond the usual context of that word. Even after his retirement Jefferson continued to advocate change, and nothing irritated him more than the veneration of ancient and useless institutions. He was seventy-three years old when he wrote, "Each generation is as independent as the one preceding, as that was of all which had gone before. . . . The dead? But the dead have no rights."

This volume includes documents which two people believe best represent a distillation of Jefferson's views on a wide variety of subjects, and we expect that many people will disagree with our choices. One consideration which guided us was that the entire document—or a considerable portion of it—be devoted to the relevant subject. This ruled out fragments expressive of Jefferson's ideas which are to be found in contexts not readily understandable to the reader. We have identified each selection by date and title or addressee so that it can be readily located in any of the large number of publications of Jefferson's writings. Of these, the following would be especially helpful to the reader who wishes to search more extensively in the Jefferson record:

The Adams-Jefferson Letters. 2 vols. Lester Cappon, ed. (Chapel Hill, N.C., 1959).

The Complete Jefferson. Saul K. Padover, ed. (New York, 1943).

Notes on the State of Virginia. William Peden, ed. (Chapel Hill, N.C., 1955).

The Papers of Thomas Jefferson. 19 vols. (to 1791). Julian P. Boyd and associates, eds. (Princeton, N.J., 1950–1974).

The Writings of Thomas Jefferson. 10 vols. Paul Leicester Ford, ed. (New York, 1892–1899).

The Writings of Thomas Jefferson. 20 vols. A. A. Lipscomb and A. E. Bergh, eds. (Washington, 1903).

It would be pretentious to say that the reproduction of these documents is without editorial errors, but in the hope that they are few enough to be insignificant we have not used "[sic]" to indicate mistakes of spelling and grammar. Some of these are attributable to outmoded eighteenth-century usages, others to the fact that the great philosopher was simply not a very good speller. Jefferson seems to have been especially confounded by "Mississippi."

We owe thanks to many people. Dr. Chris Bramlett, Associate Dean of the Graduate School of the University of Alabama, when asked for a research grant, produced one in fifteen minutes, a feat of administrative legerdemain which left us speechless. Bernard Mayo, emeritus professor of history at the University of Virginia, generously took time to check us for sins of omission and commission. Virginia Dodson, who typed the manuscript, lost neither her accuracy nor her cheerful disposition under the pressure of a deadline. James Bear, Jr., director of the Thomas Jefferson Memorial Foundation at Monticello helped us with the selection of pictures. Charley Scott, dean of the Graduate School of the University of Alabama gave us financial assistance in reproducing the manuscript. The staffs of the Amelia Gayle Gorgas Library at the University of Alabama, the Alderman Library at the University of Virginia, and the McCormick Library at Washington and Lee University were all generous with their help. This leaves the responsibility for any errors or shortcomings squarely on the shoulders of the editors, which is as it should be.

John S. Pancake
N. Sharon Summers

Portable desk on which Thomas Jefferson wrote the Declaration of Independence. Division of Political History, The National Museum of History and Technology, Smithsonian Institution. [Not in exhibition.]

CHRONOLOGY

1743 Jefferson born at Shadwell, Albemarle County, Va.

1760 Began formal education at William and Mary.

1767 Admitted to the Virginia bar.

1769 Delegate to the House of Burgesses from Albemarle.

1770 Moved to Monticello.

1772 Married Martha Wayles Skelton.

1774 Wrote *A Summary View of the Rights of British America.*

1775 Collaborated with John Dickinson to write *The Declaration . . . of the Causes and Necessity for Taking Up Arms.*

1776 Wrote the Declaration of Independence.

1776 – 1779 Served on the commission to draft the statutory code for Virginia, including the Statute for Religious Liberty.

1779 – 1781 Governor of Virginia.

1783 – 1784 Virginia delegate to the Confederation Congress, drafted the Northwest Ordinance of 1784.

1785 – 1789 U.S. minister to France.

1785 Published *Notes on Virginia.*

1790 – 1793 Secretary of State under President Washington.

1797 – 1801 Vice-president of the U.S.

1798 With Madison drafted the Virginia and Kentucky Resolutions.

1801 – 1809 President of the U.S.

1819 Founded the University of Virginia.

1826 Died at Monticello.

★
★
THOMAS JEFFERSON: 1743–1826   ★

A BIOGRAPHICAL SKETCH

If a member of the Virginia Establishment in the middle of the eighteenth century had been asked to name a family that would have produced a great man, one who would truly become a towering figure in the annals of American history, the reply would probably have been Bland or Pendleton or Carter or Randolph. Not Washington or Jefferson. Not that these latter were by any means outside the Establishment. After all, George Washington's mother was a Ball and Peter Jefferson had married a Randolph. Perhaps in another generation or two they would be numbered among the leaders of the first families of the first colony in England's American empire.

In 1741 Peter Jefferson took his family to Shadwell, a modest but comfortable home which he had built on the Rivanna River near the hamlet of Charlottesville. Albemarle County was in western—but not frontier—Virginia and if Peter Jefferson's land holdings did not rival those of the great land barons who ruled Virginia's social and political life, there was no doubt that he was of the gentry.

Thomas Jefferson was born at Shadwell on April 13, 1743, but two years later the family moved to Tuckahoe, the estate of Jane Jefferson's cousin, William Randolph, whose untimely death had left the burden of caring for his family on his good friend Peter Jefferson. So young Tom spent the earliest years of his boyhood in the company of Randolph cousins. In 1752 the family moved back to Shadwell, and nine years later, when Tom was only fourteen years old, Peter Jefferson died. He left his son two legacies. One was the land which would eventually become the estate centered around Monticello (such estates are called "plantations" in

Monticello
Thomas Jefferson Memorial Foundation, Inc.

the Deep South and "ranches" in the West, but Jefferson always called Monticello simply his "farm"; Virginia country gentlemen, perhaps in a kind of reverse snobbery, continue to use the term).

The other legacy was a determination that his son should be educated. Before his death he had sent Tom to be tutored by James Maury, a Scot who taught his young pupil a basic knowledge of the classics, but who never ceased to emphasize what he called "the Mother Tongue." Three years after his father's death Jefferson travelled to Williamsburg to enroll at the College of William and Mary.

The College had just gone through an organizational upheaval that had left its faculty greatly diminished and somewhat demoralized. His principal (and, for a time, only) professor was William Small, a gifted scholar whose range of knowledge included logic, ethics, physics, mathematics, and moral philosophy. It is possible that Small was responsible for the insatiable range of curiosity that Jefferson later developed, for he recalled that it was from Small that "I got my first view of the expansion of science & of the system of things in which we are placed."

The genius of mind and spirit that marked Thomas Jefferson does not develop spontaneously. At some point the intellect is sparked, the thirst for knowledge is instilled, and education becomes almost a personality trait which lasts as long as a man lives. Jefferson himself thought that George Wythe had the greatest influence on his early training. Although he was only 35 years old Wythe was regarded as an outstanding member of the Virginia bar who was also a great teacher. Jefferson studied law under Wythe's tutelage, and the fact that it took him five years to gain admission to the Virginia bar would seem to indicate that Jefferson studied a great deal more than the law.

In the company of Small, Wythe, Governor Francis Fauquier, Edmund Pendleton, and others of the social and political circle of the colonial capital, Jefferson matured and acquired that polish and elegance of manner which characterized the Virginia Establishment. He accepted its code and its set of values, although not always uncritically. He was in all respects a gentleman. But, as his biographer Dumas Malone remarks, "His distinction lies in the fact that he became a great deal more."

Jefferson was still a student when the colonies became embroiled with the mother country over the Stamp Act. He listened avidly to Patrick Henry's thunderous oratory in the House of Burgesses supporting the Virginia Resolves which triggered colonial opposition from Massachusetts to Georgia. The protest involved not just taxation, but a constitutional principle, "Taxation without representation is tyranny!" With his lawyer's training Jefferson quickly grasped the significance of the issue: If Parliament did not have the most basic of governmental powers, the power to tax, what power did it have in America?

The Stamp Act crisis faded when Parliament repealed the measure in 1766, but a new ministry dominated by Charles Townshend renewed the effort to tax the colonies. Again Americans were stirred to opposition and in 1769 the leaders of the resistance in Virginia signed articles of association, a pledge to boycott British goods. Jefferson, newly elected burgess from Albemarle, was one of the signers.

Parliament repealed the Townshend duties in 1770 (except for the tax on tea) and the storm subsided. Young Jefferson became preoccupied with his law practice, the family farm at Shadwell, and a new home he was building on a little mountain among the foothills of the Blue Ridge. In 1772 he brought his bride, Martha Wayles Skelton, to Monticello and the following September their first child was born, also named Martha.

He was back in Williamsburg in 1773, attending a brief session of the assembly and serving as a member of the Virginia Committee of Correspondence, organized by the Whigs to exchange information and plan strategy with similar committees in the other colonies. Jefferson was 30 years old, two inches over six feet tall, lanky—some said awkward—moving quietly and diffidently among a circle of friends and acquaintances which numbered Patrick Henry, Peter Carr, John Tyler, Richard Bland, and Thomas Ludwell Lee. His pleasant face with its hazel eyes and slightly upturned nose was surmounted by reddish hair which was rarely

powdered. He was likeable and sociable, enjoying the measured
life of the little colonial capital. He played the violin with considerable competence and his account book shows the variety of his
interests: a refracting telescope, admission charge to a puppet
show, a backgammon board, 89 bottles of wine "carried off or
broke," a fine mare, powder for his manservant's wig.

It was the tax on tea which revived the dispute between the
mother country and the colonists. Lord North, the head of the
ministry in England, induced Parliament to pass the East India
Company Act, which gave the great trading company a monopoly
on the sale of tea. North thereby hoped to recoup some of the
company's recent losses and also obtain revenue from the tax on
tea. It is a commentary on the sensitivity of the colonial spirit of
self-determination and of the effectiveness of the Whig political
organization that this act, which actually reduced the price of tea
and affected only the merchants, should have provided the spark
which lit the powder keg of colonial rebellion. The radical Whigs
convinced the colonies that the Tea Act was one more step in an
insidious ministerial effort to deprive Americans of their liberties. The Boston Tea Party in December, 1773, was followed by
similar demonstrations of colonial defiance. Parliament retaliated
with the Coercive Acts which closed the port of Boston and virtually ended self-government in Massachusetts.

Yet when the colonies sent delegates to the First Continental
Congress in Philadelphia to protest the Coercive Acts, its members were not yet talking of independence. For most of them the
issue was the preservation of their rights as Englishmen. They
petitioned the King for a redress of their grievances, looking to
their sovereign as their protector from the tyranny of Parliament.
But it was significant that the Congress also passed resolutions of
nonimportation, nonexportation and nonconsumption of British
goods, and it provided for a network of committees called the Continental Association to see that the resolutions were enforced.

Jefferson was not present at the First Continental Congress.
He had planned to attend a Whig convention at Williamsburg
which chose the Virginia delegates, but an attack of dysentery
laid him low. He did, however, forward a set of resolutions to the

convention titled *A Summary View of the Rights of British America*. Although the convention did not act on them, some of the Whig radicals arranged to have the resolutions printed. *A Summary View* swept through the colonies like wildfire and projected its author into national prominence as a spokesman for the radical cause. For Jefferson now answered the question of Parliamentary authority that had been raised by the Stamp Act. In his view the only legislative authority in America was the colonial assemblies, constituted and chosen by the people. "The British Parliament have no right to exercise authority over us." But *A Summary View* went further. The King himself was charged with usurpations and tyrannical acts. Thomas Jefferson was rushing in where moderate Whigs feared to tread. To attack the King, symbol of loyalty to the mother country, was to skirt the edge of treason.

When the Second Continental Congress assembled in the spring of 1775, the tide of events began to run with ever-increasing velocity. In April colonial militia clashed with British redcoats at Lexington and Concord and drove them back into Boston. Congress, which had met to continue its protests to the Crown, found itself raising an army and selecting George Washington as its commander in chief. By the fall of 1775 the King had declared the colonists to be rebels and it was soon evident that England intended to suppress the rebellion by force of arms. This was a momentous decision. It meant that those Whigs who hoped to preserve colonial liberties within the framework of the empire were discredited. The only way open for liberty-loving Americans was independence.

Jefferson, now a member of Congress, was in the forefront of those who convinced the delegates at Philadelphia that the creation of a new nation was the only viable alternative to their dilemma. He was not an orator and he left public persuasion to men like Richard Henry Lee and John Adams. But when independence was voted on July 1, 1776, it was the author of *A Summary View* who had prepared a declaration "of the causes which impel us to a separation," which Congress approved two days later.

It should be noted that the Declaration of Independence was a statement of goals, not of means. It does not suggest any particular form of government. It only insists that, as John Locke had postulated almost a century earlier, a social contract exists between the people and their rulers, the former giving their rights and powers to government as a trust, and the rulers exercising these powers to insure the people's right to "life, liberty, and the pursuit of happiness." George III is not indicted for being king, but for being a bad king who has failed in his duty as trustee and guardian of the rights of his subjects.

It was a momentous document, for it marked the first attempt in modern history to establish a government in which the rulers were completely accountable to the ruled. History has made the Declaration a classic statement of the proper relationship between government and the people, a warning that any system which denied "certain unalienable rights" did so at its peril.

Jefferson, like most of his contemporaries, believed that the key to the success of the new nation lay in establishing a firm foundation of republicanism in the states. Once independence was declared he hurried back to Virginia and he spent most of the war years in the service of the state. He first served on the committee charged with revising English and colonial laws into a statutory code for Virginia. Among his contributions were a plan for an educational system, provisions for abolishing laws of primogeniture and entail, and the great statute for religious freedom. He also advocated a system for the distribution of western lands which would promote the settlement of the frontier, and elimination of the death penalty, but he found that these reforms were unacceptable. He suggested to his colleagues on the commission that some system for the gradual emancipation of slaves be proposed, but became convinced that "the public mind would not yet bear the proposition. . . ."

Toward the end of the war Jefferson served two terms as governor (1779–1781). His tenure was undistinguished, partly because his powers as governor were severely limited by the constitution (all the new states were wary of strong executive power), and also because state finances were a hopeless mess under the pressure of wartime inflation. When the British sent invasion forces into the state in 1780 and 1781, he handled the emergency ineptly and the state government was finally forced to flee westward beyond the Blue Ridge. He left office amid a storm of public criticism.

Shortly afterward, in June, 1781, Martha Jefferson died, inducing a paroxysm of grief which lasted for weeks. It was an unhappy time for him and he determined to retire from public life. But his friend James Madison persuaded him to serve as a member of Congress. During his brief term (1783) he drafted a total of 30 committee reports, including a recommendation for the adoption of the metric system, and an ordinance for the government of the Old Northwest which contained a provision prohibiting slavery in the territory. If he could do nothing about the existing institution, at least he could prevent its expansion.

In 1784 Congress appointed him to succeed Benjamin Franklin as minister to France and he spent the next five years in Paris. He had already written a draft of *Notes on the State of Virginia* which contained a remarkable range of scientific, political, and philosophical observations. Although the scientific theories and speculations which it contains were antiquated by twentieth-century standards, it represented the most advanced views of Jefferson's time. More important, it revealed the tremendous range of Jefferson's intellect and reflected his conviction that scientific knowledge could be a powerful servant of mankind. He was finally persuaded to publish it, first in Paris and then in England, and it surely would have won its author the Nobel Prize had such recognition existed in the eighteenth century.

The years in France were among the happiest of his life. He attended scrupulously to his duties as minister, but he found time to travel, to talk to artists and scientists, and even to fall in love. He had a brief and tempestuous affair with Maria Cosway, the wife of an English artist. The romance cooled but the two continued to correspond for some years.

The end of Jefferson's mission to France came just as the French Revolution was erupting. He was careful to remain aloof despite his fondness for Lafayette and the group of young liberal nobles who espoused the revolutionary cause. But he detected the

vast gulf between the absolutism of the old regime and the republican aspirations of the revolutionaries, and he predicted that the
lack of experience in self-government would make the transition
too difficult. The result, he thought, would be a bloody civil war.

He was absent, then, from a milder, almost undetected revolution that took place in the United States. The Constitutional
Convention of 1787 created a new government which displaced
the inept government of the Confederation. Jefferson was critical
of some features of the Constitution but he noted that circumstances undoubtedly "called for a federal government which could
walk on its own legs, without leaning for support on the State legislatures." In the final analysis the people could be trusted; "on
their good sense we may rely with the most security for the preservation of a due degree of liberty."

In 1789 he requested a leave of absence from his post to return
to the United States to take care of family and business affairs.
When he landed at Norfolk he found that President Washington
had asked him to become Secretary of State in the new government. Once more he postponed his retirement to "my family, my
farm, and my books."

The Department of State was originally not only the department of foreign relations but also included the United States
mint, the patent office, and the depository of government records.
The secretary was also expected to act as the principal personnel
officer of the executive branch (it will be recalled that when
President Nixon resigned he addressed his letter of resignation
to the Secretary of State). Not until the spring of 1790 did Jefferson arrive in New York, and he was busy for several months
getting his department in order. The other cabinet officers were
Secretary of the Treasury Alexander Hamilton, Secretary of War
Henry Knox, and Attorney General Edmund Randolph (techni-
cally, the Justice Department was not part of the cabinet, but
Randolph attended most of the meetings).

The most pressing business of the new government was financial. A national debt of over $50,000,000, an enormous sum for
the time, had been inherited from the Confederation government.
There were few banking facilities and no circulating currency

except for the notes issued by a few private banks. The young Secretary of the Treasury set out to remedy these ills. He proposed to fund at par, not only the national debt, but also the debts incurred by the states as the result of the War of Independence, by a new federal bond issue. Since the government now had the power to tax, and therefore possessed the means of generating income, Hamilton correctly believed that the bond issue would be quickly subscribed. These bonds would be accepted in payment for taxes or other government obligations, and therefore would gain acceptability in the private sector as collateral for loans or even as payment in private business transactions. Hamilton also proposed that Congress charter a national bank which would be the depository of government funds and act as fiscal agent for the government. The bank would issue notes, extend credit (to other banks as well as individuals), and so serve the purposes of a central bank. Thus did the genius of Hamilton use "the public debt as a public blessing."

Opposition to Hamilton's measures came first from James Madison in Congress. Not only was there the objection that funding and assumption of the national and state debts would provide windfall profits for speculators, but Madison also challenged the constitutionality of the Bank of the United States. Authority for it could only be found in a very broad interpretation of the implied powers clause of Article I of the Constitution ("Congress shall have the power to make all laws which are necessary and proper for carrying into execution the foregoing powers. . . .").

The Hamiltonian program, including the Bank, passed Congress and came to the President for his approval in 1791. Washington was impressed with Madison's arguments for he was, after all, the "Father of the Constitution." Washington asked Jefferson and Hamilton to submit written opinions, and Jefferson used the occasion to express his ideas on limited government. Such a broad interpretation of the Constitution as was being invoked to justify the Bank, he said, might lead to an excess of congressional power reminiscent of the tyranny of Parliament. The powers of government should be limited and confining, supporting his oft-repeated maxim that "that government is best which governs least." Hamilton insisted that government must be energetic, a stimulus to business and commercial activity. The Bank would provide credit for the nation's expanding economy and its notes would stimulate the circulation of a sound currency which the country so badly needed. Hamilton's arguments persuaded the President, but not the Secretary of State. From this point on he became increasingly suspicious of the young financial wizard.

It soon became apparent that Hamilton's financial plans had a political purpose. The Secretary of the Treasury had little faith in the people. Men in the mass, he maintained, were governed by their "passions" by which he meant their selfish interests; "turbulent and changing, they seldom judge or determine right." Men of property and character, "the rich, the wise, and the good," ought to have the major responsibility, and therefore most of the power, in order to insure good government.

Paying off Confederation and state bonds, establishing sound credit, insuring a circulating medium, and strengthening the nation's banking system—all these would attract the political support and interest of that class of men whom Hamilton believed were most capable of wielding political power for the public good.

As Jefferson discerned the thrust of Hamiltonian politics, he began to lend his support to the opposition which was developing in Congress under Madison's leadership. To him Hamilton's philosophy smacked of the kind of elitism that was a contradiction of his own belief in the democracy. But he was hesitant about expressing his opposition only because he was part of the President's official family. He felt a deep sense of loyalty to Washington and he drew back from the idea of creating dissension in the executive branch. So his opposition, though real, was covert, but it was increasingly apparent that he and Hamilton were on a collision course.

By the beginning of Washington's second term a much more serious issue arose that eventually led to divisions not only in the government but in the whole nation. By 1793 the French Revolution had developed into a violent and bloody upheaval. Louis XVI and his family were executed and the new republican government in France commenced the savage repression of the opposition.

The Revolution also provoked a war between France and England (with most of the other nations aligning themselves on one side or the other) which was to last for the next 20 years.

Despite a Proclamation of Neutrality by the President, it soon became apparent that American opinion would not be neutral. For Hamilton the French Revolution and the Reign of Terror confirmed his worst fears of unchecked democracy. He saw Britain as the great force for the restoration of order in Europe, and he eventually came to regard England as the protector and savior of Western civilization. France must not be allowed to spread anarchy and bloody revolution through the rest of Europe. It was therefore not surprising that Hamilton worked to guide American policy so as to give every assistance to England.

Jefferson saw the Revolution as a symbol of the rise of the people against absolute monarchy. The battle against tyranny was, he thought, a continuation of the struggle for the rights of man which had begun in America. The fact that France had given indispensable aid to the American cause in 1778 constituted a very real obligation which the United States must meet. He deplored the excesses of the Reign of Terror as much as Hamilton but he regarded this as the price that must be paid for the destruction of tyranny.

It should not be forgotten that both Jefferson and Hamilton were preeminently Americans, and that they never lost sight of the fact that they shared a common goal, the safety and security of the United States. But their differences on foreign policy reflected their basically different philosophies. When men try to govern themselves there is a continuing problem of maintaining the balance between liberty and order. In other words, to what extent may people be allowed the freedom to pursue their own particular brand of happiness, and to what degree must they be restrained in order to keep them from interfering with other individuals who are pursuing divergent goals? For Jefferson and Hamilton there were no simple "either or" solutions, but Hamilton, with his abiding distrust of the people, was inclined toward a greater degree of restraint, toward tipping the scales on the side of a secure and orderly society.

Jefferson was almost as pessimistic as Hamilton about mankind's capability for evil and selfishness, but he was optimistic about people's ability to improve themselves and their society (hence his continuing emphasis on education and freedom of the press). In the last analysis he acknowledged that government by all the people would probably make mistakes. But he insisted that a broad-based democracy was the only sure safeguard against tyranny. Hamilton's orderly society controlled by "the rich, the wise, and the good" alarmed him, for he thought that it opened the way for oligarchy and statism.

Not only did these differences lead to a split between Jefferson and Hamilton but also to a division of public opinion which gave rise to the first political party system in the United States. Although there were other points of disagreement, the widening scope of the war in Europe, its increasing effect on the United States, and the emotional intensity which it generated led Jefferson to remark as early as 1793 that "the form our own government was to take depended much more on events in France than anybody before imagined."

For the rest of Washington's administration the nation steered a delicate course of neutrality between the two warring nations and their respective allies. As the largest neutral carrier of goods on the high seas, the American merchant marine was the target for restrictions and retaliation by both sides. In addition, Britain began to impress American merchant seamen to fill the ranks of her shorthanded navy. France, with increasing belligerence, pressed for the assistance to which she felt she was entitled under the terms of the Alliance of 1778, and the President was finally forced to ask for the recall of her minister, "Citizen" Genet. The crisis with France had hardly passed before England's heavy-handed conduct brought the two nations to the brink of war. Washington sent John Jay on a special mission to England in 1794. Jay concluded a treaty which avoided war but which contained concessions to Great Britain that were regarded as so degrading that it took every ounce of the President's enormous prestige to secure its approval by the Congress. Thus did the

United States discover that second-rate powers live a precarious existence when superpowers struggle for survival.

Jefferson believed that American commerce could be used as a diplomatic weapon of coercion to force England to respect the neutral rights of the United States. Through the imposition of discriminatory tariffs and other retaliatory measures, England could be made to withdraw her most obnoxious Orders in Council. The idea of an economic "cold war" appalled the Secretary of the Treasury. To his natural sympathy for England was added the deep concern for his carefully laid financial plans, which depended on a steady flow of income from tariff duties. By the end of 1793 it was obvious that Washington supported Hamilton's conciliatory policy toward Great Britain, and Jefferson resigned from the cabinet. A year later Hamilton also resigned and Washington ended his second term in the midst of bitter and recriminating public debate over Jay's Treaty.

The election of 1796 marked the first two-party contest in American political history. Although financial policy, taxation, even Jefferson's alleged atheism, were points of contention, the overriding issue was foreign policy. John Adams was the Federalist candidate and Jefferson was persuaded out of retirement by his friends to represent the Democratic-Republicans, usually called simply Republicans. Adams, who had served as Washington's vice-president, won the election and a perverse provision of the Constitution decreed that Jefferson should serve as vice-president in a Federalist administration.

The focus of tensions now shifted back to France. A hostile French government, angry over what it regarded as the betrayal of Jay's Treaty, became increasingly belligerent. American diplomatic overtures resulted in the infamous XYZ episode, which convinced many Americans that France was simply trying to blackmail the United States. Again war threatened, and the Federalists began to take measures to meet the event, increasing the navy and creating a large army commanded by Washington and Alexander Hamilton. Provisions for internal security took the form of the Alien and Sedition Acts. These laws, besides making provision against the danger of internal subversion, made it illegal for any person to write or publish anything which was intended to "defame the government, or [bring] either house of the . . . Congress, or the . . . President, or either of them into contempt or disrepute."

Jefferson and the Republicans charged that this was designed to silence criticism of the government and was a clear violation of freedom of the press. Republican protest took the form of the Virginia and Kentucky Resolutions, written by Madison and Jefferson. The Resolutions were based on the constitutional theory that the federal government derived its powers from the states; thus, the states might invoke their sovereignty to check the central government when it overstepped the constitutional limits of its powers. Although Jefferson and Madison intended the Resolutions primarily as a political weapon against the Federalists, subsequent advocates of state sovereignty in the South took their cue from these documents when they came to defend slavery.

As John Adams' presidency neared its end, the "undeclared war" with France reached its climax. The clamor for war by the Federalists was intensified by the approaching presidential election of 1800. But the corrupt government of the Directory in France was brought to an abrupt end by Napoléon's *coup d'état*, and John Adams saw his opportunity. As his party continued to thump the war drum, the President opened negotiations with the French government, negotiations that eventually ended the crisis. The Federalists thus entered the campaign as the advocates of a large army and navy—and high taxes to pay for them—but little prospect of war.

Jefferson was once again pitted against Adams. It was in this campaign that he convincingly demonstrated the political acumen that was to mark his presidency. That the philosopher and political theorist could also understand the subtleties of party politics confounded his opponents—and a good many historians. Although Jefferson had probably never heard the phrase "grass roots," he understood its implications, and the party organization which he molded during the campaign of 1800 and perfected during his term of office marked him as the first President who was also a great party leader.

The "Jeffersonian Revolution" was more one of style and technique than of radical change in national policy. Albert Gallatin, Jefferson's Secretary of the Treasury, pursued a policy with which even Hamilton could not find serious fault. Republican reforms included repeal of most of the excise taxes along with a drastic reduction in the armed forces. The defeated Federalists took refuge in the judicial branch where John Marshall was beginning his long and distinguished career as an advocate of judicial nationalism. Although Jefferson was successful in nullifying the "midnight appointments" of retiring President Adams, a last-minute attempt to increase Federalist office holders in the federal courts, the Republicans failed to convict Supreme Court Justice Samuel Chase on impeachment charges in 1805. Jefferson's outrage at what he called Marshall's "constitutional twistifications" ended in a stalemate between the President and the Chief Justice.

The crowning achievement of the first term was the purchase of Louisiana. Jefferson and Secretary of State James Madison, alarmed over the acquisition of the trans-Mississippi territory by Napoléon, played a delicate diplomatic game of thrust and parry which finally led to the treaty of acquisition in 1803.

The success of the Louisiana negotiations resulted partly because of a temporary truce in the war between France and England. But the war was shortly resumed and Jefferson's second term was a continuing struggle to maintain American rights on the high seas without becoming involved in the Napoleonic War. Britain's Orders in Council again threatened American ships and Napoléon countered with his Berlin and Milan Decrees. American ships venturing into the ports of the West Indies or southern Europe were prey for British men-of-war while those who traded with England were liable to seizure by the French. It was Britain's insistence on her right to impress seamen from American merchantmen on the pretext that they were deserters from her navy that, in the final analysis, turned most American opinion against England. In the summer of 1807 the *USS Chesapeake* refused to allow *HMS Leopard* to board her to search for deserters. The Englishman opened fire and killed several of her crew. It was a blatant act of war, yet Jefferson hesitated. He thought war was not only immoral but wasteful, and he was determined to avoid it.

He had already begun a modest employment of his favorite weapon, economic coercion, with little success. Now, in the wake of the *Chesapeake-Leopard* episode he asked Congress to impose an embargo, cutting off virtually all trade with foreign nations.

The embargo lasted fourteen months. In England its effect as a means of coercion was mitigated by the fact that the lower classes, who were most seriously affected, could not vote. In the United States the merchants were drastically affected and by the end of 1808 farmers were beginning to suffer as well. Protest became more strident not only from the Federalist opposition but from within Jefferson's own party. Although Madison had no difficulty getting elected in 1808 as Jefferson's chosen successor, the Federalists increased their seats in Congress and made considerable gains in the state legislatures.

For a brief period in the spring of 1809 it appeared that Jefferson's policy might succeed. The British envoy, David Erskine, opened negotiations with the United States and a tentative agreement was reached which contained substantial concessions on the part of Great Britain. But the political pressure on Congress became too great. In March, 1809, it repealed the embargo and the British government, having attained its goal, refused to ratify the Erskine Agreement.

Jefferson retired with his diplomatic policy nearly in ruins. But if he was unpopular in 1809, there was no lasting bitterness. Americans have always been tolerant of retired Presidents, and Jefferson was, after all, the hero of the Revolution with far more to his reputation than his presidency.

For the first time in his life he was able to devote full time to farming. Although he brought the latest scientific methods and his own inexhaustible energies to the task, he did not prosper.

His extravagances, whether at Paris, Philadelphia, or Washington had kept him from becoming a wealthy man, and the Panic of 1819 sent farm prices spiraling downward just as it appeared that his lands might produce a good profit. He was hag-ridden by an old debt incurred from his father-in-law and his friendship for Wilson Cary Nicholas led him to endorse a note which added to his burden when Nicholas defaulted. Yet he would not allow this to becloud his enjoyment of "family, farm, and books." Of his six children only two survived. Martha, his eldest and favorite, married Thomas Mann Randolph, and Mary married her cousin, John Eppes. Martha and her family lived at Monticello where she was a gracious hostess and congenial companion to the retired patriarch.

It was soon evident that he was regarded as a national hero. In the seventeen years that remained of his life, thousands of visitors found their way to the village of Charlottesville and climbed the winding road up the Little Mountain to see the author of the Declaration of Independence and his monument, Monticello. "My mornings are devoted to correspondence. From breakfast to dinner, I am in my shops, my gardens, or on horseback among my farms; from dinner to dark, I give to society and recreation with my neighbors and friends; and from candle light to bed time, I read."

He had been a close friend of John Adams during the Revolution and when they were both abroad (Adams had been in France and then England during the 1780's), but the friendship did not survive the strain of their political rivalry. In 1812 a mutual friend, Dr. Benjamin Rush, mended the breach and the two elder statesmen began a correspondence which lasted until they died. The letters read like a critique of history, although there was much speculation about the future; the two patriarchs were obviously enormously pleased with themselves as well as with each other.

In 1814, when he was 71, he undertook still another project, the establishment of a state university. He selected the site on the outskirts of Charlottesville and after more than a decade of plan-

Plan for Monticello—Accepted Elevation, 1771
Massachusetts Historical Society

ning and building he was able to write in 1825, "The Professors of our University, 8. in number, are all engaged . . . and on their arrival the whole will assemble and enter their duties."

It was as if this latest task had taken the last of his remarkable energies. On July 4, 1826, 50 years to the day after the Declaration of Independence, he died. His grave is under a simple brownstone marker at the top of the mountain of Monticello.

JEFFERSONIAN DEMOCRACY

The trouble is that Thomas Jefferson never realized that historians would coin the phrase "Jeffersonian Democracy." So there is nowhere in all his voluminous writings a philosophical discourse on democracy. Despite the attempt to fasten such labels as "visionary" and "dreamer" on him, most of his memorable statements about the problem of man governing himself are made in regard to specific problems. When he talks about freedom of speech in the First Inaugural Address, he is speaking to the particular problem of freedom to criticize the government, and his listeners understood that he was talking about "the reign of witches" carried on by the Federalists under the Sedition Act.

It was when Jefferson applied his democratic philosophy to a wide range of problems that we begin to get some insight into its meaning. His insistence on an educational system which would bring about "a general diffusion of knowledge" was an attempt to deal with the problem of selfishness and ignorance of the people. In 1776 he was not content with philosophical generalities on how the new states should govern themselves; instead, he drafted a constitution for Virginia, a project to which he devoted months of thought and energy.

Jefferson wrestled with the problem of how to make the democratic process work. He probably would have agreed with Alexander Hamilton that the mass of the democracy "were turbulent and changing. They seldom judge or determine right." But Jefferson's answer was that if man cannot govern himself "can he then be trusted with the government of others?"

The First Inaugural Address
March 4, 1801

FRIENDS AND FELLOW CITIZENS: Called upon to undertake the duties of the first executive office of our country, I
avail myself of the presence of that portion of my fellow
citizens which is here assembled, to express my grateful
thanks for the favor with which they have been pleased to
look toward me, to declare a sincere consciousness that the
task is above my talents, and that I approach it with those
anxious and awful presentiments which the greatness of the
charge and the weakness of my powers so justly inspire. A
rising nation, spread over a wide and fruitful land, travers-
ing all the seas with the rich productions of their industry,
engaged in commerce with nations who feel power and for-
get right, advancing rapidly to destinies beyond the reach
of mortal eye—when I contemplate these transcendent objects, and see the honor, the happiness, and the hopes of
this beloved country committed to the issue and the auspices
of this day, I shrink from the contemplation, and humble
myself before the magnitude of the undertaking. Utterly
indeed, should I despair, did not the presence of many whom
I here see remind me, that in the other high authorities provided by our constitution, I shall find resources of wisdom,
of virtue, and of zeal, on which to rely under all difficulties.
To you, then, gentlemen, who are charged with the sovereign functions of legislation, and to those associated with
you, I look with encouragement for that guidance and support which may enable us to steer with safety the vessel in
which we are all embarked amid the conflicting elements of
a troubled world.

During the contest of opinion through which we have
passed, the animation of discussion and of exertions has
sometimes worn an aspect which might impose on strangers
unused to think freely and to speak and to write what they
think; but this being now decided by the voice of the nation,

announced according to the rules of the constitution, all will, of course, arrange themselves under the will of the law, and unite in common efforts for the common good. All, too, will bear in mind this sacred principle, that though the will of the majority is in all cases to prevail, that will, to be rightful, must be reasonable; that the minority possess their equal rights, which equal laws must protect, and to violate which would be oppression. Let us, then, fellow citizens, unite with one heart and one mind. Let us restore to social intercourse that harmony and affection without which liberty and even life itself are but dreary things. And let us reflect that having banished from our land that religious intolerance under which mankind so long bled and suffered, we have yet gained little if we countenance a political intolerance as despotic, as wicked, and capable of as bitter and bloody persecutions. During the throes and convulsions of the ancient world, during the agonizing spasms of infuriated man, seeking through blood and slaughter his long-lost liberty, it was not wonderful that the agitation of the billows should reach even this distant and peaceful shore; that this should be more felt and feared by some and less by others; that this should divide opinions as to measures of safety. But every difference of opinion is not a difference of principle. We have called by different names brethren of the same principle. We are all republicans—we are federalists. If there be any among us who would wish to dissolve this Union or to change its republican form, let them stand undisturbed as monuments of the safety with which error of opinion may be tolerated where reason is left free to combat it. I know, indeed, that some honest men fear that a republican government cannot be strong; that this government is not strong enough. But would the honest patriot, in the full tide of successful experiment, abandon a government which has so far kept us free and firm, on the theoretic and visionary fear that this government, the world's best hope, may by possibility want energy to preserve itself? I trust not. I believe this, on the contrary, the strongest government on

earth. I believe it is the only one where every man, at the
call of the laws, would fly to the standard of the law, and
would meet invasions of the public order as his own personal
concern. Sometimes it is said that man cannot be trusted
with the government of himself. Can he, then, be trusted
with the government of others? Or have we found angels in
the forms of kings to govern him? Let history answer this
question.

Let us, then, with courage and confidence pursue our own
federal and republican principles, our attachment to our
union and representative government. Kindly separated by
nature and a wide ocean from the exterminating havoc of
one quarter of the globe; too high-minded to endure the
degradations of others; possessing a chosen country, with
room enough for our descendants to the hundredth and
thousandth generation; entertaining a due sense of our
equal right to the use of our own faculties, to the acquisitions of our industry, to honor and confidence from our
fellow citizens, resulting not from birth but from our actions and their sense of them; enlightened by a benign religion, professed, indeed, and practiced in various forms,
yet all of them including honesty, truth, temperance, gratitude, and the love of man; acknowledging and adoring an
overruling Providence, which by all its dispensations proves
that it delights in the happiness of man here and his greater
happiness hereafter; with all these blessings, what more is
necessary to make us a happy and prosperous and frugal
government, which shall restrain men from injuring one
another, which shall leave them otherwise free to regulate
their own pursuits of industry and improvement, and shall
not take from the mouth of labor the bread it has earned.
This is the sum of good government, and this is necessary
to close the circle of our felicities.

About to enter, fellow citizens, on the exercise of duties
which comprehend everything dear and valuable to you, it is
proper that you should understand what I deem the essential principles of our government, and consequently those
which ought to shape its administration. I will compress

them within the narrowest compass they will bear, stating the general principle, but not all its limitations. Equal and exact justice to all men, of whatever state or persuasion, religious or political; peace, commerce, and honest friendship with all nations—entangling alliances with none; the support of the State governments in all their rights, as the most competent administrations for our domestic concerns and the surest bulwarks against anti-republican tendencies; the preservation of the general government in its whole constitutional vigor, as the sheet anchor of our peace at home and safety abroad; a jealous care of the right of election by the people—a mild and safe corrective of abuses which are lopped by the sword of the revolution where peaceable remedies are unprovided; absolute acquiescence in the decisions of the majority—the vital principle of republics, from which there is no appeal but to force, the vital principle and immediate parent of despotism; a well-disciplined militia—our best reliance in peace and for the first moments of war, till regulars may relieve them; the supremacy of the civil over the military authority; economy in the public expense, that labor may be lightly burdened; the honest payment of our debts and sacred preservation of the public faith; encouragement of agriculture, and of commerce as its handmaid; the diffusion of information and the arraignment of all abuses at the bar of public reason; freedom of religion; freedom of the press; freedom of person under the protection of the *habeas corpus*; and trial by juries impartially selected—these principles form the bright constellation which has gone before us, and guided our steps through an age of revolution and reformation. The wisdom of our sages and the blood of our heroes have been devoted to their attainment. They should be the creed of our political faith—the text of civil instruction—the touchstone by which to try the services of those we trust; and should we wander from them in moments of error or alarm, let us hasten to retrace our steps and to regain the road which alone leads to peace, liberty, and safety.

I repair, then, fellow citizens, to the post you have as-

signed me. With experience enough in subordinate offices to
have seen the difficulties of this, the greatest of all, I have
learned to expect that it will rarely fall to the lot of imperfect man to retire from this station with the reputation and
the favor which bring him into it. Without pretensions to
that high confidence reposed in our first and great revolutionary character, whose preeminent services had entitled
him to the first place in his country's love, and destined for
him the fairest page in the volume of faithful history, I ask
so much confidence only as may give firmness and effect to
the legal administration of your affairs. I shall often go
wrong through defect of judgment. When right, I shall
often be thought wrong by those whose positions will not
command a view of the whole ground. I ask your indulgence
for my own errors, which will never be intentional; and
your support against the errors of others, who condemn
what they would not if seen in all its parts. The approbation
implied by your suffrage is a consolation to me for the past;
and my future solicitude will be to retain the good opinion
of those who have bestowed it in advance, to conciliate that
of others by doing them all the good in my power, and to be
instrumental to the happiness and freedom of all.

Relying, then, on the patronage of your good will, I advance with obedience to the work, ready to retire from it
whenever you become sensible how much better choice it is
in your power to make. And may that Infinite Power which
rules the destinies of the universe, lead our councils to what
is best, and give them a favorable issue for your peace and
prosperity.

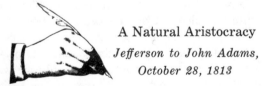

A Natural Aristocracy
*Jefferson to John Adams,
October 28, 1813*

Jefferson continually denounced the aristocracy of wealth and
birth which he claimed dominated the Federalist party. Retired

from the political wars, he proposed to his old friend and enemy, John Adams, the idea of an aristocracy of talent and virtue.

. . . For I agree with you that there is a natural aristocracy among men. The grounds of this are virtue and talents. Formerly, bodily powers gave place among the aristoi. But since the invention of gunpowder has armed the weak as well as the strong with missile death, bodily strength, like beauty, good humor, politeness and other accomplishments, has become but an auxiliary ground of distinction. There is also an artificial aristocracy, founded on wealth and birth, without either virtue or talents; for with these it would belong to the first class. The natural aristocracy I consider as the most precious gift of nature, for the institution, the trusts, and government of society. And indeed, it would have been inconsistent in creation to have formed man for the social state, and not to have provided virtue and wisdom enough to manage the concerns of the society. May we not even say, that that form of government is the best, which provides the most effectually for a pure selection of these natural aristoi into the offices of government? The artificial aristocracy is a mischievous ingredient in government, and provision should be made to prevent its ascendency. On the question, what is the best provision, you and I differ; but we differ as rational friends, using the free exercise of our own reason, and mutually indulging its errors. You think it best to put the pseudo-aristoi into a separate chamber of legislation, where they may be hindered from doing mischief by their co-ordinate branches, and where, also, they may be a protection to wealth against the Agrarian and plundering enterprises of the majority of the people. I think that to give them power in order to prevent them from doing mischief, is arming them for it, and increasing instead of remedying the evil. For if the co-ordinate branches can arrest their action, so may they that of the co-ordinates. Mischief may be done negatively as well as positively. Of this, a cabal in the Senate of the United States has furnished many proofs. Nor do I believe them necessary to protect the wealthy; because enough of these will find their way into every branch of the legislation, to protect themselves. From fifteen to twenty legislatures of our own, in action for thirty years past, have proved that no fears of an equalization of property are to be apprehended from them. I think the best remedy is exactly that provided by all our constitutions, to leave to the citizens the free election and separation of the aristoi from the pesudo-aristoi, of the wheat from the chaff. In general they will elect the really good and wise. In some instances, wealth may corrupt, and birth blind them; but not in sufficient degree to endanger the society.

It is probable that our difference of opinion may, in some measure, be produced by a difference of character in those among whom we live. From what I have seen of Massachusetts and Connecticut myself, and still more from what I have heard, and the character given of the former by yourself . . . ,who knows them so much better, there seems to be in those two States a traditionary reverence for certain families, which has rendered the offices of the government nearly hereditary in those families. I presume that from an early period of your history, members of those families happening to possess virtue and talents, have honestly exercised them for the good of the people, and by their services have endeared their names to them. In coupling Connecticut with you, I mean it politically only, not morally. For having made the Bible the common law of their land, they seem to have modeled their morality on the story of Jacob and Laban. But although this hereditary succession to office with you, may, in some degree, be founded in real family merit, yet in a much higher degree, it has proceeded from your strict alliance of Church and State. These families are canonised in the eyes of the people on common principles, "you tickle me, and I will tickle you." In Virginia we have nothing of this. Our clergy, before the revolution, having been secured against rivalship by fixed salaries, did not give themselves the trouble of acquiring influence over the people. Of wealth, there were great accumulations in particular families, handed down from generation to generation, under the English law of entails. But the only object of ambition for the wealthy was a seat in the King's Council. All their court then was paid to the crown and its creatures; and they Philipised in all collisions between the King and the people. Hence they were unpopular; and that unpopularity continues attached to their names. A Randolph, a Carter, or a Burwell must have great personal superiority over a common competitor to be elected by the people even at this day. At the first session of our legislature after the Declaration of Independence, we passed a law abolishing entails. And this was followed by one abolishing the privilege of primogeniture, and dividing the lands of intestates equally among all their children, or other representatives. These laws, drawn by myself, laid the axe to the foot of pseudo-aristocracy. And had another which I prepared been adopted by the legislature, our work would have been completed. It was a bill for the more general diffusion of learning. This proposed to divide every county into wards of five or six miles square, like your townships; to establish in each ward a free school for reading, writing and common arithmetic; to provide for the annual selection of the best subjects from these schools, who might receive, at the public expense, a higher degree of education at a district school; and from these district schools to select a certain number of the most promising subjects, to be completed at an University, where all the useful sciences should be taught. Worth and genius would thus have been sought out from every condition of life, and completely prepared by education for defeating the competition of wealth and birth for public trusts. My proposition had, for a further object, to impart to these wards those portions of self-government for which they are best qualified, by confiding to them the care of their poor, their roads, police, elections, the nomination of jurors, administration of justice in small cases, elementary exercises of militia; in short, to have made them little republics, with a warden at

the head of each, for all those concerns which, being under
their eye, they would better manage than the larger republics of the county or State. A general call of ward meetings
by their wardens on the same day through the State, would
at any time produce the genuine sense of the people on any
required point, and would enable the State to act in mass,
as your people have so often done, and with so much effect
by their town meetings. The law for religious freedom,
which made a part of this system, having put down the
aristocracy of the clergy, and restored to the citizen the
freedom of the mind, and those of entails and descents nur-
turing an equality of condition among them, this on education would have raised the mass of the people to the high
ground of moral respectability necessary to their own safety, and to orderly government; and would have completed
the great object of qualifying them to select the veritable
aristoi, for the trusts of government, to the exclusion of the
pseudalists. . . . Although this law has not yet been acted
on but in a small and inefficient degree, it is still considered
as before the legislature, with other bills of the revised code,
not yet taken up, and I have great hope that some patriotic
spirit will, at a favorable moment, call it up, and make it
the key-stone of the arch of our government.

With respect to aristocracy, we should further consider,
that before the establishment of the American States, nothing was known to history but the man of the old world,
crowded within limits either small or overcharged, and
steeped in the vices which that situation generates. A government adapted to such men would be one thing; but a
very different one, that for the man of these States. Here
everyone may have land to labor for himself, if he chooses;
or, preferring the exercise of any other industry, may exact
for it such compensation as not only to afford a comfortable
subsistence, but wherewith to provide for a cessation from
labor in old age. Everyone, by his property, or by his satisfactory situation, is interested in the support of law and
order. And such men may safely and advantageously reserve

to themselves a wholesome control over their public affairs, and a degree of freedom, which, in the hands of the *canaille* of the cities of Europe, would be instantly perverted to the demolition and destruction of everything public and private. The history of the last twenty-five years of France, and of the last forty years in America, nay of its last two hundred years, proves the truth of both parts of this observation.

But even in Europe a change has sensibly taken place in the mind of man. Science had liberated the ideas of those who read and reflect, and the American example had kindled feelings of right in the people. An insurrection has consequently begun, of science, talents, and courage, against rank and birth, which have fallen into contempt. It has failed in its first effort, because the mobs of the cities, the instrument used for its accomplishment, debased by ignorance, poverty, and vice, could not be restrained to rational action. But the world will recover from the panic of this first catastrophe. Science is progressive, and talents and enterprise on the alert. Resort may be had to the people of the country, a more governable power from their principles and subordination; and rank, and birth, and tinsel-aristocracy will finally shrink into insignificance, even there. This, however, we have no right to meddle with. It suffices for us, if the moral and physical condition of our own citizens qualifies them to select the able and good for the direction of their government, with a recurrence of elections at such short periods as will enable them to displace an unfaithful servant, before the mischief he meditates may be irremediable.

I have thus stated my opinion on a point on which we differ, not with a view to controversy, for we are both too old to change opinions which are the result of a long life of inquiry and reflection; but on the suggestions of a former letter of yours, that we ought not to die before we have explained ourselves to each other. We acted in perfect harmony, through a long and perilous contest for our liberty and independence. A constitution has been acquired, which, though neither of us thinks perfect, yet both consider as competent to render our fellow citizens the happiest and the securest on whom the sun has ever shone. If we do not think exactly alike as to its imperfections, it matters little to our country, which, after devoting to it long lives of disinterested labor, we delivered over to our successors in life, who will be able to take care of it and of themselves.

Of the pamphlet on aristocracy which has been sent to you, or who may be its author, I have heard nothing but through your letter. If the person you suspect, it may be known from the quaint, mystical, and hyperbolical ideas, involved in affected, new-tangled and pedantic terms which stamp his writings. Whatever it be, I hope your quiet is not to be affected at this day by the rudeness or intemperance of scribblers; but that you may continue in tranquillity to live and to rejoice in the prosperity of our country, until it shall be your own wish to take your seat among the aristoi who have gone before you. Ever and affectionately yours.

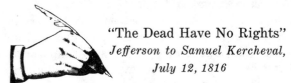

"The Dead Have No Rights"
Jefferson to Samuel Kercheval,
July 12, 1816

Note that Jefferson's philosophical discourse at the end of the letter is preceded by some very specific observations about the nuts and bolts of self-government.

SIR: I duly received your favor of June the 13th, with the copy of the letters on the calling a convention, on which you are pleased to ask my opinion. I have not been in the habit of mysterious reserve on any subject, nor of buttoning up my opinions within my own doublet. On the contrary, while in public service especially, I thought the public entitled to frankness, and intimately to know whom they employed. But I am now retired: I resign myself, as a passenger, with confidence to those at present at the helm, and ask for rest, peace and good will. The question you propose, on equal representation, has become a party one, in which I wish to take no public share. Yet, if it be asked for your own satisfaction only, and not to be quoted before the public, I have no motive to withhold it, and the less from you, as it coincides with your own. At the birth of our republic, I committed that opinion to the world, in the draught of a constitution annexed to the "Notes on Virginia," in which a provision was inserted for a representation permanently equal. The infancy of the subject at that moment, and our inexperience of self-government, occasioned gross departures in that draught from genuine republican canons. In truth, the abuses of monarchy had so much filled all the space of political contemplation, that we imagined everything republican which was not monarchy. We had not yet penetrated to the mother principle, that "governments are republican only in proportion as they embody the will of their people, and execute it." Hence, our first constitutions had really no leading principles in them. But experience and reflection have but more and more confirmed me in the particular importance of the equal representation then proposed. On that point, then, I am entirely in sentiment with your letters; and only lament that a copy-right of your pamphlet prevents their appearance in the newspapers, where alone they would be generally read, and produce general effect. The present vacancy too, of other matter, would give them place in every paper, and bring the question home to every man's conscience.

But inequality of representation in both Houses of our legislature, is not the only republican heresy in this first essay of our revolutionary patriots at forming a constitution. For let it be agreed that a government is republican in proportion as every member composing it has his equal voice in the direction of its concerns (not indeed in person, which would be impracticable beyond the limits of a city, or small township, but), by representatives chosen by himself, and responsible to him at short periods, and let us bring to the test of this canon every branch of our constitution.

In the legislature, the House of Representatives is chosen by less than half the people, and not at all in proportion to those who do choose. The Senate are still more disproportionate, and for long terms of irresponsibility. In the Executive, the Governor is entirely independent of the choice of the people, and of their control; his Council equally so, and at best but a fifth wheel to a wagon. In the Judiciary, the judges of the highest courts are dependent on none but themselves. In England, where judges were named and removable at the will of an hereditary executive, from which branch most misrule was feared, and has flowed, it was a great point gained, by fixing them for life, to make them independent of that executive. But in a government founded on the public will, this principle operates in an opposite direction, and against that will. There, too, they were still removable on a concurrence of the executive and legislative branches. But we have made them independent of the nation itself. They are irremovable, but by their own body, for any depravities of conduct, and even by their own body for the imbecilities of dotage. The justices of the inferior courts are self-chosen, are for life, and perpetuate their own body in succession forever, so that a faction once possessing themselves of the bench of a county, can never be broken up, but hold their county in chains, forever indissoluble. Yet these justices are the real executive as well as judiciary, in all our minor and most ordinary concerns. They tax us at will; fill the office of sheriff, the most important of all the executive officers of the county; name nearly all our military leaders, which leaders, once named, are removable but by themselves. The juries, our judges of all fact, and of law when they choose it, are not selected by the people, nor amenable to them. They are chosen by an officer named by the court and executive. Chosen, did I say? Picked up by the sheriff from the loungings of the court yard, after everything re-

spectable has retired from it. Where then is our republicanism to be found? Not in our constitution certainly, but
merely in the spirit of our people. That would oblige even a
despot to govern us republicanly. Owing to this spirit, and
to nothing in the form of our constitution, all things have
gone well. But this fact, so triumphantly misquoted by the
enemies of reformation, is not the fruit of our constitution,
but has prevailed in spite of it. Our functionaries have done
well, because generally honest men. If any were not so, they
feared to show it.

But it will be said, it is easier to find faults than to amend
them. I do not think their amendment so difficult as is pretended. Only lay down true principles, and adhere to them
inflexibly. Do not be frightened into their surrender by the
alarms of the timid, or the croakings of wealth against the
ascendency of the people. If experience be called for, appeal
to that of our fifteen or twenty governments for forty years,
and show me where the people have done half the mischief
in these forty years, that a single despot would have done in
a single year; or show half the riots and rebellions, the
crimes and the punishments, which have taken place in any
single nation, under kingly government, during the same
period. The true foundation of republican government is the
equal right of every citizen, in his person and property, and
in their management. Try by this, as a tally, every provision
of our constitution, and see if it hangs directly on the will of
the people. Reduce your legislature to a convenient number
for full, but orderly discussion. Let every man who fights or
pays, exercise his just and equal right in their election. Submit them to approbation or rejection at short intervals. Let
the executive be chosen in the same way, and for the same
term, by those whose agent he is to be; and leave no screen
of a council behind which to skulk from responsibility. It
has been thought that the people are not competent electors
of judges *learned in the law*. But I do not know that this is
true, and, if doubtful, we should follow principle. In this,
as in many other elections, they would be guided by reputa-

tion, which would not err oftener, perhaps, than the present mode of appointment. In one State of the Union, at least, it has long been tried, and with the most satisfactory success. The judges of Connecticut have been chosen by the people every six months, for nearly two centuries, and I believe there has hardly ever been an instance of change; so powerful is the curb of incessant responsibility. If prejudice, however, derived from a monarchical institution, is still to prevail against the vital elective principle of our own, and if the existing example among ourselves of periodical election of judges by the people be still mistrusted, let us at least not adopt the evil, and reject the good, of the English precedent; let us retain amovability on the concurrence of the executive and legislative branches, and nomination by the executive alone. Nomination to office is an executive function. To give it to the legislature, as we do, is a violation of the principle of the separation of powers. It swerves the members from correctness, by temptations to intrigue for office themselves, and to a corrupt barter of votes; and destroys responsibility by dividing it among a multitude. By leaving nomination in its proper place, among executive functions, the principle of the distribution of power is preserved, and responsibility weighs with its heaviest force on a single head.

The organization of our county administrations may be thought more difficult. But follow principle, and the knot unties itself. Divide the counties into wards of such size as that every citizen can attend, when called on, and act in person. Ascribe to them the government of their wards in all things relating to themselves exclusively. A justice, chosen by themselves, in each, a constable, a military company, a patrol, a school, the care of their own poor, their own portion of the public roads, the choice of one or more jurors to serve in some court, and the delivery, within their own wards, of their own votes for all elective officers of higher sphere, will relieve the county administration of nearly all its business, will have it better done, and by making every citizen an acting member of the government, and in the

offices nearest and most interesting to him, will attach him
by his strongest feelings to the independence of his country,
and its republican constitution. The justices thus chosen by
every ward, would constitute the county court, would do its
judiciary business, direct roads and bridges, levy county
and poor rates, and administer all the matters of common
interest to the whole country. These wards, called townships
in New England, are the vital principle of their governments, and have proved themselves the wisest invention
ever devised by the wit of man for the perfect exercise of
self-government, and for its preservation. We should thus
marshal our government into, 1, the general federal republic, for all concerns foreign and federal; 2, that of the State,
for what relates to our own citizens exclusively; 3, the
county republics, for the duties and concerns of the county;
and 4, the ward republics, for the small, and yet numerous
and interesting concerns of the neighborhood; and in government, as well as in every other business of life, it is by
division and subdivision of duties alone, that all matters,
great and small, can be managed to perfection. And the
whole is cemented by giving to every citizen, personally, a
part in the administration of the public affairs.

The sum of these amendments is, 1. General suffrage. 2.
Equal representation in the legislature. 3. An executive
chosen by the people. 4. Judges elective or amovable. 5. Justices, jurors, and sheriffs elective. 6. Ward divisions. And
7. Periodical amendments of the constitution.

I have thrown out these as loose heads of amendment, for
consideration and correction; and their object is to secure
self-government by the republicanism of our constitution,
as well as by the spirit of the people; and to nourish and
perpetuate that spirit. I am not among those who fear the
people. They, and not the rich, are our dependence for continued freedom. And to preserve their independence, we
must not let our rulers load us with perpetual debt. We
must make our election between *economy and liberty*, or
profusion and servitude. If we run into such debts, as that

we must be taxed in our meat and in our drink, in our necessaries and our comforts, in our labors and our amusements, for our callings and our creeds, as the people of England are, our people, like them, must come to labor sixteen hours in the twenty-four, give the earnings of fifteen of these to the government for their debts and daily expenses; and the sixteenth being insufficient to afford us bread, we must live, as they now do, on oatmeal and potatoes; have no time to think, no means of calling the mismanagers to account; but be glad to obtain subsistence by hiring ourselves to rivet their chains on the necks of our fellow-sufferers. Our land-holders, too, like theirs, retaining indeed the title and stewardship of estates called theirs, but held really in trust for the treasury, must wander, like theirs, in foreign countries, and be contented with penury, obscurity, exile, and the glory of the nation. This example reads to us the salutary lesson, that private fortunes are destroyed by public as well as by private extravagance. And this is the tendency of all human governments. A departure from principle in one instance becomes a precedent for a second; that second for a third; and so on, till the bulk of the society is reduced to be mere automatons of misery, to have no sensibilities left but for sinning and suffering. Then begins, indeed, the *bellum omnium in omnia*, which some philosophers observing to be so general in this world, have mistaken it for the natural, instead of the abusive state of man. And the fore horse of this frightful team is public debt. Taxation follows that, and in its train wretchedness and oppression.

Some men look at constitutions with sanctimonious reverence, and deem them like the ark of the covenant, too sacred to be touched. They ascribe to the men of the preceding age a wisdom more than human, and suppose what they did to be beyond amendment. I knew that age well; I belonged to it, and labored with it. It deserved well of its country. It was very like the present, but without the experience of the present; and forty years of experience in government is

worth a century of book-reading; and this they would say
themselves, were they to rise from the dead. I am certainly
not an advocate for frequent and untried changes in laws
and constitutions. I think moderate imperfections had better
be borne with; because, when once known, we accommodate
ourselves to them, and find practical means of correcting
their ill effects. But I know also, that laws and institutions
must go hand in hand with the progress of the human mind.
As that becomes more developed, more enlightened, as new
discoveries are made, new truths disclosed, and manners
and opinions change with the change of circumstances, institutions must advance also, and keep pace with the times.
We might as well require a man to wear still the coat which
fitted him when a boy, as civilized society to remain ever
under the regimen of their barbarous ancestors. It is this
preposterous idea which has lately deluged Europe in blood.
Their monarchs, instead of wisely yielding to the gradual
change of circumstances, of favoring progressive accommodation to progressive improvement, have clung to old abuses,
entrenched themselves behind steady habits, and obliged
their subjects to seek through blood and violence rash and
ruinous innovations, which, had they been referred to the
peaceful deliberations and collected wisdom of the nation,
would have been put into acceptable and salutary forms.
Let us follow no such examples, nor weakly believe that one
generation is not as capable as another of taking care of
itself, and of ordering its own affairs. Let us, as our sister
States have done, avail ourselves of our reason and experience, to correct the crude essays of our first and unexperi-
enced, although wise, virtuous, and well-meaning councils.
And lastly, let us provide in our constitution for its revision
at stated periods. What these periods should be, nature herself indicates. By the European tables of mortality, of the
adults living at any one moment of time, a majority will be
dead in about nineteen years. At the end of that period then,
a new majority is come into place; or, in other words, a
new generation. Each generation is as independent of the

one preceding, as that was of all which had gone before. It has then, like them, a right to choose for itself the form of government it believes most promotive to its own happiness; consequently, to accommodate to the circumstances in which it finds itself, that received from its predecessors; and it is for the peace and good of mankind, that a solemn opportunity of doing this every nineteen or twenty years, should be provided by the constitution; so that it may be handed on, with periodical repairs, from generation to generation, to the end of time, if anything human can so long endure. It is now forty years since the constitution of Virginia was formed. The same tables inform us, that, within that period, two-thirds of the adults then living are now dead. Have then the remaining third, even if they had the wish, the right to hold in obedience to their will, and to laws heretofore made by them, the other two-thirds, who, with themselves, compose the present mass of adults? If they have not, who has? The dead? But the dead have no rights. They are nothing; and nothing cannot own something. Where there is no substance, there can be no accident. This corporeal globe, and everything upon it, belong to its present corporeal inhabitants, during their generation. They alone have a right to direct what is the concern of themselves alone, and to declare the law of that direction; and this declaration can only be made by their majority. That majority, then, has a right to dispute representatives to a convention, and to make the constitution what they think will be the best for themselves. But how collect their voice? This is the real difficulty. If invited by private authority, or county or district meetings, these divisions are so large that few will attend; and their voice will be imperfectly, or falsely pronounced. Here, then, would be one of the advantages of the ward divisions I have proposed. The mayor of every ward, on a question like the present, would call his ward together, take the simple yea or nay of its members, convey these to the county court, who would hand on those of all its wards to the proper general authority; and the voice of the whole people would be thus fairly, full, and peaceably expressed, discussed, and decided by the common reason of the society. If this avenue be shut to the call of sufferance, it will make itself heard through that of force, and we shall go on, as other nations are doing, in the endless circle of oppression, rebellion, reformation; and oppression, rebellion, reformation, again; and so on forever.

These, Sir, are my opinions of the governments we see among men, and of the principles by which alone we may prevent our own from falling into the same dreadful track. I have given them at greater length than your letter called for. But I cannot say things by halves; and I confide them to your honor, so to use them as to preserve me from the gridiron of the public papers. If you shall approve and enforce them, as you have done that of equal representation, they may do some good. If not, keep them to yourself as the effusions of withered age and useless time. I shall, with not the less truth, assure you of my great respect and consideration.

Democracy in Wartime
From *Notes on Virginia*,
Query XIII, 1785

As governor of Virginia from 1779–1781, Jefferson knew at first-hand some of the problems of government by the people in wartime.

. . . In enumerating the defects of the constitution, it would be wrong to count among them what is only the errors of particular persons. In December 1776, our circumstances being much distressed, it was proposed in the house of delegates to create a *dictator*, invested with every power legislative, executive, and judiciary, civil and military, of life and of death, over our persons and over our properties; and in June 1781, again under calamity, the

same proposition was repeated, and wanted a few votes only
of being passed. One who entered into this contest from a
pure love of liberty, and a sense of injured rights, who determined to make every sacrifice, and to meet every danger,
for the re-establishment of those rights on a firm basis, who
did not mean to expend his blood and substance for the
wretched purpose of changing this matter for that, but to
place the powers of governing him in a plurality of hands
of his own choice, so that the corrupt will of no one man
might in future oppress him, must stand confounded and
dismayed when he is told, that a considerable portion of
that plurality had mediated the surrender of them into a
single hand, and, in lieu of a limited monarchy, to deliver
him over to a despotic one! How must we find his efforts
and sacrifices abused and baffled, if he may still, by a single
vote, be laid prostrate at the feet of one man! In God's
name, from whence have they derived this power? Is it
from our ancient laws? None such can be produced. Is it
from any principle in our new constitution expressed or
implied? Every lineament expressed or implied, is in full
opposition to it. Its fundamental principle is, that the State
shall be governed as a commonwealth. It provides a republican organization, proscribes under the name of *prerogative*
the exercise of all powers undefined by the laws; places on
this basis the whole system of our laws; and by consolidating them together, chooses that they should be left to stand
or fall together, never providing for any circumstances, nor
admitting that such could arise, wherein either should be
suspended; no, not for a moment. Our ancient laws expressly declare, that those who are but delegates themselves shall
not delegate to others powers which require judgment and
integrity in their exercise. Or was this proposition moved
on a supposed right in the movers, of abandoning their
posts in a moment of distress? The same laws forbid the
abandonment of that post, even on ordinary occasions; and
much more a transfer of their powers into other hands and
other forms, without consulting the people. They never ad-

mit the idea that these, like sheep or cattle, may be given from hand to hand without an appeal to their own will. Was it from the necessity of the case? Necessities which dissolve a government, do not convey its authority to an oligarchy or a monarchy. They throw back, into the hands of the people, the powers they had delegated, and leave them as individuals to shift for themselves. A leader may offer, but not impose himself, nor be imposed on them. Much less can their necks be submitted to his sword, their breath to be held at his will or caprice. The necessity which should operate these tremendous effects should at least be palpable and irresistible. Yet in both instances, where it was feared, or pretended with us, it was belied by the event. It was belied, too, by the preceding experience of our sister States, several of whom had grappled through greater difficulties without abandoning their forms of government. When the proposition was first made, Massachusetts had found even the government of committees sufficient to carry them through an invasion. But we at the time of that proposition, were under no invasion. When the second was made, there had been added to this example those of Rhode Island, New York, New Jersey, and Pennsylvania, in all of which the republican form had been found equal to the task of carrying them through the severest trials. In this State alone did there exist so little virtue, that fear was to be fixed in the hearts of the people, and to become the motive of their exertions, and principle of their government? The very thought alone was treason against the people; was treason against mankind in general; as rivetting forever the chains which bow down their necks, by giving to their oppressor a proof, which they would have trumpeted through the universe, of the imbecility of republican government, in times of pressing danger, to shield them from harm. Those who assume the right of giving away the reins of government in any case, must be sure that the herd, whom they hand on to the rods and hatchet of the dictator, will lay their necks on the block when he shall nod to them. But if our assemblies supposed such a recognition in the people, I hope they mistook their character. I am of the opinion, that the government, instead of being braced and invigorated for greater exertions under their difficulties, would have been thrown back upon the bungling machinery of county committees for administration, till a convention could have been called, and its wheels again set into regular motion. What a cruel moment was this for creating such an embarrassment, for putting to the proof the attachment of our countrymen to republican government! Those who meant well, of the advocates of this measure, (and most of them meant well, for I know them personally, had been their fellow-laborer in the common cause, and had often proved the purity of their principles,) had been seduced in their judgment by the example of an ancient republic, whose constitution and circumstances were fundamentally different. They had sought this precedent in the history of Rome, where alone it was to be found, and where at length, too, it had proved fatal. They had taken it from a republic rent by the most bitter factions and tumults, where the government was of a heavy-handed unfeeling aristocracy, over a people ferocious, and rendered desperate by poverty and wretchedness; tumults which could not be allayed under the most trying circumstances, but by the omnipotent hand of a single despot. Their constitution, therefore, allowed a temporary tyrant to be erected, under the name of a dictator; and that temporary tyrant, after a few examples, became perpetual. They misapplied this precedent to a people mild in their dispositions, patient under their trial, united for the public liberty, and affectionate to their leaders. But if from the constitution of the Roman government there resulted to their senate a power of submitting all their rights to the will of one man, does it follow that the assembly of Virginia have the same authority? What clause in our constitution has substituted that of Rome, by way of residuary provision, for all cases not otherwise provided for? Or if they may step *ad libitum* into any other form of government for precedents to rule us by, for what oppression may not a precedent be found in this world of the *ballum omnium in omnia*? Searching for the foundations of this proposition, I can find none which may pretend a color of right or reason, but the defect before developed, that there being no barrier between the legislative, executive, and judiciary departments, the legislature may seize the whole; that having seized it, and possessing a right to fix their own quorum, they may reduce that quorum to one, whom they may call a chairman, speaker, dictator, or by any other name they please. Our situation is indeed perilous, and I hope my countrymen will be sensible of it, and will apply, at a proper season, the proper remedy; which is a convention to fix the constitution, to amend its defects, to bind up the several branches of government by certain laws, which, when they transgress, their acts shall become nullities; to render unnecessary an appeal to the people, or in other words a rebellion, on every infraction of their rights, on the peril that their acquiescence shall be construed into an intention to surrender those rights.

 A Government for the Northwest Territory
March 22, 1784

The Old Northwest was an extensive "colonial territory." Jefferson wanted to be sure that these people were not denied first-class citizenship.

The Committee to whom was recommitted the report of a plan for a temporary government of the Western territory have agreed to the following resolutions.

Resolved, that so much of the territory ceded or to be ceded by individual states to the United States as is already purchased or shall be purchased of the Indian inhabitants and offered for sale by Congress, shall be divided into distinct states, in the following manner, as nearly as such cessions will admit; that is to say, by parallels of latitude, so that each state shall comprehend from South to North two degrees of latitude beginning to count from the completion of thirty-one degrees North of the Equator; and by meridians of longitude, one of which shall pass through the lowest point of the rapids of Ohio, and the other through the Western Cape of the mouth of the Great Kanhaway, but the territory Eastward of this last meridian, between the Ohio, Lake Erie, and Pennsylvania shall be one state, whatsoever may be its comprehension of latitude. That which may lie beyond the completion of the 45th degree between the said meridians shall make part of the state adjoining it on the South, and that part of the Ohio which is between the same meridians coinciding nearly with the parallel of 39° shall be substituted so far in lieu of that parallel as a boundary line.

That the settlers on any territory so purchased and offered for sale shall, either on their own petition, or on the order of Congress, receive authority from them with appointments of time and place for their free males of full age, within the limits of their state to meet together for the purpose of establishing a temporary government, to adopt the constitution and laws of any one of the original states, so that such laws nevertheless shall be subject to alteration by their ordinary legislature; and to erect, subject to a like alteration, counties or townships for the election of members of their legislature.

That such temporary government shall only continue in force in any state until it shall have acquired 20,000 free inhabitants, when giving due proof thereof to Congress, they shall receive from them authority with appointment of time and place to call a convention of representatives to establish a permanent Constitution and Government for themselves. Provided that both the temporary and permanent governments be established on these principles as their basis. 1. That they shall forever remain a part of this confederacy of the United States of America. 2. That in their persons, property and territory they shall be subject to the Government of the United States in Congress assembled, and to the articles of Confederation in all those cases in which the original states shall be so subject. 3. That they shall be subject to pay a part of the federal debts contracted or to be contracted, to be apportioned on them by Congress, according to the same common rule and measure, by which apportionments thereof shall be made on the other states. 4. That their respective Governments shall be in republican forms and shall admit no person to be a citizen who holds any hereditary title. 5. That after the year 1800 of the Christian era, there shall be neither slavery nor involuntary servitude in any of the said states, otherwise than in punishment of crimes whereof the party shall have been convicted to have been personally guilty.

That whensoever any of the said states shall have, of free inhabitants, as many as shall then be in any one the least numerous, of the thirteen original states, such state shall be admitted by its delegates into the Congress of the United States on an equal footing with the said original states: provided nine States agree to such admission according to the reservation of the 11th of the articles of Confederation, and in order to adopt the said articles of Confederation to the state of Congress when its members shall be thus increased, it shall be proposed to the legislatures of the states originally parties thereto, to require the assent of two thirds of the United States in Congress assembled in all those cases wherein by the said articles the assent of nine states is now required; which being agreed to by them shall be binding on the new states. Until such admission by their delegates into Congress, any of the said states after the establishment of their temporary government shall have authority to keep a sitting member in Congress, with a right of debating, but not of voting.

That the preceding articles shall be formed into a charter of compact, shall be duly executed by the president of the United States in Congress assembled, under his hand and the seal of the United States, shall be promulgated and shall stand as fundamental constitutions between the thirteen original states and each of the several states now newly described, unalterable but by the joint consent of the United States in Congress assembled, and of the particular state within which such alteration is proposed to be made.

That measures not inconsistent with the principles of the Confederation and necessary for the preservation of peace and good order among the settlers in any of the said new states until they shall assume a temporary Government as aforesaid, may from time to time be taken by the United States in Congress assembled.

JEFFERSON AS REVOLUTIONIST

A comparative study of revolutions reveals the rather surprising fact that most of the successful ones go through several stages. The first, defiance to the established government, is usually a demand for reform within the existing institutions. In the case of the French Revolution the fall of the Bastille was followed by an attempt to persuade Louis XVI to become a constitutional monarch. Only when the King refused to compromise did the radicals win ascendency and demand the end of the monarchy and the establishment of a republic. In Russia the overthrow of the tsar in 1917 was followed by a brief experiment with constitutional monarchy and then the democratic government of Alexander Kerensky. Only after these had failed did Lenin and "the dictatorship of the proletariat" triumph.

In the American Revolution a great many Whigs stoutly opposed various acts of Parliament, but were reluctant to make a complete break with England. Even as the Second Continental Congress organized an army and appointed Washington as commander in chief, it was addressing another petition to George III asking for a redress of their grievances. The war went on for more than a year before the colonies finally committed themselves to independence.

This reluctance stemmed from the fact that the revolutionists realized that they were (as in all revolutions) a minority. It was necessary that, within their ranks, they demonstrate a solid front to the opposition by a unanimous vote in support of independence. So, while Jefferson and the Adamses may have seen the break with England coming, they held themselves on a tight rein because of the need, as Jefferson noted, "to keep front and rear together."

It should be remembered that Jefferson and his colleagues were children of the Age of Reason. They argued their case on rational and legal grounds, accusing the ministry and Parliament of illegal acts. Parliament had no authority over the colonies, for they were bound to the mother country by a social contract with their ruler, the king. He agreed to be their protector and rule in behalf of their interests and they agreed to be faithful subjects. The terms of the contract were contained in the colonial charters, which also created the colonial assemblies, who alone had the right to pass laws for the governing of their internal affairs. This is why the first attacks are directed against Parliament. (Jefferson's attack on the king in the *Summary View* was probably the reason why it failed to pass the Virginia Assembly. He had let "the front" get ahead of "the rear.")

Faced with the momentous step of independence—which was treason—these orderly and reasonable men did not desert their legal stance. Instead, they invoked "the law of nature and nature's God," which later freedom fighters would refer to as "a higher law."

A Summary View of
the Rights of British America
*(With a foreword from
Jefferson's Autobiography, 1774)*

. . . Before I left home, to attend the Convention, I prepared what I thought might be given, in instruction, to the Delegates who should be appointed to attend the General Congress proposed. They were drawn in haste, with a number of blanks, with some uncertainties and inaccuracies of historical facts, which I neglected at the moment, knowing they could be readily corrected at the meeting. I set out on my journey, but was taken sick on the road, and was unable to proceed. I therefore sent on, by express, two copies, one under cover to Patrick Henry, the other to Peyton Randolph, who I knew would be in the chair of the Convention. Of the former, no more was ever heard or known. Mr. Henry probably thought it too bold, as a first measure, as the majority of the members did. On the other copy being laid on the table of the Convention, by Peyton Randolph, as the proposition of a member, who was prevented from attendance by sickness on the road, tamer sentiments were preferred, and, I believe, wisely preferred; the leap I proposed being too long, as yet, for the mass of our citizens. The distance between these, and the instructions actually adopted, is of some curiosity, however, as it shews the inequality of pace with which we moved, and the prudence required to keep front and rear together. My creed had been formed on unsheathing the sword at Lexington. They printed the paper, however, and gave it the title of "A Summary view of the rights of British America." In this form it got to London, where the opposition took it up, shaped it to opposition views, and, in that form, it ran rapidly through several editions:

Resolved, That it be an instruction to the said deputies, when assembled in General Congress, with the deputies from the other states of British America, to propose to the said Congress, that an humble and dutiful address be presented to his Majesty, begging leave to say before him as chief magistrate of the British empire the united complaints of his majesty's subjects in America; complaints which are excited by many unwarrantable incroachments and usurpations, attempted to be made by the legislature of one part of the empire, upon those rights which god and the laws have given equally and independently to all. To represent to his majesty that these his states have often individually made humble application to his imperial throne, to obtain thro' it's intervention some redress of their injured rights; to none of which was ever even an answer condescended. Humbly to hope that this their joint address, penned in the language of truth, and divested of those expressions of servility which would persuade his majesty that we are asking favors and not rights, shall obtain from his majesty a more respectful acceptance. And this his majesty will think we have reason to expect when he reflects that he is no more than the chief officer of the people, appointed by the laws, and circumscribed with definite powers, to assist in working the great machine of government erected for their use, and consequently subject to their superintendance. . . .

[There follows a lengthy summary of the evolution of English law and of the development of the crisis in America down to the passage of the Coercive Acts.]

. . . One free and independent legislature hereby takes upon itself to suspend the powers of another, free and independent as itself, thus exhibiting a phaenomenon, unknown in nature, the creator and creature of it's own power. Not only the principles of common sense, but the common feelings of human nature must be surrendered up, before his majesty's subjects here can be persuaded to believe that they hold their political existence at the will of a British parliament. Shall these governments be dissolved, their property annhilated, and their people reduced to a state of nature, at the imperious breath of a body of men whom they never saw, in whom they never confided, and over whom they have no powers of punishment or removal, let their crimes against the American public be ever so great? Can any one reason be assigned why 160,000 electors in the island of Great Britain should give law to four millions in the states of America, every individual of whom is equal to every individual of them in virtue, in understanding, and in bodily strength? Were this to be admitted, instead of being a free people, as we have hitherto supposed, and mean to continue, ourselves, we should suddenly be found the slaves, not of one, but of 160,000 tyrants, distinguished too from all others by this singular circumstance that they are removed from the reach of fear, the only restraining motive which may hold the hand of a tyrant.

That by 'an act to discontinue in such manner and for such time as are therein mentioned the landing and discharging lading or shipping of goods wares and merchandize at the town and within the harbor of Boston in the province of Massachusett's bay in North America' which was passed at the last session of British parliament, a large and populous town, whose trade was their sole subsistence, was deprived of that trade, and involved in utter ruin. Let us for a while suppose the question of right suspended, in order to examine this act on principles of justice. An act of parliament had been passed imposing duties on teas to be paid in America, against which act the Americans had protested as inauthoritative. The East India company, who till that time had never sent a pound of tea to America on their own account, step forth on that occasion the asserters of parliamentary right, and send hither many ship loads of that obnoxious commodity. The masters of their several vessels however, on their arrival in America, wisely attended to admonition, and returned with their cargoes. In the province of New England alone the remonstrances of the people were disregarded, and a compliance, after being many days waited for, was flatly refused. Whether in this the master of the vessel was governed by his obstinacy or his instructions, let those who know, say. There are extraordinary situations which require extraordinary interposition. An exasperated people, who feel that they possess power, are not easily restrained within limits strictly regular. A number of them assembled in the town of Boston, threw the tea into the ocean and dispersed without doing any other act of violence. If in this they did wrong, they were known, and were amenable to the laws of the land, against which it could not be objected that they had ever in any instance been obstructed or diverted from their regular course in favor of popular offenders. They should therefore not have been distrusted on this occasion. But that ill-fated colony had formerly been bold in their enmities against the house of Stuart, and were now devoted to ruin by that unseen hand which governs the momentous affairs of this great empire. On the partial representations of a few worthless ministerial dependants, whose constant office it has been to keep that government embroiled, and who by their treacheries hope to obtain the dignity of the British knighthood, without calling for a party accused, without asking a proof, without attempting a distinction between the guilty and the innocent, the whole of that antient and wealthy town is in a moment reduced from opulence to beggary. Men who had spent their lives in extending the British commerce, who had invested in that place the wealth their honest endeavors had merited, found themselves and their families thrown at once on the world for subsistence by it's charities. Not the hundredth part of the inhabitants of that town had been concerned in the act complained of; many of them were in Great Britain and in other parts beyond sea; yet all were involved in one indiscriminate ruin, by a new executive power unheard of till then, that of a British parliament. A property of the value of many millions of money was sacrifised to revenge, not repay, the loss of a few thousands. This is administering justice with a heavy hand indeed! And when is this tempest to be arrested in it's course? Two wharfs are to be opened again when his majesty shall think proper: the residue which lined the extensive shores of the bay of Boston are forever interdicted the exercise of commerce. This little exception seems to have been thrown in for no other purpose than that of setting a precedent for investing his majesty with legislative powers. If the pulse of his people shall beat calmly under this experiment, another and another will be tried till the measure of despotism be filled up. It would be an insult on common sense to pretend that this exception was made in order to restore it's commerce to that great town. The trade which cannot be received at two wharfs alone, must of necessity be transferred to some other place; to which it will soon be followed by that of the two wharfs. Considered in this light it would be an insolent and cruel mockery at the annihilation of the town of Boston.

By the act for the suppression of riots and tumults in the town of Boston, passed also in the last session of parliament, a murder committed there is, if the governor pleases, to be tried in the court of King's bench in the island of Great Britain, by a jury of Middlesex. The witnesses too, on receipt of such a sum as the Governor shall think it reasonable for them to expend, are to enter into recognisance to appear at the trial. This is in other words taxing them to the amount of their recognisance; and that amount may be whatever a Governor pleases. For who does his majesty think can be prevailed on to cross the Atlantick for the sole purpose of bearing evidence to a fact? His expences are to be borne indeed as they shall be estimated by a Governor; but who are to feed the wife and children whom he leaves behind, and who have had no other subsistence but his daily labor? Those epidemical disorders too, so terrible in a foreign climate, is the cure of them to be estimated among the articles of expence, and their danger to be warded off by the almighty power of a parliament? And the wretched criminal, if he happen to have offended on the American side, stripped of his privilege of trial by peers, of his vicinage, removed from the place where alone full evidence could be obtained, without money, without counsel, without friends, without exculpatory proof, is tried before judges predetermined to condemn. The cowards who would suffer a countryman to be torn from the bowels of their society in order to be thus offered a sacrifice to parliamentary tyranny, would merit that everlasting infamy now fixed on the authors of the act! A clause for a similar purpose had been introduced into an act passed in the 12th. year of his majesty's reign entitled 'an act for the better securing and preserving his majesty's dock-yards, magazines, ships, ammunition and stores,' against which as merited the same censures the several colonies have already protested.

That these are the acts of power assumed by a body of men foreign to our constitutions, and unacknowledged by our laws; against which we do, on behalf of the inhabitants of British America, enter this our solemn and determined

protest. And we do earnestly intreat his majesty, as yet the
only mediatory power between the several states of the
British empire, to recommend to his parliament of Great
Britain the total revocation of these acts, which however
nugatory they be, may yet prove the cause of further dis-
contents and jealousies among us.

That we next proceed to consider the conduct of his
majesty, as holding the executive powers of the laws of
these states, and mark out his deviations from the line of
duty. By the constitution of Great Britain as well as of the
several American states, his majesty possesses the power of
refusing to pass into a law any bill which has already
passed the other two branches of legislature. His majesty
however and his ancestors, conscious of the impropriety of
opposing their single opinion to the united wisdom of two
houses of parliament, while their proceedings were un-
biased by interested principles, for several ages past have
modestly declined the exercise of this power in that part of
his empire called Great Britain. But by change of circumstances, other principles than those of justice simply have
obtained an influence on their determinations. The addition
of new states to the British empire has produced an addition of new, and sometimes opposite interests. It is now
therefore the great office of his majesty to resume the exercise of his negative power, and to prevent the passage of
laws by any one legislature of the empire which might bear
injuriously on the rights and interests of another. Yet this
will not excuse the wanton exercise of this power which we
have seen his majesty practice on the laws of the American
legislatures. For the most trifling reasons, and sometimes
for no conceivable reason at all, his majesty has rejected
laws of the most salutary tendency. The abolition of domestic slavery is the great object of desire in those colonies
where it was unhappily introduced in their infant state.
But previous to the infranchisement of the slaves we have,
it is necessary to exclude all further importations from
Africa. Yet our repeated attempts to effect this by prohibi-

tions, and by imposing duties which might amount to a prohibition, have been hitherto defeated by his majesty's negative: thus preferring the immediate advantages of a few British corsairs to the lasting interests of the American states, and to the rights of human nature deeply wounded by this infamous practice. Nay the single interposition of an interested individual against a law was scarcely ever known to fail of success, tho' in the opposite scale were placed the interests of a whole country. That this is so shameful an abuse of a power trusted with his majesty for other purposes, as if not reformed would call for some legal restrictions.

With equal inattention to the necessities of his people here, has his majesty permitted our laws to lie neglected in England for years, neither confirming them by his assent, nor annulling them by his negative: so that such of them as have no suspending clause, we hold on the most precarious of all tenures, his majesty's will, and such of them as suspend themselves till his majesty's assent be obtained we have feared might be called into existence at some future and distant period, when time and change of circumstances shall have rendered them destructive to his people here. And to render this grievance still more oppressive, his majesty by his instructions has laid his governors under such restrictions that they can pass no law of any moment unless it have such suspending clause: so that, however immediate may be the call for legislative interposition, the law cannot be executed till it has twice crossed the Atlantic, by which time the evil may have spent it's whole force.

But in what terms reconcileable to majesty and at the same time to truth, shall we speak of a late instruction to his majesty's governor of the colony of Virginia, by which he is forbidden to assent to any law for the division of a county, unless the new county will consent to have no representative in assembly? That colony has as yet affixed no boundary to the Westward. Their Western counties therefore are of indefinite extent. Some of them are actually

seated many hundred miles from their Eastern limits. Is it
possible then that his majesty can have bestowed a single
thought on the situation of those people, who, in order to
obtain justice for injuries however great or small, must,
by the laws of that colony, attend their county court at
such a distance, with all their witnesses, monthly, till their
litigation be determined? Or does his majesty seriously
wish, and publish it to the world, that his subjects should
give up the glorious right of representation, with all the
benefits derived from that, and submit themselves the absolute slaves of his sovereign will? Or is it rather meant to
confine the legislative body to their present numbers, that
they may be the cheaper bargain whenever they shall become worth a purchase?

One of the articles of impeachment against Tresilian and
the other judges of Westminster Hall in the reign of Richard the second, for which they suffered death as traitors
to their country, was that they had advised the king that
he might dissolve his parliament at any time: and succeeding kings have adopted the opinion of these unjust judges.
Since the establishment however of the British constitution
at the glorious Revolution on it's free and ancient principles, neither his majesty nor his ancestors have exercised
such a power of dissolution in the island of Great Britain;
and when his majesty was petitioned by the united voice
of his people there to dissolve the present parliament, who
had become obnoxious to them, his ministers were heard to
declare in open parliament that his majesty possessed no
such power by the constitution. But how different their
language and his practice here! To declare as their duty
required the known rights of their country, to oppose the
usurpation of every foreign judicature, to disregard the
imperious mandates of a minister or governor, have been
the avowed causes of dissolving houses of representatives
in America. But if such powers be really vested in his majesty, can he suppose they are there placed to awe the members from such purposes as these? When the representative

body have lost the confidence of their constituents, when they have notoriously made sale of their most valuable rights, when they have assumed to themselves powers which the people never put into their hands, then indeed their continuing in office becomes dangerous to the state, and calls for an exercise of the power of dissolution. Such being the causes for which the representative body should and should not be dissolved, will it not appear strange to an unbiassed observer that that of Great Britain was not dissolved, while those of the colonies have repeatedly incurred that sentence?

But your majesty or your Governors have carried this power beyond every limit known or provided for by the laws. After dissolving one house of representatives, they have refused to call another, so that for a great length of time the legislature provided by the laws has been out of existence. From the nature of things, every society must at all times possess within itself the sovereign powers of legislation. The feelings of human nature revolt against the supposition of a state so situated as that it may not in any emergency provide against dangers which perhaps threaten immediate ruin. While those bodies are in existence to whom the people have delegated the powers of legislation, they alone possess and may exercise those powers. But when they are dissolved by the lopping off one or more of their branches, the power reverts to the people, who may use it to unlimited extent, either assembling together in person, sending deputies, or in any other way they may think proper. We forbear to trace consequences further; the dangers are conspicuous with which this practice is replete.

That we shall at this time also take notice of an error in the nature of our landholdings, which crept in at a very early period of our settlement. The introduction of the Feudal tenures into the kingdom of England, though antient, is well enough understood to set this matter in a proper light. In the earlier ages of the Saxon settlement feudal holdings were certainly altogether unknown, and very few, if any, had been introduced at the time of the Norman conquest. Our Saxon ancestors held their lands, as they did their personal property, in absolute dominion, disencumbered with any superior, answering nearly to the nature of those possessions which the Feudalists term Allodial: William the Norman first introduced that system generally. The lands which had belonged to those who fell in the battle of Hastings, and in the subsequent insurrections of his reign, formed a considerable proportion of the lands of the whole kingdom. These he granted out, subject to feudal duties, as did he also those of a great number of his new subjects, who by persuasions or threats were induced to surrender them for that purpose. But still much was left in the hands of his Saxon subjects, held of no superior, and not subject to feudal conditions. These therefore by express laws, enacted to render uniform the system of military defence, were made liable to the same military duties as if they had been feuds: and the Norman lawyers soon found means to straddle them also with all the other feudal burthens. But still they had not been surrendered to the king, they were not derived from his grant, and therefore they were not holden of him. A general principle indeed was introduced that 'all lands in England were held either mediately or immediately of the crown': but this was borrowed from those holdings which were truly feudal, and only applied to others for the purposes of illustration. Feudal holdings were therefore but exceptions out of the Saxon laws of possession, under which all lands were held in absolute right. These therefore still form the basis or groundwork of the Common law, to prevail wheresoever the exceptions have not taken place. America was not conquered by William the Norman, nor it's lands surrendered to him or any of his successors. Possessions there are undoubtedly of the Allodial nature. Our ancestors however, who migrated hither, were laborers, not lawyers. The fictitious principle that all lands belong originally to the king, they were early persuaded to believe real, and accordingly took grants of their own lands from the crown. And while the crown continued to grant for small sums and on reasonable rents, there was no inducement to arrest the error and lay it open to public view. But his majesty has lately taken on him to advance the terms of purchase and of holding to the double of what they were, by which means the acquisition of lands being rendered difficult, the population of our country is likely to be checked. It is time therefore for us to lay this matter before his majesty, and to declare that he has no right to grant lands of himself. From the nature and purpose of civil institutions, all the lands within the limits which any particular society has circumscribed around itself, are assumed by that society, and subject to their allotment only. This may be done by themselves assembled collectively, or by their legislature to whom they may have delegated sovereign authority: and, if they are allotted in neither of these ways, each individual of the society may appropriate to himself such lands as he finds vacant, and occupancy will give him title.

That, in order to inforce the arbitrary measures before complained of, his majesty has from time to time sent among us large bodies of armed forces, not made up of the people here, nor raised by the authority of our laws. Did his majesty possess such a right as this, it might swallow up all our other rights whenever he should think proper. But his majesty has no right to land a single armed man on our shores; and those whom he sends here are liable to our laws for the suppression and punishment of Riots, Routs, and unlawful assemblies, or are hostile bodies invading us in defiance of law. When in the course of the late war it became expedient that a body of Hanoverian troops should be brought over for the defence of Great Britain, his majesty's grandfather, our late sovereign, did not pretend to introduce them under any authority he possessed. Such a measure would have given just alarm to his subjects in Great Britain, whose liberties would not be safe if armed

men of another country, and of another spirit, might be
brought into the realm at any time without the consent of
their legislature. He therefore applied to parliament who
passed an act for that purpose, limiting the number to be
brought in and the time they were to continue. In like
manner is his majesty restrained in every part of the empire. He possesses indeed the executive power of the laws
in every state; but they are the laws of the particular state
which he is to administer within that state, and not those
of any one within the limits of another. Every state must
judge for itself the number of armed men which they may
safely trust among them, of whom they are to consist, and
under what restrictions they are to be laid. To render these
proceedings still more criminal against our laws, instead of
subjecting the military to the civil power, his majesty has
expressly made the civil subordinate to the military. But
can his majesty thus put down all law under his feet? Can
he erect a power superior to that which erected itself? He
has done it indeed by force; but let him remember that
force cannot give right.

That these are our grievances which we have thus laid
before his majesty with that freedom of language and sentiment which becomes a free people, claiming their rights
as derived from the laws of nature, and not as the gift of
their chief magistrate. Let those flatter, who fear: it is not
an American art. To give praise where it is not due, might
be well from the venal, but would ill beseem those who are
asserting the rights of human nature. They know, and will
therefore say, that kings are the servants, not the proprietors of the people. Open your breast Sire, to liberal and
expanded thought. Let not the name of George the third be
a blot in the page of history. You are surrounded by British counsellors, but remember that they are parties. You
have no ministers for American affairs, because you have
none taken from among us, nor amenable to the laws on
which they are to give you advice. It behoves you therefore
to think and to act for yourself and your people. The great

principles of right and wrong are legible to every reader:
to pursue them requires not the aid of many counsellors.
The whole art of government consists in the art of being
honest. Only aim to do your duty, and mankind will give
you credit where you fail. No longer persevere in sacrificing
the rights of one part of the empire to the inordinate de-
sires of another: but deal out to all equal and impartial
right. Let no act be passed by any one legislature which
may infringe on the rights and liberties of another. This
is the important post in which fortune has placed you,
holding the balance of a great, if a well poised empire.
This, Sire, is the advice of your great American council, on
the observance of which may perhaps depend your felicity
and future fame, and the preservation of that harmony
which alone can continue both to Great Britain and America the reciprocal advantages of their connection. It is
neither our wish nor our interest to separate from her. We
are willing on our part to sacrifice every thing which reason can ask to the restoration of that tranquility for which
all must wish. On their part let them be ready to establish
union on a generous plan. Let them name their terms, but
let them be just. Accept of every commercial preference it
is in our power to give for such things as we can raise for
their use, or they make for ours. But let them not think to
exclude us from going to other markets, to dispose of those
commodities which they cannot use, nor to supply those
wants which they cannot supply. Still less let it be proposed
that our properties within our own territories shall be
taxed or regulated by any power on earth but our own. The
god who gave us life, gave us liberty at the same time: the
hand of force may destroy, but cannot disjoin them. This,
Sire, is our last, our determined resolution: and that you
will be pleased to interpose with that efficacy which your
earnest endeavors may insure to procure redress of these
our great grievances, to quiet the minds of your subjects in
British America against any apprehensions of future in-
croachment, to establish fraternal love and harmony thro'

the whole empire, and that that may continue to the latest ages of time, is the fervent prayer of all British America.

Declaration of Taking Up Arms
July 6, 1775

Jefferson and John Dickinson were appointed to a committee to draw up a declaration of the Congress, setting forth "the causes of . . . taking up arms." Jefferson's language was too strong for Congress and it adopted a milder version by Dickinson, who borrowed much of Jefferson's language. Compare the charges against George III with the Declaration of Independence.

A Declaration by the representatives of the United colonies of America now sitting in General Congress, setting forth the causes and necessity of their taking up arms.

The large strides of late taken by the *legislature of Great Britain* towards establishing over these colonies their absolute rule, and the hardiness of the present attempt to effect by force of arms what by law or right they could never effect, render it necessary for us also to change the ground of opposition, and to close with their last appeal from reason to arms. And it behooves those, who *are called to this great decision*, to be assured that their cause is approved before supreme reason; so is it of great avail that its justice be made known to the world, whose affections will ever take part with those encountering oppression. Our forefathers, inhabitants of the island of Great Britain, left their native lands to seek on these shores a residence for civil and religious freedom. At the expence of their blood, to the ruin of their fortunes, with the relinquishment of everything quiet and comfortable in life, they effected settlements in the hospitable wilds of America; and there established civil societies with various forms of constitution. To continue their connection with the friends whom they had left, they arranged themselves by charters of compact under the same common king, who thus completed their powers of full and perfect legislation and became the link of union between the several parts of the empire. Some occasional assumptions of power by the parliament of Great Britain, however unacknowledged by the constitution of our government, were finally acquiesced in through warmth of affection. Proceeding thus in the fullness of mutual harmony and confidence, both parts of the empire increased in population and wealth with a rapidity unknown in the history of man. The political institutions of America, its various soils and climates opened a certain resource to the unfortunate and to the enterprising of every country, and ensured to them the acquisition and free possession of property. Great Britain too acquired a lustre and a weight among the powers of the earth which her internal resources could never have given her. To a communication of the wealth and power of every part of the empire we may surely ascribe in some measure the illustrious character she sustained through her last European war, and its successful event. At the close of that war it pleased our sovereign to make a change in his counsels. The new ministry finding all the foes of Britain subdued she took up the unfortunate idea of subduing her friends also. By them and her parliament then for the first time assumed a power of unbounded legislation over the colonies of America; and in the course of ten years have given such decisive specimens of the spirit of this new legislation, as leaves no room to doubt the consequence of acquiescence under it. By several acts of parliament passed within that time they have undertaken to give and grant our money without our consent: a right of which we have ever had the exclusive exercise: they have interdicted all commerce to one of our principal towns, thereby annihilating its property in the hands of the holders; they have cut off the commercial intercourse of whole colonies with foreign countries; they have extended the jurisdiction of courts of admiralty beyond their ancient

limits; they have deprived us of the inestimable privilege
of trial by a jury of the vicinage, in cases affecting both
life and property; they have declared that American Subjects charged with certain offenses shall be transported
beyond sea to be tried before the very persons against
whose pretended sovereignty the offense is supposed to be
committed; they have attempted fundamentally to alter the
form of government in one of these colonies, a form secured
by charters on the part of the crown and confirmed by acts
of its own legislature; they have erected in a neighboring
province acquired by the joint arms of Great Britain and
America, a tyranny dangerous to the very existence of all
these colonies. But why should we enumerate their injuries
in the detail? By one act they have suspended the powers
of one American legislature, and by another have declared
they may legislate for us themselves in all cases whatsoever.
These two acts alone form a basis broad enough whereon to
erect a despotism of unlimited extent. And what is to secure
us against this dreaded evil? The persons assuming these
powers are not chosen by us, are not subject to our controul
or influence, are exempted by their situation from the operation of these laws, and lighten their own burthens in proportion as they increase ours. These temptations might put
to trial the severest characters of ancient virtue: with what
new armour then shall a British parliament encounter the
rude assault? towards these deadly injuries from the tender
plant of liberty which we have brought over, and with so
much affection fostered on these our own shores, we have
pursued every temperate, every respectful measure. We
have supplicated our king at various times, in terms almost
disgraceful to freedom; we have reasoned, we have remon-
strated with parliament in the most mild and decent language; we have even proceeded to break off our commercial
intercourse with our fellow subjects, as the last peaceful
admonition that our attachment to no nation on earth
should supplant our attachment to liberty. And here we had
well hoped was the ultimate step of the controversy. But

subsequent events have shewn how vain was even this last remain of confidence in the moderation of the British ministry. During the course of the last year their troops in a hostile manner invested the town of Boston in the province of Massachusets bay, and from that time have held the same beleaguered by sea and land. On the 19th day of April in the present year they made an unprovoked assault on the inhabitants of the said province at the town of Lexington, murdered eight of them on the spot and wounded many others. From thence they proceeded in all the array of war to the town of Concord, where they set upon another party of the inhabitants of the same province, killing many of them also, burning houses, and laying waste property, until repressed by the people suddenly assembled to oppose this cruel aggression. Hostilities thus commenced on the part of the ministerial army have been since by them pursued without regard to faith or to fame. The inhabitants of the town of Boston in order to procure their enlargement having entered into treaty with General Gage their Governor it was stipulated that the said inhabitants, having first deposited their arms with their own magistrates should have liberty to depart from out of the said town taking with them their other effects. But in open violation of plighted faith and honour, in defiance of the sacred obligations of treaty which even savage nations observe, their arms and warlike stores deposited with their own magistrates to be preserved as their property, were immediately seized by a body of armed men under orders from the said General, the greater part of the inhabitants were detained in the town, and the few permitted to depart were compelled to leave their most valuable effects behind. We leave the world to its own reflections on this atrocious perfidy. That we might no longer doubt the ultimate aim of these ministerial maneuvers General Gage, by proclamation bearing date the 12th of June, after reciting the grossest falsehoods and calumnies against the good people of these colonies, proceeds to declare them all, either by name or description, to be rebels and traitors, to supersede the exercise of the common law of the said province, and to proclaim and order instead thereof the use and exercise of the law martial. This bloody edict issued, he had proceeded to commit further ravages and murders in the same province, burning the town of Charlestown, attacking and killing great numbers of the people residing or assembling therein; and is now going on in an avowed course of murder and devastation, taking every occasion to destroy the lives and properties of the inhabitants. To oppose his arms we also have taken up arms. We should be wanting to ourselves, we should be perfidious to posterity, we should be unworthy that free ancestry from which we derive our descent, should we submit with folded arms to military butchery and depredation, to gratify the lordly ambition, or sate the avarice of a British ministry. We do then most solemnly, before God and the world declare that, regardless of every consequence, at the risk of every distress, the arms we have been compelled to assume we will use with the perserverance, exerting to their utmost energies all those powers which our creator hath given us, to preserve that liberty which he committed to us in sacred deposit and to protect from every hostile hand our lives and our properties. But that this declaration may not disquiet the minds of our good fellow subjects in any parts of the empire, we do further assure them that we mean not in any wise to affect that union with them in which we have so long and so happily lived and which we wish so much to see again restored. That necessity must be hard indeed which may force upon us that desperate measure, or induce us to avail ourselves of any aid which their enemies might proffer. We did not embody a soldiery to commit aggression on them; we did not raise armies for glory or for conquest; we did not invade their island carrying death or slavery to its inhabitants. In defence of our persons and properties under actual violation, we took up arms. When that violence shall be removed, when hostilities shall cease on the part of the aggressors, hostilities shall cease on our part also. For the achievement of this happy event, we call for and confide in the good offices of our fellow subjects beyond the Atlantic. Of their friendly dispositions we do not cease to hope; aware, as they must be, that they have nothing more to expect from the same common enemy, than the humble favour of being last devoured. And we devoutly implore assistance of Almighty God to conduct us happily through this great conflict, to dispose his majesty, his ministers, and parliament to reconciliation with us on reasonable terms, and to deliver us from the evils of a civil war.

The preceding document is the only piece of Jefferson's writing that was drastically altered by someone else. What follows is Dickinson's version as adopted by Congress.

If it was possible for men, who exercise their reason, to believe, that the Divine Author of our existence intended a part of the human race to hold an absolute property in, and an unbounded power over others, marked out by his infinite goodness and wisdom, as the objects of a legal domination never rightfully resistible, however severe and oppressive, the Inhabitants of these colonies might at least require from the Parliament of Great Britain some evidence, that this dreadful authority over them, has been granted to that body. But a reverence for our great Creator, principles of humanity, and the dictates of common sense, must convince all those who reflect upon the subject, that government was instituted to promote the welfare of mankind, and ought to be administered for the attainment of that end. The legislature of Great Britain, however, stimulated by an inordinate passion for a power, not only unjustifiable, but which they know to be peculiarly reprobated by the very constitution of that kingdom, and desperate of success in any mode of contest, where regard should be had to truth, law, or right, have at length, deserting those, attempted to effect their cruel and impolitic purpose of enslaving these Colonies by violence, and have thereby rendered it necessary for us to close with their last appeal from Reason to Arms.—Yet, however blinded that assembly may be, by their intemperate rage for unlimited domination, so to slight justice and the opinion of mankind, we esteem ourselves bound, by obligations of respect to the rest of the world, to make known the justice of our cause.

Our forefathers, inhabitants of the island of Great Britain, left their native land, to seek on these shores a residence for civil and religious freedom. At the expense of their blood, at the hazard of their fortunes, without the least charge to the country from which they removed, by unceasing labour, and an unconquerable spirit, they effected settlements in the distant and inhospitable wilds of America, then filled with numerous and warlike nations of barbarians. Societies or governments, vested with perfect legislatures, were formed under charters from the crown, and an harmonious intercourse was established between the colonies and the kingdom from which they derived their origin. The mutual benefits of this union became in a short time so extraordinary, as to excite astonishment. It is universally confessed, that the amazing increase of the wealth, strength, and navigation of the realm, arose from this source; and the minister, who so wisely and successfully directed the measures of Great Britain in the late war, publicly declared, that these colonies enabled her to triumph over her enemies. Towards the conclusion of that war, it pleased our sovereign to make a change in his counsels. From that fatal moment, the affairs of the British empire began to fall into confusion, and gradually sliding from the summit of glorious prosperity, to which they had been advanced by the virtues and abilities of one man, are at length distracted by the convulsions, that now shake it to its deepest foundations. The new ministry finding the brave foes of Britain, though frequently defeated, yet still contending, took up the unfortunate idea of granting them a hasty peace, and of then subduing her faithful friends.

These devoted colonies were judged to be in such a state, as to present victories without bloodshed, and all easy emoluments of statuteable plunder.—The uninterrupted tenor of their peaceable and respectful behavior from the beginning of colonization, their dutiful, zealous, and useful services during the war, though so recently and amply acknowledged in the most honorable manner by his majesty, by the late king, and by Parliament, could not save them from the meditated innovations.—Parliament was influenced to adopt the pernicious project, and assuming a new power over them, have, in the course of eleven years, given such decisive specimens of the spirit and consequences attending this power, as to leave no doubt concerning the effects of acquiescence under it. They have undertaken to give and grant our money without our consent, though we have ever exercised an exclusive right to dispose of our own property; statutes have been passed for extending the jurisdiction of courts of Admiralty and Vice-Admiralty beyond their ancient limits; for depriving us of the accustomed and inestimable privilege of trial by jury, in cases affecting both life and property; for suspending the legislature of one of the colonies; for interdicting all commerce to the capital of another; and for altering fundamentally the form of government established by charter, and secured by acts of its own legislature solemnly confirmed by the crown; for exempting the "murderers" of colonists from legal trial, and in effect, from punishment; for erecting in a neighboring province, acquired by the joint arms of Great Britain and America, a despotism dangerous to our very existence; and for quartering soldiers upon the colonists in time of profound peace. It has also been resolved in parliament, that colonists charged with committing certain offenses, shall be transported to England to be tried.

But why should we enumerate our injuries in detail? By one statute it is declared, that parliament can "of right make laws to bind us IN ALL CASES WHATSOEVER." What is to defend us against so enormous, so unlimited a power? Not a single man of those who assume it, is chosen by us; or is subject to our control or influence; but, on the

contrary, they are all of them exempt from the operation of
such laws, and an American revenue, if not diverted from
the ostensible purposes for which it is raised, would actually
lighten their own burdens in proportion, as they increase
ours. We saw the misery to which such despotism would
reduce us. We for ten years incessantly and ineffectually
besieged the Throne as supplicants; we reasoned, we rem-
onstrated with parliament, in the most mild and decent
language. But Administration, sensible that we should regard these oppressive measures as freemen ought to do,
sent over fleets and armies to enforce them. The indignation
of the Americans was roused, it is true; but it was the indignation of a virtuous, loyal, and affectionate people. A
Congress of Delegates from the United Colonies was assembled at Philadelphia, on the fifth day of last September.
We resolved again to offer an humble and dutiful petition
to the King, and also addressed our fellow-subjects of Great
Britain. We have pursued every temperate, every respectful
measure: we have even proceeded to break off our commercial intercourse with our fellow-subjects as the last peaceable admonition, that our attachment to no nation upon
earth should supplant our attachment to liberty.—This, we
flattered ourselves, was the ultimate step of the controversy:
But subsequent events have shewn, how vain was this hope
of finding moderation in our enemies.

Several threatening expressions against the colonies were
inserted in his Majesty's speech; our petition, though we
were told it was a decent one, and that his Majesty had been
pleased to receive it graciously, and to promise laying it
before his Parliament, was huddled into both houses among
a bundle of American papers, and there neglected. The
Lords and Commons in their address, in the month of February, said, that "a rebellion at that time actually existed
within the province of Massachusetts bay; and that those
concerned in it, had been countenanced and encouraged by
unlawful combinations and engagements, entered into by
his Majesty's subjects in several of the other colonies; and

therefore they besought his Majesty, that he would take the most effectual measures to enforce due obedience to the laws and authority of the supreme legislature."—Soon after, the commercial intercourse of whole colonies, with foreign countries, and with each other, was cut off by an act of Parliament; by another, several of them were entirely prohibited from the fisheries in the seas near their coasts, on which they always depended for their sustenance; and large re-inforcements of ships and troops were immediately sent over to General Gage.

Fruitless were all the entreaties, arguments, and eloquence of an illustrious band of the most distinguished Peers, and Commoners, who nobly and strenuously asserted the justice of our cause, to stay, or even to mitigate the heedless fury with which these accumulated and unexampled outrages were hurried on. . . .

. . . General Gage, who in the course of the last year had taken possession of the town of Boston, in the province of Massachusetts-Bay, and still occupied it as a garrison, on the 19th day of April, sent out from that place a large detachment of his army, who made an unprovoked assault on the inhabitants of the said province, at the town of Lexington, as appears by the affidavits of a great number of persons, some of whom were officers and soldiers of that detachment, murdered eight of the inhabitants, and wounded many others. From thence the troops proceeded in warlike array to the town of Concord, where they set upon another party of the inhabitants of the same province, killing several and wounding more, until compelled to retreat by the country people suddenly assembled to repel this cruel aggression. Hostilities, thus commenced by the British troops, have been since prosecuted by them without regard to faith or reputation.—The inhabitants of Boston being confined within that town by the General their Governor, and having, in order to procure their dismission, entered into a treaty with him, it was stipulated that the said inhabitants having deposited their arms with their own magistrates, should have liberty to depart, taking with them their other effects. They accordingly delivered up their arms, but in open violation of honor, in defiance of the obligation of treaties, which even savage nations esteemed sacred, the Governor ordered the arms deposited as aforesaid, that they might be preserved for their owners, to be seized by a body of soldiers; detained the greatest part of the inhabitants in the town, and compelled the few who were permitted to retire, to leave their most valuable effects behind. . . .

The General, further emulating his ministerial masters, by a proclamation bearing date on the 12th day of June, after venting the grossest falsehoods and calumnies against the good people of these colonies, proceeds to "declare them all, either by name or description, to be rebels and traitors, to supersede the course of the common law, and instead thereof to publish and order the use and exercise of the law martial."—His troops have butchered our countrymen, have wantonly burnt Charles-Town, besides a considerable number of houses in other places; our ships and vessels are seized; the necessary supplies of provisions are intercepted, and he is exerting his utmost power to spread destruction and devastation around him.

We have received certain intelligence, that General Carleton, the Governor of Canada, is instigating the people of that province and the Indians to fall upon us; and we have but too much reason to apprehend, that schemes have been formed to excite domestic enemies against us. In brief, a part of these colonies now feels, and all of them are sure of feeling, as far as the vengeance of administration can inflict them, the complicated calamities of fire, swored, and famine.—We are reduced to the alternative of chusing an unconditional submission to the tyranny of irritated ministers, or resistance by force.—The latter is our choice.—We have counted the cost of this contest, and find nothing so dreadful as voluntary slavery.—Honor, justice, and humanity, forbid us tamely to surrender that freedom which we received from our gallant ancestors, and which our innocent

posterity have a right to receive from us. We cannot endure
the infamy and guilt of resigning succeeding generations to
that wretchedness which inevitably awaits them, if we
basely entail hereditary bondage upon them.

Our cause is just. Our union is perfect. Our internal resources are great, and, if necessary, foreign assistance is
undoubtedly attainable.—We gratefully acknowledge, as
signal instances of the Divine favor towards us, that his
Providence would not permit us to be called into this severe controversy, until we were grown up to our present
strength, had been previously exercised in warlike operation, and possessed of the means of defending ourselves.—
With hearts fortified with these animating reflections, we
most solemnly, before God and the world, declare, that,
exerting the utmost energy of those powers, which our
beneficent Creator hath graciously bestowed upon us, the
arms we have been compelled by our enemies to assume, we
will, in defiance of every hazard, with unabating firmness
and perseverance, employ for the preservation of our liberties; being with our [one] mind resolved to dye (*sic*) Freemen rather than to live Slaves.

Lest this declaration should disquiet the minds of our
friends and fellow-subjects in any part of the empire, we
assure them that we mean not to dissolve that Union which
has so long and so happily subsisted between us, and which
we sincerely wish to see restored.—Necessity has not yet
driven us into that desperate measure, or induced us to
excite any other nation to war against them.—We have not
raised armies with ambitious designs of separating from
Great Britain, and establishing independent states. We fight
not for glory or for conquest. We exhibit to mankind the
remarkable spectacle of a people attacked by unprovoked
enemies, without any imputation or even suspicion of offense. They boast of their privileges and civilization, and
yet proffer no milder conditions than servitude or death.

In our own native land, in defence of the freedom that is
our birth-right, and which we ever enjoyed till the late vio-

lation of it—for the protection of our property, acquired solely by the honest industry of our fore-fathers and ourselves, against violence actually offered, we have taken up arms. We shall lay them down when hostilities cease on the part of the aggressors, and all danger of their being renewed shall be removed, and not before.

With an humble confidence in the mercies of the supreme and impartial Judge and Ruler of the universe, we most devoutly implore his divine goodness to protect us happily through this great conflict, to dispose our adversaries to reconciliation on reasonable terms, and thereby to relieve the empire from the calamities of civil war.

The Declaration of Independence
July 4, 1776

Notice that the Declaration does not condemn George III for being king, but for being a bad king. The twenty-eight charges of misrule "proves" that he has betrayed his trust and so the compact with his American subjects is dissolved.

When in the Course of human events, it becomes necessary for one people to dissolve the political bands which have connected them with another, and to assume among the powers of the earth, the separate and equal station to which the Laws of Nature and of Nature's God entitle them, a decent respect to the opinions of mankind requires that they should declare the causes which impel them to the separation. We hold these truths to be self-evident, that all men are created equal, that they are endowed by their Creator with certain unalienable Rights, that among these are Life, Liberty and the pursuit of Happiness. That to secure these rights, Governments are instituted among Men, deriving their just powers from the consent of the governed, That whenever any Form of Government becomes destructive of these ends, it is the Right of the People to alter or to abolish it, and to institute new Government, laying its foundation on such principles and organizing its powers in such form, as to them shall seem most likely to effect their Safety and Happiness. Prudence, indeed, will dictate that Governments long established should not be changed for light and transient causes; and accordingly all experience hath shewn, that mankind are more disposed to suffer, while evils are sufferable, than to right themselves by abolishing the forms to which they are accustomed. But when a long train of abuses and usurpations, pursuing invariably the same Object evinces a design to reduce them under absolute Despotism, it is their right, it is their duty, to throw off such Government, and to provide new Guards for their future security. Such has been the patient sufferance of these Colonies; and such is now the necessity which constrains them to alter their former Systems of Government. The history of the present King of Great Britain is a history of repeated injuries and usurpations, all having in direct object the establishment of an absolute Tyranny over these States. To prove this, let Facts be submitted to a candid world. He has refused his Assent to Laws, the most wholesome and necessary for the public good. He has forbidden his Governors to pass Laws of immediate and pressing importance, unless suspended in their operation till his Assent should be obtained; and when so suspended, he has utterly neglected to attend to them. He has refused to pass other Laws for the accommodation of large districts of people, unless those people would relinquish the right of Representation in the Legislature, a right inestimable to them and formidable to tyrants only. He has called together legislative bodies at places unusual, uncomfortable, and distant from the depository of their public Records, for the sole purpose of fatiguing them into compliance with his measures. He has dissolved Representative Houses repeatedly, for opposing with manly firmness his invasions on the rights of the people. He has refused for a long time, after

John Trumbull's The Declaration of Independence, 1797
Yale University Art Gallery

In CONGR

The unanimous Declaration

When in the Course of human events, it becomes n
assume among the Powers of the earth, the separate and equal Station to which the Laws of Natur
should declare the causes which impel them to the Separation. ——————— We ho
with certain unalienable Rights, that among these are Life, Liberty and the pursuit of H
Powers from the consent of the governed, — That whenever any Form of Government becomes
Government, laying its foundation on such principles and organizing its Powers in such f
will dictate that Governments long established should not be changed for light and transient
evils are sufferable, than to right themselves by abolishing the forms to which they are accus
evinces a design to reduce them under absolute Despotism, it is their right, it is their duty,
been the patient sufferance of these Colonies; and such is now the necessity which constrains t
Britain is a history of repeated injuries and usurpations, all having in direct object the establi
world. ——————— He has refused his Assent to Laws, the most wholesome and nec
and pressing importance, unless suspended in their operation till his Assent should be obta
pass other Laws for the accommodation of large districts of people, unless those people would rel
to tyrants only. ——————— He has called together legislative bodies at places unusual, uncomfor
compliance with his measures. ——————— He has dissolved Representative Houses repeatedly, f
along time, after such dissolutions, to cause others to be elected; whereby the Legislative Powers
ing in the mean time exposed to all the dangers of invasion from without, and convulsions w
ting the Laws for Naturalization of Foreigners; refusing to pass others to encourage their migrati
Administration of Justice, by refusing his Assent to Laws for establishing Judiciary Powers ——————
and payment of their salaries. ——————— He has erected a multitude of New Offices, and sent
us, in times of peace, Standing Armies without the Consent of our legislatures. ——————— He has
with others to subject us to a jurisdiction foreign to our constitution, and unacknowledged by o
armed troops among us: — For protecting them, by a mock Trial, from punishment for an
our Trade with all parts of the world: — For imposing Taxes on us without our Consent
Seas to be tried for pretended offences ——————— For abolishing the free System of English Laws in
so as to render it at once an example and fit instrument for introducing the same absolute ru
altering fundamentally the Forms of our Governments: — For suspending our own Legislat
He has abdicated Government here, by declaring us out of his Protection and waging War ag
of our people. ——————— He is at this time transporting large Armies of foreign Mercenaries to comp
scarcely paralleled in the most barbarous ages, and totally unworthy the Head of a civilized nation

SS, JULY 4, 1776.

hirteen united States of America.

on one people to dissolve the political bands which have connected them with another, and to
Nature's God entitle them, a decent respect to the opinions of mankind requires that they
uths to be self-evident, that all men are created equal, that they are endowed by their Creator
That to secure these rights, Governments are instituted among Men, deriving their just
e of these ends, it is the Right of the People to alter or to abolish it, and to institute new
to them shall seem most likely to effect their Safety and Happiness. Prudence, indeed,
nd accordingly all experience hath shewn, that mankind are more disposed to suffer, while
Best when a long train of abuses and usurpations, pursuing invariably the same Object
f such Government, and to provide new Guards for their future security. — Such has
er their former Systems of Government. The history of the present King of Great
f an absolute Tyranny over these States. To prove this, let Facts be submitted to a candid
the public good. ——— He has forbidden his Governors to pass Laws of immediate
d when so suspended, he has utterly neglected to attend to them ——— He has refused to
he right of Representation in the Legislature, a right inestimable to them and formidable
d distant from the depository of their Public Records, for the sole purpose of fatiguing them into
ng with manly firmness his invasions on the rights of the people. ——— He has refused for
ble of Annihilation, have returned to the People at large for their exercise; the State remain-
——— He has endeavoured to prevent the Population of these States; for that purpose obstruc-
and raising the conditions of new Appropriations of Lands. ——— He has obstructed the
He has made Judges dependent on his Will alone, for the tenure of their offices, and the amount
arms of Officers to harass our people, and eat out their substance ——— He has kept among
unds the Military independent of and superior to the Civil power. ——— He has combined
giving his Assent to their Acts of pretended Legislation: — For Quartering large bodies of
rs which they should commit on the Inhabitants of these States: — For cutting off
depriving us in many cases, of the benefits of Trial by Jury: — For transporting us beyond
ouring Province, establishing therein an Arbitrary government, and enlarging its Boundaries
hese Colonies: ——— For taking away our Charters, abolishing our most valuable Laws, and
d declaring themselves invested with power to legislate for us in all cases whatsoever. —
——— He has plundered our seas, ravaged our Coasts, burnt our towns, and destroyed the lives
ks of death, desolation and tyranny, already begun with circumstances of Cruelty & perfidy
He has constrained our fellow Citizens taken Captive on the high Seas to bear Arms against

their country, to become the executioners of their friends and Brethren, or to fall themselves by their
inhabitants of our frontiers, the merciless Indian Savages, whose known rule of warfare, is an und
have Petitioned for Redress in the most humble terms: Our repeated Petitions have been answered
is unfit to be the ruler of a free people.   Nor have We been wanting in attentions to our Britt
able jurisdiction over us. We have reminded them of the circumstances of our emigration and f
by the ties of our common kindred to disavow these usurpations, which, would inevitably in
consanguinity. We must, therefore, acquiesce in the necessity, which denounces our Separa

We, therefore, the Representatives of the united States of America, in
tentions, do, in the Name, and by Authority of the good People of these Colonies, solemnly publis
States; that they are Absolved from all Allegiance to the British Crown, and that all politi
that as Free and Independent States, they have full Power to levy War, conclude Peace, c
States may of right do. —— And for the support of this Declaration, with a firm
and our sacred Honor

Wm Hooper   John
Joseph Hewes,
John Penn   Samuel
                                       Wm Pac
Button Gwinnett   Thos. St
Lyman Hall   Chas. Caroll
Geo Walton.

                    Edward Rutledge.

                    Thos Heyward Junr.   Georg
                    Thomas Lynch Junr.   Richard
                    Arthur Middleton   Th Jeff
                                                Benj Ha
                                                Thos Nelso
                                                Francis Ligh
                                                Carter Bra

— He has excited domestic insurrections amongst us, and has endeavoured to bring on the
destruction of all ages, sexes and conditions. In every stage of these Oppressions We
injury. A Prince, whose character is thus marked by every act which may define a Tyrant,
We have warned them from time to time of attempts by their legislature to extend an unwarrant-
. We have appealed to their native justice and magnanimity, and we have conjured them
connections and correspondence They too have been deaf to the voice of justice and of
ld them, as we hold the rest of mankind, Enemies in War, in Peace Friends.———
ngress, Assembled, appealing to the Supreme Judge of the world for the rectitude of our in-
ate, That these United Colonies are, and of Right ought to be Free and Independent
n between them and the State of Great Britain, is and ought to be totally dissolved; and
nces, establish Commerce, and to do all other Acts and Things which Independent
protection of divine Providence, we mutually pledge to each other our Lives, our Fortunes

Rob Morris
Benjamin Rush
Benj. Franklin
John Morton
Geo Clymer
Ja. Smith
Geo Taylor
James Wilson
Geo. Ross
Casar Rodney
Geo Read
Tho M. Kean

Wm Floyd
Phil. Livingston
Fran. Lewis
Lewis Morris

Rich. Stockton
Jno Witherspoon
Fras. Hopkinson
John Hart
Abra Clark

Josiah Bartlett
Wm Whipple
Sam. Adams
John Adams
Robt Treat Paine
Elbridge Gerry
Step. Hopkins
William Ellery
Roger Sherman
Sam. Huntington
Wm Williams
Oliver Wolcott
Matthew Thornton

such dissolutions, to cause others to be elected; whereby the
Legislative powers, incapable of Annihilation, have returned to the people at large for their exercise; the State
remaining in the mean time exposed to all the dangers of
invasion from without, and convulsions within. He has endeavoured to prevent the population of these States; for
that purpose obstructing the Laws for Naturalization of
Foreigners; refusing to pass others to encourage their mi-
grations hither, and raising the conditions of new Appropriations of Lands. He has obstructed the Administration
of Justice, by refusing his Assent to Laws for establishing
Judiciary powers. He has made Judges dependent on his
Will alone, for the tenure of their offices, and the amount
and payment of their salaries. He has erected a multitude
of New Offices, and sent hither swarms of Officers to
harrass our people, and eat out their substance. He has
kept among us, in times of peace, standing Armies without the Consent of our legislatures. He has affected to
render the Military independent of and superior to the
Civil power. He has combined with others to subject us
to a jurisdiction foreign to our constitution, and unacknowledged by our laws; giving his Assent to their Acts
of pretended Legislation: For Quartering large bodies of
armed troops among us: For protecting them, by a mock
Trial, from punishment for any Murders which they should
commit on the Inhabitants of these States: For cutting off
our Trade with all parts of the world: For imposing Taxes
on us without our Consent: For depriving us in many cases
of the benefits of Trial by Jury: For transporting us beyond
Seas to be tried for pretended offences: For abolishing the
free System of English Laws in a neighbouring Province,
establishing therein an Arbitrary government, and enlarging its Boundaries so as to render it at once an example and
fit instrument for introducing the same absolute rule into
these Colonies: For taking away our Charters, abolishing
our most valuable Laws, and altering fundamentally the
Forms of our Governments: For suspending our own Legis-

latures, and declaring themselves invested with power to legislate for us in all cases whatsoever. He has abdicated Government here, by declaring us out of his Protection and waging War against us. He has plundered our seas, ravaged our Coasts, burnt our towns, and destroyed the Lives of our people. He is at this time transporting large Armies of foreign Mercenaries to compleat the works of death, desolation and tyranny, already begun with circumstances of Cruelty & perfidy scarcely paralleled in the most barbarous ages, and totally unworthy the Head of a civilized nation. He has constrained our fellow Citizens taken Captive on the high Seas to bear Arms against their Country, to become the executioners of their friends and Brethren, or to fall themselves by their Hands. He has excited domestic insurrections amongst us, and has endeavoured to bring on the inhabitants of our frontiers, the merciless Indian Savages, whose known rule of warfare, is an undistinguished destruction of all ages, sexes and conditions. In every stage of these Oppressions We have Petitioned for Redress in the most humble terms: Our repeated Petitions have been answered only by repeated injury. A Prince, whose character is thus marked by every act which may define a Tyrant, is unfit to be the ruler of a free people. Nor have We been wanting in attentions to our British brethren. We have warned them from time to time of attempts by their legislature to extend an unwarrantable jurisdiction over us. We have reminded them of the circumstances of our emigration and settlement here. We have appealed to their native justice and magnanimity, and we have conjured them by the ties of our common kindred to disavow these usurpations, which, would inevitably interrupt our connections and correspondence. They too have been deaf to the voice of justice and consanguinity. We must, therefore, acquiesce in the necessity, which denounces our Separation, and hold them, as we hold the rest of mankind, Enemies in War, in Peace Friends.

We, therefore, the Representatives of the united States

of America, in General Congress, Assembled, appealing to the Supreme Judge of the world for the rectitude of our intentions, do, in the Name, and by Authority of the good People of these Colonies, solemnly publish and declare, That these United Colonies are, and of Right ought to be Free and Independent States; that they are Absolved from all Allegiance to the British Crown, and that all political connection between them and the State of Great Britain, is and ought to be totally dissolved; and that as Free and Independent States, they have full Power to levy War, conclude Peace, contract Alliances, establish Commerce, and to do all other Acts and Things which Independent States may of right do. And for the support of this Declaration, with a firm reliance of the protection of divine Providence, we mutually pledge to each other our Lives, our Fortunes and our sacred Honor.

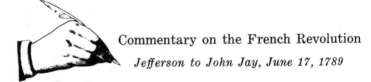

Commentary on the French Revolution

Jefferson to John Jay, June 17, 1789

It may seem strange that Jefferson appears sympathetic to the king and an advocate of constitutional monarchy, but he thought that there would have to be a transitional period from absolutism to republicanism in order to avoid the violence of a civil war.

. . . You will have seen by my former letters that the question whether the States general should vote by Persons, or by Orders, had stopped their proceedings in the very first instance in which it could occur, that is, as to the verification of their powers, and that they had appointed committees to try if there were any means of accomodation. These could do nothing. The king then proposed that they should appoint others, to meet persons whom he should name, on the same subject. These conferences also proved ineffectual. He then proposed a specific mode of verifying. The Clergy accepted it unconditionally: the Noblesse with such conditions and modifications as did away their acceptance altogether. The commons, considering this as a refusal came to the resolution of the 10th. inst. (which I have the honor to send you) inviting the two other orders to come and take their places in the common room, and notifying that they should proceed to the verification of powers, and to the affairs of the nation either with or without them. The clergy have as yet given no answer. A few of their members have accepted the invitation of the Commons, and have presented themselves in their room to have their powers verified, but how many it will detach in the whole from that body, cannot be known till an answer be decided on. The Noblesse adhered to their former resolutions, and even the minority, well disposed to the commons, thought they could do more good in their own chamber by endeavoring to increase their numbers, and bettering the measures of the majority, than by joining the Commons. An intrigue was set on foot between the leaders of the Majority in that house, the *queen* and *princes*.* They persuaded *the king to go for some time to Marly. He went on the same day. The leaders* moved in the chamber of Nobles that they should address the king to declare his own sentiments on the great question between the orders. It was intended that this address should be delivered to him *at Marly, where separated from his ministers, and surrounded by the queen and princes, he might be surprized into a declaration for the nobles*. The motion was lost however by a very great majority, that chamber being not yet quite ripe for throwing themselves into the *arms of despotism. Necker and Montmorin who had discovered this intrigue, had warned some of the minority to defeat it, or they could not answer for what would happen. These two and St. Priest are the only members of the Council* in favor of the commons. *Luzerne, Puy-Segur and the others are high aristocrats*. The commons having verified their powers,

---

*The italicized words were encoded in the original.

a motion was made the day before yesterday to declare
themselves constituted and to proceed to business. I left
them at two oclock yesterday, the debates not then finished.
They differed only about forms of expression, but agreed in
the substance, and probably decided yesterday, or will decide to-day. Their next move I fancy will be to suppress all
taxes, and instantly reestablish them till the end of their
session in order to prevent a premature dissolution: and
then they will go to work on a Declaration of rights and a
constitution. The Noblesse I suppose will be employed altogether in counter operations; the Clergy, that is to say the
higher clergy, and such of the Cures as they can bring over
to their side will be waiting and watching merely to keep
themselves in their saddles. Their deportment hitherto is
that of meekness and cunning. The fate of the nation depends on the conduct of the king and his ministers. Were
they to side openly with the Commons the revolution would
be completed without a convulsion, by the establishment of
a constitution, tolerably free, and in which the distinction
of Noble and Commoner would be suppressed. But this is
scarcely possible. *The king is honest and wishes the good
of his people, but the expediency of an hereditary aristocracy is too difficult a question for him.*—On the contrary *his
prejudices, his habits and his connections decide him in his
heart to support it.* Should they decide openly for the Noblesse, the Commons, after suppressing taxes, and finishing
their Declaration of rights, would probably go home, a
bankruptcy takes place in the instant, Mr. Necker must go
out, a resistance to the tax gatherers follows, and probably
a civil war. These consequences are too evident and violent
to render this issue likely. Tho' *the queen and princes* are
infatuated enough to hazard it, *their party in the ministry*
would not. Something therefore like what I hinted in my
letter of May 12. is still the most likely to take place. While
the Commons, either with or without their friends of the
other two houses, shall be employed in framing a constitution, perhaps the government may set the other two houses

to work on the same subject: and when the three schemes shall be ready, joint committees may be negociated to compare them together, to see in what parts they agree, and probably they will agree in all except the organisation of the future states general. As to this, it may be endeavored, by the aid of wheedling and intimidation, to induce the two privileged chambers to melt themselves into one, and the commons, instead of one, to agree to two houses of legislation. I see no other middle ground to which they can be brought. It is a tremendous cloud indeed which hovers over this nation, and he at the helm has neither the courage nor the skill necessary to weather it. Eloquence in a high degree, knoledge on matters of account, and order, are distinguishing traits in his character. Ambition is his first passion, Virtue his second. He has not discovered that sublime truth that a bold, unequivocal virtue is the best handmaid, even to Ambition, and would carry him further in the end than the temporizing wavering policy he pursues. His judgment is not of the first order, scarcely even of the second, his resolution frail, and upon the whole it is rare to meet an instance of a person so much below the reputation he has obtained. As this character, by the post and times in which providence has placed it, is important to be known, I send it to you as drawn by a person of my acquaintance who knows him well. He is not indeed his friend, and allowance must therefore be made for the high colouring. But this being abated, the facts and ground work of the drawing are just. If the Tiers separate, he goes at the same time: if they stay together and succeed in establishing a constitution to their mind, as soon as that is placed in safety, they will abandon him to the mercy of the court, unless he can recover the confidence which he has lost at present, and which indeed seems to be irrecoverable. . . .

Alexander Hamilton by John Trumbull
Frick Art Reference Library

JEFFERSON AND THE
CONSTITUTION

3 ★
★
★
★

Because his public life was spent primarily as a diplomat and chief executive, we sometimes lose sight of the fact that Thomas Jefferson was a thorough student of constitutions and constitutional law. Once Congress adopted the Declaration of Independence in 1776, Jefferson was in a fever of impatience to get back to Virginia where the state constitutional convention was meeting. Although he was held in Philadelphia by his position as congressman, he sent his draft of a constitution to his friends in Williamsburg, and a few of his ideas were adopted. When the Constitutional Convention met in 1787, he was in Paris as the American minister. (John Adams was also absent, representing the United States in England. It may have been just as well, for if democratic Jefferson and conservative Adams had both been in Philadelphia, the Convention might never have finished its work.) Jefferson therefore missed two great opportunities for putting his lawyer's talent to use. When his close friend James Madison failed to write him promptly of the proceedings, Jefferson sent several angry notes which betrayed his impatience at the lack of news. When a copy finally reached him, he fired off a number of impulsive letters in which he made exaggerated criticisms of the work of the Convention, especially the omission of a bill of rights. This gave rise to the impression, then and later, that Jefferson opposed the Constitution. The letter quoted below was written after he had had time to study the document more carefully, and after he had received explanatory letters from Madison.

Jefferson never confused ends and means. For him constitutions and governments merely provided a framework for a society in which individuals were left as free as possible to engage in the

pursuit of happiness. When men govern themselves, they are constantly confronted with the problem of the free individual in an
orderly society. To what extent must he be restrained in order to
prevent him from injuring the other members of the society who
are pursuing their particular brand of happiness? This attempt
to balance liberty and order is the oldest and most constant problem in societies in which the people rule. The only consolation is
that the very existence of the problem is evidence that we are
still a free people.

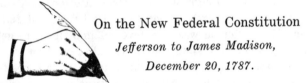

On the New Federal Constitution

Jefferson to James Madison,
December 20, 1787.

... I like much the general idea of framing a government
which should go on of itself peaceably, without needing continual recurrence to the state legislatures. I like the organization of the government into Legislative, Judiciary and
Executive. I like the power given the Legislature to levy
taxes; and for that reason solely approve of the greater
house being chosen by the people directly. For tho' I think
a house chosen by them will be very illy qualified to legislate
for the Union, for foreign nations &c. yet this evil does not
weigh against the good of preserving inviolate the fundamental principle that the people are not to be taxed but by
representatives chosen immediately by themselves. I am
captivated by the compromise of the opposite claims of the
great and little states, of the latter to equal, and the former
to proportional influence. I am much pleased too with the
substitution of the method of voting by persons, instead of
that of voting by states: and I like the negative given to
the Executive with a third of either house, though I should
have liked it better had the Judiciary been associated for
that purpose, or invested with a similar and separate power.
There are other good things of less moment. I will now add
what I do not like. First the omission of a bill of rights pro-

viding clearly and without the aid of sophisms for freedom
of religion, freedom of the press, protection against standing armies, restriction against monopolies, the eternal and
unremitting force of the habeas corpus laws, and trials by
jury in all matters of fact triable by the laws of the land
and not by the law of Nations. To say, as Mr. Wilson does
that a bill of rights was not necessary because all is reserved in the case of the general government which is not
given, while in the particular ones all is given which is not
reserved might do for the Audience to whom it was addressed, but is surely gratis dictum, opposed by strong in-
ferences from the body of the instrument, as well as from
the omission of the clause of our present confederation
which had declared that in express terms. It was a hard
conclusion to say because there has been no uniformity
among the states as to the cases triable by jury, because
some have been so incautious as to abandon this mode of
trial, therefore the more prudent states shall be reduced to
the same level of calamity. It would have been much more
just and wise to have concluded the other way that as most
of the states had judiciously preserved this palladium, those
who had wandered should be brought back to it, and to have
established general right instead of general wrong. Let me
add that a bill of rights is what the people are entitled to
against every government on earth, general or particular,
and what no just government should refuse, or rest on inference. The second feature I dislike, and greatly dislike, is
the abandonment in every instance of the necessity of rota-
tion in office, and most particularly in the case of the President. Experience concurs with reason in concluding that the
first magistrate will always be re-elected if the constitution
permits it. He is then an officer for life. This once observed
it becomes of so much consequence to certain nations to
have a friend or a foe at the head of our affairs that they
will interfere with money and with arms. A Galloman or an
Angloman will be supported by the nation he befriends. If
once elected, and at a second or third election outvoted by

one or two votes, he will pretend false votes, foul play, hold
possession of the reins of government, be supported by the
states voting for him, especially if they are the central ones
lying in a compact body themselves and separating their
opponents: and they will be aided by one nation of Europe,
while the majority are aided by another. The election of a
President of America some years hence will be much more
interesting to certain nations of Europe than ever the election of a king of Poland was. Reflect on all the instances in
history antient and modern, of elective monarchies, and say
if they do not give foundation for my fears, the Roman
emperors, the popes, while they were of any importance, the
German emperors till they became hereditary in practice,
the kings of Poland, the Deys of the Ottoman dependancies.
It may be said that if elections are to be attended with
these disorders, the seldomer they are renewed the better.
But experience shews that the only way to prevent disorder
is to render them uninteresting by frequent changes. As
incapacity to be elected a second time would have been the
only effectual preventative. The power of removing him
every fourth year by the vote of the people is a power which
will not be exercised. The king of Poland is removable every
day by the Diet, yet he is never removed.—Smaller objections are the Appeal in fact as well as law, and the binding
all persons Legislative, Executive and Judiciary by oath to
maintain that constitution. I do not pretend to decide what
would be the best method of procuring the establishment of
the manifold good things in this constitution, and of getting
rid of the bad. Whether by adopting it in hopes of future
amendment, or, after it has been duly weighed and can-
vassed by the people, after seeing the parts they generally
dislike, and those they generally approve, to say to them
'We see now what you wish. Send together your deputies
again, let them frame a constitution for you omitting what
you have condemned, and establishing the powers you approve. Even these will be a great addition to the energy of
your government.'—At all events I hope you will not be dis-

couraged from other trials, if the present one should fail of it's full effect.—I have thus told you freely what I like and dislike: merely as a matter of curiosity for I know your own judgment has been formed on all these points after having heard every thing which could be urged on them. I own I am not a friend to a very energetic government. It is always oppressive. The late rebellion in Massachusetts has given more alarm than I think it should have done. Calculate that one rebellion in 13 states in the course of 11 years, is but one for each state in a century and a half. No country should be so long without one. Nor will any degree of power in the hands of government prevent insurrections. France with all it's despotism, and two or three hundred thousand men always in arms has had three insurrections in the three years I have been here in every one of which greater numbers were engaged than in Massachusets and a great deal more blood was spilt. In Turkey, which Montesquieu supposes more despotic, insurrections are the events of every day. In England, where the hand of power is lighter than here, but heavier than with us they happen every half dozen years. Compare again the ferocious depredations of their insurgents with the order, the moderation and the almost self extinguishment of ours.—After all, it is my principle that the will of the Majority should always prevail. If they approve the proposed Convention in all it's parts, I shall concur in it chearfully, in hopes that they will amend it whenever they shall find it work wrong. I think our governments will remain virtuous for many centuries; as long as they are chiefly agricultural; and this will be as long as there shall be vacant lands in any part of America. When they get piled upon one another in large cities, as in Europe, they will become corrupt as in Europe. Above all things I hope the education of the common people will be attended to; convinced that on their good sense we may rely with the most security for the preservation of a due degree of liberty. I have tired you by this time with my disquisitions and will therefore only add assurances of the sincerity

*Thomas Rossiter's painting of the Constitutional
Convention of 1787
Independence National Historical Park Collection*

of those sentiments of esteem and attachment with which I
am Dear Sir your affectionate friend & servant,

                                                    TH: JEFFERSON

P.S.   The instability of our laws is really an immense evil.
I think it would be well to provide in our constitutions that
there shall always be a twelvemonth between the ingrossing
a bill and passing it: that it should then be offered to it's
passage without changing a word: and that if circumstances
should be thought to require a speedier passage, it should
take two thirds of both houses instead of a bare majority.

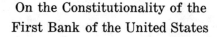

On the Constitutionality of the
First Bank of the United States

*An Opinion Written at the
Request of President Washington,
February 15, 1791*

Jefferson disagreed with Alexander Hamilton's government of
energy and stimulus, and especially with Hamilton's broad or
"loose construction" interpretation of the implied powers clause
of the Constitution, under which he justified the charter of the
Bank.

The bill for establishing a National Bank undertakes,
among other things
1. to form the subscribers into a Corporation.
2. to enable them, in their corporate capacities to receive
    grants of land; and so far is against the laws of *Mort-
    main.*
3. to make *alien* subscribers capable of holding lands, and
    so far is against the laws of *Alienage.*
4. to transmit these lands, on the death of a proprietor, to
    a certain line of successors: and so far changes the
    course of *Descents.*

5. to put the lands out of the reach of forfeiture or escheat and so far is against the laws of *Forfeiture and Escheat*.
6. to transmit personal chattels to successors in a certain line: and so far is against the laws of *Distribution*.
7. to give them the sole and exclusive right of banking under the national authority: and so far is against the laws of *Monopoly*.
8. to communicate to them a power to make laws paramount to the laws of the states: for so they must be construed, to protect the institution from the controul of the state legislatures; and so, probably they will be construed.

I consider the foundation of the Constitution as laid on this ground that 'all powers not delegated to the U.S. by the Constitution, not prohibited by it to the states, are reserved to the states or to the people' (XIIth. Amendmt.). To take a single step beyond the boundaries thus specially drawn around the powers of Congress, is to take possession of a boundless field of power, no longer susceptible of any definition.

The incorporation of a bank, and other powers assumed by this bill have not, in my opinion, been delegated to the U.S. by the Constitution.

I. They are not among the powers specially enumerated, for these are

1. A power to *lay taxes* for the purpose of paying the debts of the U.S. But no debt is paid by this bill, nor any tax laid. Were it a bill to raise money, it's origination in the Senate would condemn it by the constitution.
2. 'to borrow money.' But this bill neither borrows money, nor ensures the borrowing it. The proprietors of the bank will be just as free as any other money holders, to lend or not to lend their money to the public. The operation proposed in the bill, first to lend them two millions, and then borrow them back again, cannot change the nature of the latter act, which will still be a payment, and not a loan, call it by what name you please.

3. 'to regulate commerce with foreign nations, and among
    the states, and with the Indian tribes.' To erect a bank,
    and to regulate commerce, are very different acts. He
    who erects a bank creates a subject of commerce in it's
    bills: so does he who makes a bushel of wheat, or digs a
    dollar out of the mines. Yet neither of these persons
    regulates commerce thereby. To erect a thing which may
    be bought and sold, is not to prescribe regulations for
    buying and selling. Besides; if this was an exercise of
    the power of regulating commerce, it would be void, as
    extending as much to the internal commerce of every
    state, as to it's external. For the power given to Con-
    gress by the Constitution, does not extend to the internal
    regulation of the commerce of a state (that is to say of
    the commerce between citizen and citizen) which re-
    mains exclusively with it's own legislature; but to its'
    external commerce only, that is to say, it's commerce
    with another state, or with foreign nations or with the
    Indian tribes. Accordingly the bill does not propose the
    measure as a 'regulation of trade,' but as 'productive
    of considerable advantage to trade.'

Still less are these powers covered by any other of the
special enumerations.

II. Nor are they within either of the general phrases,
which are the two following.

1. 'To lay taxes to provide for the general welfare of the
    U.S.' that is to say 'to lay taxes *for the purpose* of pro-
    viding for the general welfare.' For the laying of taxes
    is the *power* and the general welfare the *purpose* for
    which the power is to be exercised. They are not to lay
    taxes ad libitum *for any purpose they please*; but only to
    pay the debts or provide for the welfare of the Union.
    In like manner they are not *to do anything they please*
    to provide for the general welfare, but only *to lay taxes*
    for that purpose. To consider the latter phrase, not as
    describing the purpose of the first, but as giving a dis-
    tinct and independent power to do any act they please,

which might be for the good of the Union, would render all the preceding and subsequent enumerations of power completely useless. It would reduce the whole instrument to a single phrase, that of instituting a Congress with power to do whatever would be for the good of the U.S. and as they would be the sole judges of the good or evil, it would be also a power to do whatever evil they pleased. It is an established rule of construction, where a phrase will bear either of two meanings, to give it that which will allow some meaning to the other parts of the instrument, and not that which would render all the others useless. Certainly no such universal power was meant to be given them. It was intended to lace them up straitly within the enumerated powers, and those without which, as means, these powers could not be carried into effect. It is known that the very power now proposed *as a means*, was rejected *as an end*, by the Convention which formed the constitution. A proposition was made to them to authorize Congress to open canals, and an amendatory one to empower them to incorporate. But the whole was rejected, and one of the reasons of rejection urged in debate was that then they would have a power to erect a bank, which would render the great cities, where there were prejudices and jealousies on that subject adverse to the reception of the constitution.

2. The second general phrase is 'to make all laws *necessary* and proper for carrying into execution the enumerated powers.' But they can all be carried into execution without a bank. A bank therefore is not *necessary*, and consequently not authorised by this phrase.

It has been much urged that a bank will give great facility, or convenience in the collection of taxes. Suppose this were true: yet the constitution allows only the means which are 'necessary' not those which are merely 'convenient' for effecting the enumerated powers. If such a latitude of construction be allowed to this phrase as to give any non-enumerated power, it will go to every one, for there is no one which ingenuity may not torture into a *convenience, in some way or other,* to *some one* of so long a list of enumerated powers. It would swallow up all the delegated powers, and reduce the whole to one phrase as before observed. Therefore it was that the constitution restrained them to the *necessary* means, that is to say, to those means without which the grant of the power would be nugatory.

But let us examine this *convenience,* and see what it is. The report on this subject, page 3. states the only *general* convenience to be the preventing the transportation and re-transportation of money between the states and the treasury. (For I pass over the increase of circulating medium ascribed to it as a merit, and which, according to my ideas of paper money is clearly a demerit.) Every state will have to pay a sum of tax-money into the treasury: and the treasury will have to pay, in every state, a part of the interest on the public debt, and salaries to the officers of government resident in that state. In most states there will still be a surplus of tax-money to come up to the seat of government for the officers residing there. The payments of interest and salary in each state may be made by treasury-orders on the state collector. This will take up the greater part of the money he has collected in his state, and consequently prevent the mass of it from being drawn out of the state. If there be a balance of commerce in favour of that state against the one in which the government resides, the surplus of taxes will be remitted by the bills of exchange drawn for that commercial balance. And so it must be if there was a bank. But if there be no balance of commerce, either direct or circuitous, all the banks in the world could not bring up the surplus of taxes but in the form of money. Treasury orders then and bills of exchange may prevent the displacement of the main mass of the money collected, without the aid of any bank: and where these fail, it cannot be prevented even with that aid.

Perhaps indeed bank bills may be a more *convenient* vehicle than treasury orders. But a little *difference* in the degree of *convenience*, cannot constitute the necessity which the constitution makes the ground for assuming any non-enumerated power.

Besides; the existing banks will without a doubt, enter into arrangements for lending their agency: and the more favourable, as there will be a competition among them for it: whereas the bill delivers us up bound to the national bank, who are free to refuse all arrangement, but on their own terms, and the public not free, on such refusal, to employ any other bank. That of Philadelphia, I believe, now does this business, by their post-notes, which by an arrangement with the treasury, are paid by any state collector to whom they are presented. This expedient alone suffices to prevent the existence of that *necessity* which may justify the assumption of a non-enumerated power as a means for carrying into effect an enumerated one. The thing may be done, and has been done, and well done without this assumption; therefore it does not stand on that degree of *necessity* which can honestly justify it.

It may be said that a bank, whose bills would have a currency all over the states, would be more convenient than one whose currency is limited to a single state. So it would be still more convenient that there should be a bank whose bills should have a currency all over the world. But it does not follow from this superior conveniency that there exists anywhere a power to establish such a bank; or that the world may not go on very well without it.

Can it be thought that the Constitution intended that for a shade or two of *convenience*, more or less, Congress should be authorised to break down the most antient and fundamental laws of the several states, such as those against Mortmain, the laws of alienage, the rules of descent, the acts of distribution, the laws of escheat and forfeiture, the laws of monopoly? Nothing but a necessity invincible by any other means, can justify such a prostration of laws which constitute the pillars of our whole system of jurisprudence. Will Congress be too strait-laced to carry the constitution into honest effect, unless they may pass over the foundation-laws of the state-governments for the slightest convenience to theirs?

The Negative of the President is the shield provided by the constitution to protect against the invasions of the legislature 1. the rights of the Executive 2. of the Judiciary 3. of the states and state legislatures. The present is the case of a right remaining exclusively with the states and is consequently one of those intended by the constitution to be placed under his protection.

It must be added however, that unless the President's mind on a view of every thing which is urged for and against this bill, is tolerably clear that it is unauthorised by the constitution, if the pro and con hang so even as to balance his judgment, a just respect for the wisdom of the legislature would naturally decide the balance in favour of their opinion. It is chiefly for cases where they are clearly misled by error, ambition, or interest, that the constitution has placed a check in the negative of the President.

The Kentucky Resolutions
November 16, 1798

In 1798, threatened by the possibility of war with France, Congress made its first attempt to deal with the problem of internal security. The Sedition Act appeared to Jefferson and other Republicans to be an outrageous attempt on the part of the Federalist majority to silence political opposition. The resolutions of the Kentucky legislature, secretly written by Jefferson, theorized that the states had originally granted to the federal government whatever power it possessed, and so it was proper that the states should intervene against this unconstitutional exercise of federal authority.

1. *Resolved,* That the several States composing the United

States of America, are not united on the principle of
unlimited submission to their general government; but
that, by a compact under the style and title of a Constitution for the United States, and of amendments thereto, they constituted a general government for special
purposes—delegated to that government certain definite
powers, reserving, each State to itself, the residuary
mass of right to their own self-government; and that
whensoever the general government assumes undelegated powers, its acts are unauthoritative, void, and of
no force: that to this compact each State acceded as a
State, and is an integral party, its co-States forming, as
to itself, the other party: that the government created
by this compact was not made the exclusive or final judge
of the extent of the powers delegated to itself; since
that would have made its discretion, and not the Constitution, the measure of its powers; but that, as in all
other cases of compact among powers having no common judge, each party has an equal right to judge for
itself, as well as infractions as of the mode and measure
of redress.

2. *Resolved*, That the Constitution of the United States,
having delegated to Congress a power to punish treason,
counterfeiting the securities and current coin of the
United States, piracies, and felonies committed on the
high seas, and offences against the law of nations, and
no other crimes whatsoever; and it being true as a general principle, and one of the amendments to the Constitution having also declared, that "the powers not
delegated to the United States by the Constitution, nor
prohibited by it to the States, are reserved to the States
respectively, or to the people," therefore the act of Congress, passed on the 14th day of July, 1798, and intituled
"An Act in addition to the act intituled An Act for
the punishment of certain crimes against the United
States," as also the act passed by them on the—day of
June, 1798, intituled "An Act to punish frauds com-

mitted on the bank of the United States," (and all their other acts which assume to create, define, or punish crimes, other than those so enumerated in the Constitution,) are altogether void, and of no force; and that the power to create, define, and punish such other crimes is reserved, and, of right, appertains solely and exclusively to the respective States, each within its own territory.

3. *Resolved*, That it is true as a general principle, and is also expressly declared by one of the amendments to the Constitution, that "the powers not delegated to the United States by the Constitution, nor prohibited by it to the States, are reserved to the States respectively, or to the people"; and that no power over the freedom of religion, freedom of speech, or freedom of the press being delegated to the United States by the Constitution, not prohibited by it to the States, all lawful powers respecting the same did of right remain, and were reserved to the States or the people: that thus was manifested their determination to retain to themselves the right of judging how far the licentiousness of speech and of the press may be abridged without lessening their useful freedom, and how far those abuses which cannot be separated from their use should be tolerated, rather than the use be destroyed. And thus also they guarded against all abridgment by the United States of the freedom of religious opinions and exercises, and retained to themselves the right of protecting the same, as this State, by a law passed on the general demand of its citizens, had already protected them from all human restraint or interference. And that in addition to this general principle and express declaration, another and more special provision has been made by one of the amendments to the Constitution, which expressly declares, that "Congress shall make no law respecting an establishment of religion, or prohibiting the free exercise thereof, or abridging the freedom of speech or of the press": thereby guarding in the same sentence, and

under the same words, the freedom of religion, of speech, and of the press: insomuch, that whatever violated either, throws down the sanctuary which covers the others, and that libels, falsehood, and defamation, equally with heresy and false religion, are withheld from the cognizance of federal tribunals. That, therefore, the act of Congress of the United States, passed on the 14th day of July, 1798, intituled "An Act in addition to the act intituled An Act for the punishment of certain crimes against the United States," which does abridge the freedom of the press, is not law, but is altogether void, and of no force.

4. *Resolved,* That alien friends are under the jurisdiction and protection of the laws of the State wherein they are: that no power over them has been delegated to the United States, nor prohibited to the individual States, distinct from their power over citizens. And it being true as a general principle, and one of the amendments to the Constitution having also declared, that "the powers not delegated to the United States by the Constitution, nor prohibited by it to the States, are reserved to the States respectively, or to the people," the act of Congress of the United States, passed on the —day of July, 1798, intituled "An Act concerning aliens," which assumes powers over alien friends, not delegated by the Constitution, is not law, but is altogether void, and of no force.

5. *Resolved,* That in addition to the general principle, as well as the express declaration, that powers not delegated are reserved, another and more special provision, inserted in the Constitution from abundant caution, has declared that "the migration or importation of such persons as any of the States now existing shall think proper to admit, shall not be prohibited by the Congress prior to the year 1808": that this commonwealth does admit the migration of alien friends, described as the subject of the said act concerning aliens: that a provi-

sion against prohibiting their migration, is a provision against all acts equivalent thereto, or it would be nugatory: that to remove them when migrated, is equivalent to a prohibition of their migration, and is, therefore, contrary to the said provision of the Constitution, and void.

6. *Resolved*, That the imprisonment of a person under the protection of the laws of this commonwealth, on his failure to obey the simple *order* of the President to depart out of the United States, as is undertaken by said act intituled "An Act concerning aliens," is contrary to the Constitution, one amendment to which has provided that "no person shall be deprived of liberty without due progress of law"; and that another having provided that "in all criminal prosecutions the accused shall enjoy the right to public trial by an impartial jury, to be informed of the nature and cause of the accusation, to be confronted with the witnesses against him, to have compulsory process for obtaining witnesses in his favor, and to have the assistance of counsel for his defence," the same act, undertaking to authorize the President to remove a person out of the United States, who is under the protection of the law, on his own suspicion, without accusation, without jury, without public trial, without confrontation of the witnesses against him, without hearing witnesses in his favor, without defence, without counsel, is contrary to the provision also of the Constitution, is therefore not law, but utterly void, and of no force: that transferring the power of judging any person, who is under the protection of the laws, from the courts to the President of the United States, as is undertaken by the same act concerning aliens, is against the article of the Constitution which provides that "the judicial power of the United States shall be vested in courts, the judges of which shall hold their offices during good behavior"; and that the said act is void for that reason also. And it is further to be noted, that this trans-

fer of judiciary power is to that magistrate of the general government who already possesses all the Executive and a negative on all Legislative powers.

7. *Resolved,* That the construction applied by the General Government (as is evidenced by sundry of their proceedings) to those parts of the Constitution of the United States which delegate to Congress a power "to lay and collect taxes, duties, imports, and excises, to pay the debts, and provide for the common defence and general welfare of the United States," and "to make all laws which shall be necessary and proper for carrying into execution the powers vested by the Constitution in the government of the United States, or in any department or officer thereof," goes to the destruction of all limits prescribed to their power by the Constitution: that words meant by the instrument to be subsidiary only to the execution of limited powers ought not to be so construed as themselves to give unlimited powers, nor a part to be so taken as to destroy the whole residue of that instrument: that the proceedings of the General Government under color of these articles, will be a fit and necessary subject of revisal and correction, at a time of greater tranquillity, while those specified in the preceding resolutions call for immediate redress.

8. *Resolved,* That a committee of conference and correspondence be appointed, who shall have in charge to communicate the preceding resolutions to the Legislatures of the several States; to assure them that this commonwealth continues in the same esteem of their friendship and union which it has manifested from that moment at which a common danger first suggested a common union: that it considers union, for specified national purposes, and particularly to those specified in their late federal compact, to be friendly to the peace, happiness and prosperity of all the States: that faithful to that compact, according to the plain intent and meaning in which it was understood and acceded to by the several

parties, it is sincerely anxious for its preservation: that
it does also believe, that to take from the States all the
powers of self-government and transfer them to a general and consolidated government, without regard to the
special delegations and reservations solemnly agreed to
in that compact, is not for the peace, happiness or prosperity of these States; and that therefore this commonwealth is determined, as it doubts not its co-States are,
to submit to undelegated, and consequently unlimited
powers in no man, or body of men on earth: that in
cases of an abuse of the delegated powers, the members
of the general government, being chosen by the people,
a change by the people would be the constitutional remedy; but, where powers are assumed which have not
been delegated, a nullification of the act is the rightful
remedy: that every State has a natural right in cases
not within the compact, (*casus non foederis*,) to nullify
of their own authority all assumptions of power by others within their limits: that without this right, they
would be under the dominion, absolute and unlimited, or
whosoever might exercise this right of judgment for
them: that nevertheless, this commonwealth, from motives of regard and respect for its co-States, has wished
to communicate with them on the subject: that with
them alone it is proper to communicate, they alone being
parties to the compact, and solely authorized to judge in
the last resort of the powers exercised under it, Congress being not a party, but merely the creature of the
compact, and subject as to its assumptions of power to
the final judgment of those by whom, and for whose use
itself and its powers were all created and modified: that
if the acts before specified should stand, these conclusions would flow from them; that the general government may place any act they think proper on the list of
crimes, and punish it themselves whether enumerated or
not enumerated by the constitution as cognizable by
them: that they may transfer its cognizance to the Pres-

ident, or any other person, who may himself be the accuser, counsel, judge and jury, whose *suspicions* may be the evidence, his *order* the sentence, his *officer* the executioner, and his breast the sole record of the transaction: that a very numerous and valuable description of the inhabitants of these States being, by this precedent, reduced, as outlaws, to the absolute dominion of one man, and the barrier of the Constitution thus swept away from us all, no rampart now remains against the passions and the powers of a majority in Congress to protect from a like exportation, or other more grievous punishment, the minority of the same body, the legislatures, judges, governors and counsellors of the States, nor their other peaceable inhabitants, who may venture to reclaim the constitutional rights and liberties of the States and people, or who for other causes, good or bad, may be obnoxious to the views, or marked by the suspicions of the President, or be thought dangerous to his or her election, or other interests, public or personal: that the friendless alien has indeed been selected as the safest subject of the first experiment; but the citizen will soon follow, or rather, has already followed, for already sedition has marked him as its prey: that these and successive acts of the same character, unless arrested at the threshold, necessarily drive these States into revolution and blood, and will furnish new calumnies against republican government, and new pretexts for those who wish it to be believed that man cannot be governed by a rod of iron: that it would be a dangerous delusion were a confidence in the men of our choice to silence our fears for the safety of our rights: that confidence is everywhere the parent of despotism—free government is founded in jealousy, not confidence; it is jealousy, not confidence which prescribes limited constitutions, to bind down those whom we are obliged to trust with power: that our Constitution has accordingly fixed the limits to which, and no further, our confidence may

go; and let the honest advocate of confidence read the
Alien and Sedition acts, and say if the Constitution has
not been wise in fixing limits to the government it created, and whether we should be wise in destroying those
limits. Let him say what the government is, if it be not
a tyranny, which the men of our choice have conferred
on our President, and the President of our choice has
assented to, and accepted over the friendly strangers to
whom the mild spirit of our country and its laws have
pledged hospitality and protection: that the men of our
choice have more respected the bare *suspicions* of the
President, than the solid right of innocence, the claims
of justification, the sacred force of truth, and the forms
and substance of law and justice. In questions of power,
then, let no more be heard of confidence in man, but bind
him down from mischief by the chains of the Constitution. That this commonwealth does therefore call on its
co-States for an expression of their sentiments on the
acts concerning aliens, and for the punishment of certain crimes herein before specified, plainly declaring
whether these acts are or are not authorized by the federal compact. And it doubts not that their sense will be
so announced as to prove their attachment unaltered to
limited government, whether general or particular. And
that the rights and liberties of their co-States will be
exposed to no dangers by remaining embarked in a common bottom with their own. That they will concur with
this commonwealth in considering the said acts as so
palpably against the Constitution as to amount to an
undisguised declaration that that compact is not meant
to be the measure of the powers of the General Government, but that it will proceed in the exercise over these
States, of all powers whatsoever: that they will view
this as seizing the rights of the States, and consolidating
them in the hands of the General Government, with a
power assumed to bind the States (not merely as the
cases made federal, *casus foederis* but), in all cases

whatsoever, by laws made, not with their consent, but by others against their consent: that this would be to surrender the form of government we have chosen, and live under one deriving its powers from its own will, and not from our authority; and that the co-States, recurring to their natural right in cases not made federal, will concur in declaring these acts void, and of no force, and will each take measures of its own for providing that neither these acts, nor any others of the General Government not plainly and intentionally authorized by the Constitution, shall be exercised within their respective territories.

9. *Resolved,* That the said committee be authorized to communicate by writing or personal conferences, at any times or places whatever, with any person or persons who may be appointed by any one or more co-States to correspond or confer with them; and that they lay their proceedings before the next session of Assembly.

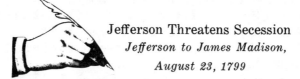

Jefferson Threatens Secession
Jefferson to James Madison,
August 23, 1799

The appeal of the Virginia and Kentucky Resolutions failed. Determined not to abandon the fight and convinced that the threat was a grave one, Jefferson wrote to Madison suggesting that the Union itself was not worth the price of liberty. The letter so alarmed Madison that he went to Monticello to calm his friend (Jefferson, after all, was Vice-President of the United States). A second set of Kentucky Resolutions, prepared by the collaboration of the author of the Declaration of Independence and the father of the Constitution, produced a more moderate tone.

I inclose you a letter I received from W. C. Nicholas three days ago. It is so advantageous that Virginia & Kentucky

should pursue the same tract on this occasion, & a difference
of plan would give such advantage to the Consolidationers
that I would immediately see you at your own house, but
that we have a stranger lying ill here, whose state has been
very critical, & who would suffer in spirits at least if not
substantially by my absence. I shall not answer Mr. N's
letter till Thursday next. Perhaps you could take a ride
about that time, so as to have a meeting here with him on
Sunday sennight, the day preceding our court. I dare say he
will not go before court, and if you could drop him a line by
post he would certainly meet you, and let us consider a little
together what is to be done. Not that I should prepare anything, but the opportunity is certainly a valuable one of
producing a concert of action. I will in the mean time give
you my ideas to reflect on. That the principles already advanced by Virginia & Kentucky are not to be yielded in
silence, I presume we all agree. I should propose a declaration or Resolution by their legislatures on this plan. 1st.
Answer the reasonings of such of the states as have ven-
tured into the field of reason, & that of the Committee of
Congress. Here they have given us all the advantage we
could wish. Take some notice of those states who have either
not answered at all, or answered without reasoning. 2. Make
a firm protestation against the principle & the precedent;
and a reservation of the rights resulting to us from these
palpable violations of the constitutional compact by the Federal government, and the approbation or acquiescence of
the several co-states; so that we may hereafter do, what we
might now rightfully do, whenever repetitions of these and
other violations shall make it evident that the Federal government, disregarding the limitations of the federal compact, mean to exercise powers over us to which we have
never assented. 3. Express in affectionate & conciliatory
language our warm attachment to union with our sister-
states, and to the instrument & principles by which we are
united; that we are willing to sacrifice to this every thing
except those rights of self government the securing of

which was the object of that compact; that not at all disposed to make every measure of error or wrong a cause of scission, we are willing to view with indulgence to wait with patience till those passions & delusions shall have passed over which the federal government have artfully & successfully excited to cover it's own abuses & to conceal it's designs; fully confident that the good sense of the American

D R A U G H T

O F *A*

FUNDAMENTAL CONSTITUTION

F O R T H E

COMMONWEALTH OF VIRGINIA.

T O the citizens of the Commonwealth of Virginia, and all others whom it may concern, the Delegates for the said Commonwealth in Convention assembled, send greeting.

It is known to you and to the world, that the government of Great Britain, with which the American states were not long since connected, assumed over them an authority unwarrantable and oppressive ; that they endeavored to enforce this authority by arms, and that the states of New Hampshire, Massachusets, Rhode island, Connecticut, New York, New Jersey, Pennsylvania, Delaware, Maryland, Virginia, North Carolina, South Carolina, and Georgia, considering resistance, with all its train of horrors, as a lesser evil than abject submission, closed in the appeal to arms. It hath pleased the sovereign disposer of all human events to give to this appeal an issue favourable to the rights of the states ; to enable them to reject for ever all dependance on a government which had shewn itself so capable of abusing the trusts reposed in it ; and to obtain from that government a solemn and explicit acknowledgment that they are free, sovereign, and independant states. During the progress of that war through which we had to labour for the establishment of our rights, the legislature of the commonwealth of Virginia, found it necessary to make a temporary organization of government for preventing anarchy, and pointing our efforts to the two important objects of war

First page of Jefferson's 1783 draft of Virginia's constitution
Beinecke Rare Book and Manuscript Library, Yale University

people and their attachment to those very rights which we are now vindicating will, before it shall be too late, rally with us round the true principles of our federal compact. But determined, were we to be disappointed in this, to sever ourselves from that union we so much value, rather than give up the rights of self government which we have reserved, & in which alone we see liberty, safety & happiness.

These things I sketch hastily, only as topics to be enlarged on, and wishing you to consider on them or what else is best to be done. At any rate let me hear from you by the post or before it if you can. Adieu affectionately.

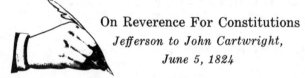

On Reverence For Constitutions
Jefferson to John Cartwright,
June 5, 1824

In this excerpt Jefferson underscores the fact that constitutions and governments should never become petrified by time into rigid and unchanging institutions. He also defines his concept of the federal-state relationship.

DEAR AND VENERABLE SIR: 1 am much indebted for your kind letter of February 29th, and for your valuable volume on the English constitution. I have read this with pleasure and much approbation, and think it has deduced the constitution of the English nation from its rightful root, the Anglo-Saxon. It is really wonderful, that so many able and learned men should have failed in their attempts to define it with correctness. No wonder then, that Paine, who thought more than he read, should have credited the great authorities who have declared, that the will of parliament is the constitution of England. So Marbois, before the French revolution, observed to me, that the Almanac Royal was the constitution of France. Your derivation of it from the Anglo-Saxons, seems to be made on legitimate principles. Having driven out the former inhabitants of that part of the island called England, they became aborigines as to you, and your lineal ancestors. They doubtless had a constitution; and although they have not left it in a written formula, to the precise text of which you may always appeal, yet they have left fragments of their history and laws, from which it may be inferred with considerable certainty. Whatever their history and laws show to have been practised with approbation, we may presume was permitted by their constitution; whatever was not so practised, was not permitted. And although this constitution was violated and set at naught by Norman force, yet force cannot change right. A perpetual claim was kept up by the nation, by their perpetual demand of a restoration of their Saxon laws, which shows they were never relinquished by the will of the nation. In the pullings and haulings of these ancient rights, between the nation, and its kings of the races of Plantagenets, Tudors and Stuarts, there was sometimes gain, and sometimes loss, until the final re-conquest of their rights from the Stuarts. The destitution and expulsion of this race broke the thread of pretended inheritance, extinguished all regal usurpations, and the nation re-entered into all its rights; and although in their bill of rights they specifically reclaimed some only, yet the omission of the others was no renunciation of the right to assume their exercise also, whenever occasion should occur. The new King received no rights or powers, but those expressly granted to him. It has ever appeared to me, that the difference between the whig and the tory of England is, that the whig deduces his rights from the Anglo-Saxon source, and the tory from the Norman. And Hume, the great apostle of toryism, says, in so many words, note AA to chapter 42, that, in the reign of the Stuarts, "it was the people who encroached upon the sovereign, not the sovereign who attempted, as is pretended, to usurp upon the people." This supposes the Norman usurpations to be rights in his successors. And again, C, 159, "the commons established a principle, which is noble in itself, and seems specious, but is belied by all history and experience, *that the people are the origin of all just power.*"

And where else will this degenerate son of science, this traitor to his fellow men, find the origin of *just* powers, if not in the majority of the society? Will it be in the minority? Or in an individual of that minority?

Our Revolution commenced on more favorable ground. It presented us an album on which we were free to write what we pleased. We had no occasion to search into musty records, to hunt up royal parchments, or to investigate the laws and institutions of a semi-barbarous ancestry. We appealed to those of nature, and found them engraved on our hearts. Yet we did not avail ourselves of all the advantages of our position. We had never been permitted to exercise self-government. When forced to assume it, we were novices in its science. Its principles and forms had entered little into our former education. We established however some, although not all its important principles. The constitutions of most of our States assert, that all power is inherent in the people; that they may exercise it by themselves, in all cases to which they think themselves competent (as in electing their functionaries executive and legislative, and deciding by a jury of themselves, in all judiciary cases in which any fact is involved), or they may act by representatives, freely and equally chosen; that it is their right and duty to be at all times armed; that they are entitled to freedom of person, freedom of religion, freedom of property, and freedom of the press. In the structure of our legislatures, we think experience has proved the benefit of subjecting questions to two separate bodies of deliberants; but in constituting these, natural right has been mistaken, some making one of these bodies, and some both, the representatives of property instead of persons; whereas the double deliberation might be as well obtained without any violation of true principle, either by requiring a greater age in one of the bodies, or by electing a proper number of representatives of persons, dividing them by lots into two chambers, and renewing the division at frequent intervals, in order to break up all cabals. Virginia, of which I am myself a native and resi-

dent, was not only the first of the States, but, I believe I
may say, the first of the nations of the earth, which assembled its wise men peaceably together to form a fundamental constitution, to commit it to writing, and place it
among their archives, where everyone should be free to
appeal to its text. But this act was very imperfect. The
other States, as they proceeded successively to the same
work, made successive improvements; and several of them,
still further corrected by experience, have, by conventions,
still further amended their first forms. My own State has
gone on so far with its *première ébauche*; but it is now
proposing to call a convention for amendment. Among other
improvements, I hope they will adopt the subdivision of our
counties into wards. The former may be estimated at an
average of twenty-four miles square; the latter should be
about six miles square each, and would answer to the hundreds of your Saxon Alfred. In each of these might be, 1st.
An elementary school; 2d. A company of militia, with its
officers; 3d. A justice of the peace and constable; 4th. Each
ward should take care of their own poor; 5th. Their own
roads; 6th. Their own police; 7th. Elect within themselves
one or more jurors to attend the courts of justice; and 8th.
Give in at their Folk-house, their votes for all functionaries
reserved to their election. Each ward would thus be a small
republic within itself, and every man in the State would
thus become an acting member of the common government,
transacting in person a great portion of its rights and
duties, subordinate indeed, yet important, and entirely within his competence. The wit of man cannot devise a more
solid basis for a free, durable and well-administered republic.

With respect to our State and federal governments, I do
not think their relations correctly understood by foreigners.
They generally suppose the former subordinate to the latter.
But this is not the case. They are co-ordinate departments
of one simple and integral whole. To the State governments
are reserved all legislation and administration, in affairs

which concern their own citizens only, and to the federal government is given whatever concerns foreigners, or the citizens of other States; these functions alone being made federal. The one is the domestic, the other the foreign branch of the same government; neither having control over the other, but within its own department. There are one or two exceptions only to this partition of power. But, you may ask, if the two departments should claim each the same subject of power, where is the common umpire to decide ultimately between them? In cases of little importance or urgency, the prudence of both parties will keep them aloof from the questionable ground; but if it can neither be avoided nor compromised, a convention of the States must be called, to ascribe the doubtful power to that department which they may think best. You will perceive by these details, that we have not yet so far perfected our constitutions as to venture to make them unchangeable. But still, in their present state, we consider them not otherwise changeable than by the authority of the people, on a special election of representatives for that purpose expressly: they are until then the *lex legum*.

But can they be made unchangeable? Can one generation bind another, and all others, in succession forever? I think not. The Creator has made the earth for the living, not the dead. Rights and powers can only belong to the persons, not to things, not to mere matter, unendowed with will. The dead are not even things. The particles of matter which composed their bodies, make part now of the bodies of other animals, vegetables, or minerals, of a thousand forms. To what then are attached the rights and powers they held while in the form of men? A generation may bind itself as long as its majority continues in life; when that has disappeared, another majority is in place, holds all the rights and powers their predecessors once held, and may change their laws and institutions to suit themselves. Nothing then is unchangeable but the inherent and unalienable rights of man. . . .

JEFFERSONIAN ECONOMICS

4 ★
★
★

Neither Jefferson nor his colleagues ever developed anything that could be called an economic system or philosophy. Jefferson himself would be the first to admit that the economic measures which he proposed or, more often, opposed, were important because of their political or diplomatic implications. As we have already seen, the bank charter was much more important because of the constitutional implications of "loose construction" interpretation than for the fiscal effects of the Bank itself. Indeed, when Jefferson became President, he followed Albert Gallatin's advice and made no effort to disturb the Bank's operation.

Again, where Alexander Hamilton regarded the prosperity of American commerce as necessary to a sound fiscal system, Jefferson saw it as a weapon of coercion which could be wielded to subdue America's enemies abroad.

Jefferson was not a doctrinaire physiocrat. In fact, by 1805 the goals he sought to achieve were distinctly Hamiltonian, although the methods he used revealed a greater concern for constitutional legitimacy. Even so, his tenure as President may have convinced him that energetic executive action was necessary, although this was incompatible with his idea of limited government and contradicted earlier strictures on executive power.

By the end of the War of 1812 he had recognized that the United States must free itself from dependence on industrial goods from Europe, and he briefly became an advocate of protective tariffs. But he never really foreswore his belief that agriculture was the bedrock of the nation's economy and "those who labor in the earth are the chosen people of God. . . ."

The Evils of Industry
From Notes on Virginia,
Query XIX, 1785

We never had an interior trade of any importance. Our exterior commerce has suffered very much from the beginning of the present contest. During this time we have manufactured within our families the most necessary articles of clothing. Those of cotton will bear some comparison with the same kinds of manufacture in Europe; but those of wool, flax and hemp are very coarse, unsightly, and unpleasant; and such is our attachment to agriculture, and such our preference for foreign manufactures, that be it wise or unwise, our people will certainly return as soon as they can, to the raising raw materials, and exchanging them for finer manufactures than they are able to execute themselves.

The political economists of Europe have established it as a principle, that every State should endeavor to manufacture for itself; and this principle, like many others, we transfer to America, without calculating the difference of circumstance which should often produce a difference of result. In Europe the lands are either cultivated, or locked up against the cultivator. Manufacture must therefore be resorted to of necessity not of choice, to support the surplus of their people. But we have an immensity of land courting the industry of the husbandman. Is it best then that all our citizens should be employed in its improvement, or that one half should be called off from that to exercise manufactures and handicraft arts for the other? Those who labor in the earth are the chosen people of God, if ever He had a chosen people, whose breasts He has made His peculiar deposit for substantial and genuine virtue. It is the focus in which he keeps alive that sacred fire, which otherwise might escape from the face of the earth. Corruption of morals in the mass of cultivators is a phenomenon of which no age nor nation has furnished an example. It is the mark set on those, who,

not looking up to heaven, to their own soil and industry, as
does the husbandman, for their subsistence, depend for it
on casualties and caprice of customers. Dependence begets
subservience and venality, suffocates the germ of virtue,
and prepares fit tools for the designs of ambition. This, the
natural progress and consequence of the arts, has sometimes
perhaps been retarded by accidental circumstances; but,
generally speaking, the proportion which the aggregate of
the other classes of citizens bears in any State to that of its
husbandmen, is the proportion of its unsound to its healthy
parts, and is a good enough barometer whereby to measure
its degree of corruption. While we have land to labor then,
let us never wish to see our citizens occupied at a work-
bench, or twirling a distaff. Carpenters, masons, smiths, are
wanting in husbandry; but, for the general operations of
manufacture, let our workshops remain in Europe. It is
better to carry provisions and materials to workmen there,
than bring them to the provisions and materials, and with
them their manners and principles. The loss by the transportation of commodities across the Atlantic will be made
up in happiness and permanence of government. The mobs
of great cities add just so much to the support of pure government, as sores do to the strength of the human body. It
is the manners and spirit of a people which preserve a republic in vigor. A degeneracy in these is a canker which
soon eats to the heart of its laws and constitution.

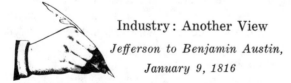

Industry: Another View

Jefferson to Benjamin Austin,
January 9, 1816

The shortage of manufactured goods from abroad, resulting
from the economic restrictions of 1809 to 1815, convinced Jefferson of the necessity for developing America's industrial capacity.

You tell me I am quoted by those who wish to continue

our dependence on England for manufactures. There was a time when I might have been so quoted with more candor, but within the thirty years which have since elapsed, how are circumstances changed! We were then in peace. Our independent place among nations was acknowledged. A commerce which offered the raw material in exchange for the same material after receiving the last touch of industry, was worthy of welcome to all nations. It was expected that those especially to whom manufacturing industry was important, would cherish the friendship of such customers by every favor, by every inducement, and particularly cultivate their peace by every act of justice and friendship. Under this prospect the question seemed legitimate, whether with such an immensity of unimproved land, courting the hand of husbandry, the industry of agriculture, or that of manufactures, would add most to the national wealth? And the doubt was entertained on this consideration chiefly, that to the labor of the husbandman a vast addition is made by the spontaneous energies of the earth on which it is employed: for one grain of wheat committed to the earth, she renders twenty, thirty, and even fifty fold, whereas to the labor of the manufacturer nothing is added. Pounds of flax, in his hands, yield, on the contrary, but pennyweights of lace. This exchange, too, laborious as it might seem, what a field did it promise for the occupations of the ocean; what a nursery for that class of citizens who were to exercise and maintain our equal rights on that element? This was the state of things in 1785, when the "Notes on Virginia" were first printed; when, the ocean being open to all nations, and their common right in it acknowledged and exercised under regulations sanctioned by the assent and usage of all, it was thought that the doubt might claim some consideration. But who in 1785 could foresee the rapid depravity which was to render the close of that century the disgrace of the history of man? Who could have imagined that the two most distinguished in the rank of nations, for science and civilization, would have suddenly descended from that honorable

eminence, and setting at defiance all those moral laws established by the Author of nature between nation and nation,
as between man and man, would cover earth and sea with
robberies and piracies, merely because strong enough to do
it with temporal impunity; and that under this disbandment
of nations from social order, we should have been despoiled
of a thousand ships, and have thousands of our citizens reduced to Algerine slavery. Yet all this has taken place. One
of these nations interdicted to our vessels all harbors of the
globe without having first proceeded to some one of hers,
there paid a tribute proportioned to the cargo, and obtained
her license to proceed to the port of destination. The other
declared them to be lawful prize if they had touched at the
port, or been visited by a ship of the enemy nation. Thus
were we completely excluded from the ocean.

Compare this state of things with that of '85, and say
whether an opinion founded in the circumstances of that
day can be fairly applied to those of the present. We have
experienced what we did not then believe, that there exists
both profligacy and power enough to exclude us from the
field of interchange with other nations: that to be independent for the comforts of life we must fabricate them ourselves. We must now place the manufacturer by the side
of the agriculturist. The former question is suppressed, or
rather assumes a new form. Shall we make our own comforts, or go without them, at the will of a foreign nation?
He, therefore, who is now against domestic manufacture,
must be for reducing us either to dependence on that foreign nation, or to be clothed in skins, and to live like wild
beasts in dens and caverns. I am not one of these; experience has taught me that manufactures are now as necessary
to our independence as to our comfort; and if those who
quote me as of a different opinion, will keep pace with me
in purchasing nothing foreign where an equivalent of domestic fabric can be obtained, without regard to difference
of price, it will not be our fault if we do not soon have a
supply at home equal to our demand, and wrest that weapon

of distress from the hand which has wielded it. If it shall
be proposed to go beyond our own supply, the question of
'85 will then recur, will our *surplus* labor be then most bene-
ficially employed in the culture of the earth, or in the fabri-
cations of art? We have time yet for consideration, before
that question will press upon us; and the maxim to be applied will depend on the circumstances which shall then
exist; for in so complicated a science as political economy,
no one axiom can be laid down as wise and expedient for
all times and circumstances, and for their contraries.

Republican Frugality
Message to Congress, December 8, 1801

The Jeffersonians were determined to reduce federal spending,
reduce taxes, and balance the budget.

. . . Other circumstances, combined with the increase of
numbers [population], have produced an augmentation of
revenue arising from consumption, in a ratio far beyond
that of population alone, and though the changes of foreign
relations now taking place so desirably for the world, may
for a season affect this branch of revenue, yet, weighing all
probabilities of expense, as well as of income, there is reasonable ground of confidence that we may now safely dispense with all the internal taxes, comprehending excises,
stamps, auctions, licenses, carriages, and refined sugars, to
which the postage on newspapers may be added, to facilitate
the progress of information, and that the remaining sources
of revenue will be sufficient to provide for the support of
government, to pay the interest on the public debts, and to
discharge the principals in shorter periods than the laws
or the general expectations had contemplated. War, indeed,
and untoward events, may change this prospect of things,
and call for expenses which the imposts could not meet; but

sound principles will not justify our taxing the industry of
our fellow citizens to accumulate treasure for wars to happen we know not when, and which might not perhaps happen but from the temptations offered by that treasure.

These views, however, of reducing our burdens, are
formed on the expectation that a sensible, and at the same
time salutary reduction, may take place in our habitual
expenditures. For this purpose, those of the civil government, the army, and navy, will need revisal.

When we consider that this government is charged with
the external and mutual relations only of these states; that
the states themselves have principal care of our persons,
our property, and our reputation, constituting the great
field of human concerns, we may well doubt whether our
organization is not too complicated, too expensive; whether
officers have not been multiplied unnecessarily, and sometimes injuriously to the service they were meant to promote.
I will cause to be laid before you an essay toward a statement of those who, under public employment of various
kinds, draw money from the treasury or from our citizens.
Time has not permitted a perfect enumeration, the ram-
ifications of office being too multiplied and remote to be
completely traced in a first trial. Among those who are
dependent on executive discretion, I have begun the reduction of what was deemed necessary. The expenses of diplomatic agency have been considerably diminished. The in-
spectors of internal revenue who were found to obstruct the
accountability of the institution, have been discontinued.
Several agencies created by executive authority, on salaries
fixed by that also, have been suppressed, and should suggest
the expediency of regulating that power by law, so as to
subject its exercises to legislative inspection and sanction.
Other reformations of the same kind will be pursued with
that caution which is requisite in removing useless things,
not to injure what is retained. But the great mass of public
offices is established by law, and, therefore, by law alone
can be abolished. Should the legislature think it expedient

to pass this roll in review, and try all its parts by the test of public utility, they may be assured of every aid and light which executive information can yield. Considering the general tendency to multiply offices and dependencies, and to increase expense to the ultimate term of burden which the citizen can bear, it behooves us to avail ourselves of every occasion which presents itself for taking off the surcharge; that it never may be seen here that, after leaving to labor the smallest portion of its earnings on which it can subsist, government shall itself consume the residue of what it was instituted to guard.

In our care, too, of the public contributions intrusted to our direction, it would be prudent to multiply barriers against their dissipation, by appropriating specific sums to every specific purpose susceptible of definition; by disallowing all applications of money varying from the appropriation in object, or transcending it in amount; by reducing the undefined field of contingencies, and thereby circumscribing discretionary powers over money; and by bringing back to a single department all accountabilities for money where the examination may be prompt, efficacious, and uniform.

An account of the receipts and expenditures of the last year, as prepared by the Secretary of the Treasury, will as usual be laid before you. The success which has attended the late sales of the public lands, shows that with attention they may be made an important source of receipt. Among the payments, those made in discharge of the principal and interest of the national debt, will show that the public faith has been exactly maintained. To these will be added an estimate of appropriations necessary for the ensuing year. This last will of course be effected by such modifications of the systems of expense, as you shall think proper to adopt.

A statement has been formed by the Secretary of War, on mature consideration, of all the posts and stations where garrisons will be expedient, and of the number of men requisite for each garrison. The whole amount is considerably short of the present military establishment. For the surplus no particular use can be pointed out. For defense against invasion, their number is as nothing; nor is it conceived needful or safe that a standing army should be kept up in time of peace for that purpose. Uncertain as we must ever be of the particular point in our circumference where an enemy may choose to invade us, the only force which can be ready at every point and competent to oppose them, is the body of neighboring citizens as formed into a militia. On these collected from the parts most convenient, in numbers proportioned to the invading foe, it is best to rely, not only to meet the first attack, but if it threatens to be permanent, to maintain the defence until regulars may be engaged to relieve them. These considerations render it important that we should at every session continue to amend the defects which from time to time show themselves in the laws for regulating the militia, until they are sufficiently perfect. Nor should we now or at any time separate, until we can say we have done everything for the militia which we could do were an enemy at our door.

The provisions of military stores on hand will be laid before you, that you may judge of the additions still requisite.

With respect to the extent to which our naval preparations should be carried, some difference of opinion may be expected to appear; but just attention to the circumstances of every part of the Union will doubtless reconcile all. A small force will probably continue to be wanted for actual service in the Mediterranean. Whatever annual sum beyond that you may think proper to appropriate to naval preparations, would perhaps be better employed in providing those articles which may be kept without waste or consumption, and be in readiness when any exigence calls them into use. Progress has been made, as will appear by papers now communicated, in providing materials for seventy-four gun ships as directed by law.

How far the authority given by the legislature for procuring and establishing sites for naval purposes has been

perfectly understood and pursued in the execution, admits
of some doubt. A statement of the expenses already incurred
on that subject, shall be laid before you. I have in certain
cases suspended or slackened these expenditures, that the
legislature might determine whether so many yards are
necessary as have been contemplated. The works at this
place are among those permitted to go on; and five of the
seven frigates directed to be laid up, have been brought and
laid up here, where, besides the safety of their position, they
are under the eye of the executive administration, as well as
of its agents, and where yourselves also will be guided by
your own view in the legislative provisions respecting them
which may from time to time be necessary. They are preserved in such condition, as well the vessels as whatever
belongs to them, as to be at all times ready for sea on a
short warning. Two others are yet to be laid up so soon as
they shall have received the repairs requisite to put them
also into sound condition. As a superintending officer will
be necessary at each yard, his duties and emoluments, hitherto fixed by the executive, will be a more proper subject
for legislation. A communication will also be made of our
progress in the execution of the law respecting the vessels
directed to be sold. . . .

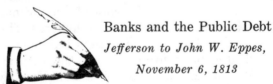

Banks and the Public Debt
Jefferson to John W. Eppes,
November 6, 1813

The Bank of the United States failed to secure a recharter in
1811. Sentiment for the renewal of the charter provoked an extensive dissertation on banking and the public debt. Though the
theories of finance are outmoded by modern standards, it is clear
that Jefferson understood the financial questions of his day very
well.

. . . After the solemn decision of Congress against the

renewal of the charter of the Bank of the United States, and the grounds of that decision (the want of constitutional power), I had imagined that question at rest, and that no more applications would be made to them for the incorporation of banks. The opposition on that ground to its first establishment, the small majority by which it was overborne, and the means practiced for obtaining it, cannot be already forgotten. The law having passed, however, by a majority, its opponents, true to the sacred principle of submission to a majority, suffered the law to flow through its term without obstruction. During this, the nation had time to consider the constitutional question, and when the renewal was proposed, they condemned it, not by their representatives in Congress only, but by express instructions from different organs of their will. Here then we might stop, and consider the memorial as answered. But, setting authority apart, we will examine whether the Legislature ought to comply with it, even if they had the power.

Proceeding to reason on this subject, some principles must be premised as forming its basis. The adequate price of a thing depends on the capital and labor necessary to produce it (In the term *capital*, I mean to include science, because capital as well as labor has been employed to acquire it.) Two things requiring the same capital and labor, should be of the same price. If a gallon of wine requires for its production the same capital and labor with a bushel of wheat, they should be expressed by the same price, derived from the application of a common measure, we may proceed to observe, that were a country so insulated as to have no commercial intercourse with any other, to confine the interchange of all its wants and supplies within itself, the amount of circulating medium, as a common measure for adjusting these exchanges, would be quite immaterial. If their circulation, for instance, were of a million dollars, and the annual produce of their industry equivalent to ten millions of bushels of wheat, the price of a bushel of wheat might be one dollar. If, then, by a progressive coinage, their medium should be doubled, the price of a bushel of wheat might become progressively two dollars, and without inconvenience. Whatever be the proportion of the circulating medium to the value of the annual produce of industry, it may be considered as the representative of that industry. In the first case, a bushel of wheat will be represented by one dollar; in the second, by two dollars. This is well explained by Hume, and seems admitted by Adam Smith. . . . But where a nation is in a full course of interchange of wants and supplies with all others, the proportion of its medium to its produce is no longer indifferent. . . . To trade on equal terms, the common measure of values should be as nearly as possible on a par with that of its corresponding nations, whose medium is in a sound state; that is to say, not in an accidental state of excess or deficiency. Now, one of the great advantages of specie as a medium is, that being of universal value, it will keep itself at a general level, flowing out from where it is too high into parts where it is lower. Whereas, if the medium be of local value only, as paper money, if too little, indeed, gold and silver will flow in to supply the deficiency; but if too much, it accumulates, banishes the gold and silver not locked up in vaults and hoards, and depreciates itself; that is to say, its proportion to the annual produce of industry being raised, more of it is required to represent any particular article of produce than in the other countries. This is agreed by Smith, . . . the principal advocate for a paper circulation; but advocating it on the sole condition that it be strictly regulated. He admits, nevertheless, that "the commerce and industry of a country cannot be so secure when suspended on the Daedalian wings of paper money, as on the solid ground of gold and silver; and that in time of war, the insecurity is greatly increased, and great confusion possible where the circulation is for the greater part in paper." . . . But in a country where loans are uncertain, and a specie circulation the only sure resource for them, the preference of that circulation assumes a far different degree of importance, as is explained in my former letters.

The only advantage which Smith proposes by substituting paper in the room of gold and silver money, . . . is "to replace an expensive instrument with one much less costly, and *sometimes* equally convenient;" that is to say, . . . "to allow the gold and silver to be sent abroad and converted into foreign goods," and to substitute paper as being a cheaper measure. But this makes no addition to the stock or capital of the nation. The coin sent out was worth as much, while in the country, as the goods imported and taking its place. It is only, then, a change of form in a part of the national capital, from that of gold and silver to other goods. He admits, too, that while a part of the goods received in exchange for the coin exported may be materials, tools and provisions for the employment of an additional industry, a part, also, may be taken back in foreign wines, silks, &c., to be consumed by idle people who produce nothing; and so far the substitution promotes prodigality, increases expense and corruption, without increasing production. So far also, then, it lessens the capital of the nation. What may be the amount which the conversion of the part exchanged for productive goods may add to the former productive mass, it is not easy to ascertain, because, as he says, . . . "it is impossible to determine what is the proportion which the circulating money of any country bears to the whole value of the annual produce. It has been computed by different authors, from a fifth to a thirtieth of that value." In the United States it must be less than in any other part of the commercial world; because the great mass of their inhabitants being in responsible circumstances, the great mass of their exchanges in the country is effected on credit, in their merchant's ledger, who supplies all their wants through the year, and at the end of it receives the produce of their farms, or other articles of their industry. It is a fact, that a farmer with a revenue of ten thousand

dollars a year, may obtain all his supplies from his merchant, and liquidate them at the end of the year, by the sale
of his produce to him, without the intervention of a single
dollar of cash. This, then, is merely barter, and in this way
of barter a great portion of the annual produce of the
United States is exchanged without the intermediation of
cash. We might safely, then, state our medium at the minimum of one-thirtieth. But what is one-thirtieth of the value
of the annual produce of the industry of the United States?
Or what is the whole value of the annual produce of the
United States? An able writer and competent judge of the
subject, in 1799, on as good grounds as probably could be
taken, estimated it, on the then population of four and a
half millions of inhabitants, to be thirty-seven and a half
millions sterling, or one hundred and sixty-eight and three-
fourths millions of dollars. . . . According to the same estimate for our present population, it will be three hundred
millions of dollars, one thirtieth of which, Smith's minimum, would be ten millions, and one-fifth, his maximum,
would be sixty millions for the quantum of circulation. But
suppose that instead of our needing the least circulating
medium of any nation, from the circumstance before mentioned, we should place ourselves in the middle term of the
calculation, to-wit: at thirty-five millions. One-fifth of this,
at the least, Smith thinks should be retained in specie, which
would leave twenty-eight millions in specie to be exported
in exchange for other commodities; and if fifteen millions
of that should be returned in productive goods, and not in
articles of prodigality, that would be the amount of capital
which this operation would add to the existing mass. But to
what mass? Not that of the three hundred millions, which
is only its gross annual produce, and is deemed its net profit,
and twenty times that its fee simple value. The profits on
landed capital may, with accuracy enough for our purpose,
be supposed on a par with those of other capital. This
would give us then for the United States, a capital of
two thousand millions, all in active employment, and exclu-

sive of unimproved lands laying in a great degree dormant. Of this, fifteen millions would be the hundred and thirty-third part. And it is for this petty addition to the capital of the nation, this minimum of one dollar, added to one hundred and thirty-three and a third, or three-fourths per cent, that we are to give up our gold and silver medium, its intrinsic solidity, its universal value, and its saving powers in time of war, and to substitute for it paper, with all its train of evils, moral, political and physical, which I will not pretend to enumerate.

There is another authority to which we may appeal for the proper quantity of circulating medium for the United States. The old Congress, when we were estimated at about two millions of people, on a long and able discussion, June 22d, 1775, decided the sufficient quantity to be two millions of dollars, which sum they then emitted. According to this, it should be eight millions, now that we are eight millions of people. This differs little from Smith's minimum of ten millions, and strengthens our respect for that estimate.

There is, indeed, a convenience in paper; its easy transmission from one place to another. But this may be mainly supplied by bills of exchange, so as to prevent any great displacement of actual coin. Two places trading together balance their dealings, for the most part, by their mutual supplies, and the debtor individuals of either may, instead of cash, remit the bills of those who are creditors in the same dealings; or may obtain them through some third place with which both have dealings. The cases would be rare where such bills could not be obtained, either directly or circuitously, and too unimportant to the nation to overweigh the train of evils flowing from paper circulation.

From eight to thirty-five millions then being our proper circulation, and two hundred millions the actual one, the memorial proposes to issue ninety millions more, because, it says, a great scarcity of money is proved by the numerous applications for banks; to wit, New York for eighteen millions, Pennsylvania ten millions, &c. The answer to this

shall be quoted from Adam Smith; . . . where speaking of
the complaints of the trader against the Scotch bankers,
who had already gone too far in their issues of paper, he
says, "those traders and other undertakers having got so
much assistance from banks, wished to get still more. The
banks, they seem to have thought, could extend their credits
to whatever sum might be wanted, without incurring any
other expense besides that of a few reams of paper. They
complained of the contracted views and dastardly spirit of
the directors of those banks, which did not, they said, extend their credits in proportion to the extension of the trade
of the country; meaning, no doubt, by the extension of that
trade, the extension of their own projects beyond what they
could carry on, either *with their own capital*, or with what
they had credit to borrow of private people in the usual
way of bond or mortgage. The banks, they seem to have
thought, were in honor bound to supply the deficiency, and
to provide them with all the capital which they wanted to
trade with." And again, . . . "when bankers discovered that
certain projectors were trading, not with any capital of
their own, but with that which they advanced them, they
endeavored to withdraw gradually, making every day greater and greater difficulties about discounting. These difficulties alarmed and enraged in the highest degree those
projectors. Their own distress, of which this prudent and
necessary reserve of the banks was no doubt the immediate
occasion, they called the distress of the country; and this
distress of the country, they said, was altogether owing to
the ignorance, pusillanimity, and bad conduct of the banks,
which did not give a sufficiently liberal aid to the spirited
undertakings of those who exerted themselves in order to
beautify, improve and enrich the country. It was the duty
of the banks, they seemed to think, to lend for as long a
time, and to as great an extent, as they might wish to borrow." It is, probably, the *good paper* of these projectors
which the memorial says, the bank being *unable* to discount, goes into the hands of brokers, who (knowing the

risk of this *good paper*) discount it at a much higher rate
than legal interest, to the great distress of the enterprising
adventurers, who had rather try trade on borrowed capital,
than go to the plough or other laborious calling. Smith again
says, . . . "that the industry of Scotland languished for want
of money to employ it, was the opinion of the famous Mr.
Law. By establishing a bank of a particular kind, which, he
seems to have imagined might issue paper to the amount of
the whole value of all the lands in the country, he proposed
to remedy this want of money. It was afterwards adopted,
with some variations, by the Duke of Orleans, at that time
Regent of France. The idea of the possibility of multiplying
paper to almost any extent, was the real foundation of what
is called the Mississippi scheme, the most extravagant project both of banking and stock jobbing, that perhaps the
world ever saw. The principles upon which it was founded
are explained by Mr. Law himself, in a discourse concerning
money and trade, which he published in Scotland when he
first proposed his project. The splendid but visionary ideas
which are set forth in that and some other works upon the
same principles, still continue to make an impression upon
many people, and have perhaps, in part, contributed to that
excess of banking which has of late been complained of both
in Scotland and in other places." The Mississippi scheme,
it is well known, ended in France in the bankruptcy of the
public treasury, the crush of thousands and thousands of
private fortunes, and scenes of desolation and distress equal
to those of an invading army, burning and laying waste
all before it.

At the time we were funding our national debt, we heard
much about "a public debt being a public blessing;" that
the stock representing it was a creation of active capital for
the aliment of commerce, manufacture and agriculture. This
paradox was well adapted to the minds of believers in
dreams, and the gulls of that size entered *bôna fide* into it.
But the art and mystery of banks is a wonderful improvement on that. It is established on the principle that *"private*

debts are a public blessing." That the evidences of those
private debts, called bank notes, become active capital, and
aliment the whole commerce, manufacturers, and agriculture of the United States. Here are a set of people, for instance, who have bestowed on us the great blessing of
running in our debt about two hundred millions of dollars,
without our knowing who they are, where they are, or what
property they have to pay this debt when called on; nay,
who have made us so sensible of the blessings of letting
them run in our debt, that we have exempted them by law
from the repayment of these debts beyond a given proportion (generally estimated at one-third). And to fill up the
measure of blessing, instead of paying, they receive an interest on what they owe from those to whom they owe; for
all the notes, or evidences of what they owe, which we see
in circulation, have been lent to somebody on an interest
which is levied again on us through the medium of commerce. And they are so ready still to deal out their liberalities to us, that they are now willing to let themselves run
in our debt ninety millions more, on our paying them the
same premium of six or eight per cent interest, and on the
same legal exemption from the repayment of more than
thirty millions of the debt, when it shall be called for. But
let us look at this principle in its original form, and its
copy will then be equally understood. "A public debt is a
public blessing." That our debt was juggled from forty-
three up to eighty millions, and funded at that amount,
according to this opinion was a great public blessing, because the evidences of it could be vested in commerce, and
thus converted into active capital, and then the more the
debt was made to be, the more active capital was created.
That is to say, the creditors could now employ in commerce
the money due them from the public, and make from it an
annual profit of five per cent, of four millions of dollars. But
observe, that the public were at the same time paying on it
an interest of exactly the same amount of four millions of
dollars. Where then is the gain to either party, which makes

it a public blessing? There is no change in the state of things, but of persons only. A has a debt due to him from the public, of which he holds their certificate as evidence, and on which he is receiving an annual interest. He wishes, however, to have the money itself, and to go into business with it. B has an equal sum of money in business, but wishes to retire, and live on the interest. He therefore gives it to A in exchange for A's certificates of public stock. Now, then, A has the money to employ in business, which B so employed before. B has the money on interest to live on, which A lived on before; and the public pays the interest to B which they paid to A before. Here is no new creation of capital, no additional money employed, nor even a change in the employment of a single dollar. The only change is of place between A and B in which we discover no creation of capital, nor public blessing. Suppose, again, the public owe nothing. Then A not having lent his money to the public, would be in possession of it himself, and would go into business without the previous operation of selling stock. Here again, the same quantity of capital is employed as in the former case, though no public debt exists. In neither case is there any creation of active capital, nor other difference than that there is a public debt in the first case, and none in the last; and we may safely ask which of the two situations is most truly a public blessing? If, then, a *public* debt be no public blessing, we may pronounce, *à fortiori*, that a private one cannot be so. If the debt which the banking companies owe be a blessing to anybody, it is to themselves alone, who are realizing a solid interest of eight or ten per cent on it. As to the public, these companies have banished all our gold and silver medium, which, before their institution, we had without interest, which never could have perished in our hands, and would have been our salvation now in the hour of war; instead of which they have given us two hundred million of froth and bubble, on which we are to pay them heavy interest, until it shall vanish into air, as Morris' notes did. We are warranted, then, in affirming that this parody on the principle of "a public debt being a public blessing," and its mutation into the blessing of private instead of public debts, is as ridiculous as the original principle itself. In both cases, the truth is, that capital may be produced by industry, and accumulated by economy; but jugglers only will propose to create it by legerdemain tricks with paper.

I have called the actual circulation of bank paper in the United States, two hundred millions of dollars. I do not recollect where I have seen this estimate; but I retain the impression that I thought it just at the time. It may be tested, however, by a list of the banks now in the United States, and the amount of their capital. I have no means of recurring to such a list for the present day; but I turn to two lists in my possession for the years of 1803 and 1804.

In 1803, there were thirty-four banks, whose capital was $28,902,000. In 1804, there were sixty-six, consequently thirty-two additional ones. Their capital is not stated, but at the average of the others (excluding the highest, that of the United States, which was of ten millions), they would be of six hundred thousand dollars each, and add 19,200,000. Making a total of $48,102,000 or say of fifty millions in round numbers. Now, everyone knows the immense multiplication of these institutions since 1804. If they have only doubled, their capital will be of one hundred millions, and if trebled, as I think probable, it will be one hundred and fifty millions, on which they are at liberty to circulate treble the amount. I should sooner, therefore, believe two hundred millions to be far below than above the actual circulation. In England, by a late parliamentary document (see *Virginia Argus* of October the 18th, 1813, and other public papers of about that date), it appears that six years ago the Bank of England had twelve millions of pounds sterling in circulation, which had increased to forty-two millions in 1812, or to one hundred and eighty-nine millions of dollars. What proportion all the other banks may add to this, I do not know; if we were allowed to suppose they equal it, this would give a circulation of three hundred and seventy-eight millions, or the double of ours on a double population. But that nation is essentially commercial, ours essentially agricultural, and needing, therefore, less circulating medium, because the produce of the husbandman comes but once a year, and is then partly consumed at home, partly exchanged by barter. The dollar, which was of four shilling and six-pence sterling, was, by the same document, stated to be then six shillings and nine pence, a depreciation of exactly fifty per cent. The average price of wheat on the continent of Europe, at the commencement of its present war with England, was about a French crown, of one hundred and ten cents, the bushel. With us it was one hundred cents, and consequently we could send it there in competition with their own. That ordinary price has now doubled with us, and more than doubled in England; and although a part of this augmentation may proceed from the war demand, yet from the extraordinary nominal rise in the prices of land and labor here, both of which have nearly doubled in that period, and are still rising with every new bank, it is evident that were a general peace to take place tomorrow, and time allowed for the re-establishment of commerce, justice, and order, we could not afford to raise wheat for much less than two dollars, while the continent of Europe, having no paper circulation, and that of its specie not being augmented, would raise it at their former price of one hundred and ten cents. It follows, then, that with our redundancy of paper, we cannot, after peace, send a bushel of wheat to Europe, unless extraordinary circumstances double its price in particular places, and that then the exporting countries of Europe could undersell us.

It is said that our paper is as good as silver, because we may have silver for it at the bank where it issues. This is not true. One, two, or three persons might have it; but a general application would soon exhaust their vaults, and leave a ruinous proportion of their paper in its intrinsic

worthless form. It is a fallacious pretence, for another reason. The inhabitants of the banking cities might obtain cash
for their paper, as far as the cash of the vaults would hold
out, but distance puts it out of the power of the country to
do this. A farmer having a note of a Boston or Charleston
bank, distant hundreds of miles, has no means of calling for
the cash. And while these calls are impracticable for the
country, the banks have no fear of their being made from
the towns; because their inhabitants are mostly on their
books, and there on sufferance only, and during good behavior.

In this state of things, we are called on to add ninety
millions more to the circulation. Proceeding in this career,
it is infallible, that we must end where the revolutionary
paper ended. Two hundred millions was the whole amount
of all the emissions of the old Congress, at which point their
bills ceased to circulate. We are now at that sum, but with
treble the population, and of course a longer tether. Our
depreciation is, as yet, but about two for one. Owing to the
support its credit receives from the small reservoirs of
specie in the vaults of the banks, it is impossible to say at
what point their notes will stop. Nothing is necessary to
effect it but a general alarm; and that may take place whenever the public shall begin to reflect on, and perceive the
impossibility that the banks should repay this sum. At
present, caution is inspired no farther than to keep prudent
men from selling property on long payments. Let us suppose the panic to arise at three hundred millions, a point to
which every session of the legislatures hasten us by long
strides. Nobody dreams that they would have three hundred
millions of specie to satisfy the holders of their notes. Were
they even to stop now, no one supposes they have two hundred millions in cash, or even the sixty-six and two-third
millions, to which amount alone the law compels them to
repay. One hundred and thirty-three and one-third millions
of loss, then, is thrown on the public by law; and as to the
sixty-six and two-thirds, which they are legally bound to

pay, and ought to have in their vaults, everyone knows there is no such amount of cash in the United States, and what would be the course with what they really have there? Their notes are refused. Cash is called for. The inhabitants of the banking towns will get what is in the vaults, until a few banks declare their insolvency; when, the general crush becoming evident, the others will withdraw even the cash they have, declare their bankruptcy at once, and leave an empty house and empty coffers for the holders of their notes. In this scramble of creditors, the country gets nothing, the towns but little. What are they to do? Bring suits? A million of creditors bring a million of suits against John Nokes and Robert Styles, wheresoever to be found? All nonsense. The loss is total. And a sum is thus swindled from our citizens, of seven times the amount of the real debt, and four times that of the fictitious one of the United States, at the close of the war. All this they will justly charge on their legislatures; but this will be poor satisfaction for the two or three hundred millions they will have lost. It is time, then, for the public functionaries to look to this. Perhaps it may not be too late. Perhaps, by giving time to the banks, they may call in and pay off their paper by degrees. But no remedy is ever to be expected while it rests with the State legislatures. Personal motive can be excited through so many avenues to their will, that, in their hands, it will continue to go on from bad to worse, until the catastrophe overwhelms us. I still believe, however, that on proper representations of the subject, a great proportion of these legislatures would cede to Congress their power of establishing banks, saving the charter rights already granted. And this should be asked, not by way of amendment to the constitution, because until three-fourths should consent, nothing could be done; but accepted from them one by one, singly, as their consent might be obtained. Any single State, even if no other should come into the measure, would find its interest in arresting foreign bank paper immediately, and its own by degrees. Specie would flow in on them as paper disappeared. Their own banks would call in and pay off their notes gradually, and their constituents would thus be saved from the general wreck. Should the greater part of the States concede, as is expected, their power over banks to Congress, besides insuring their own safety, the paper of the non-conceding States might be checked and circumscribed, by prohibiting its receipt in any of the conceding States, and even in the non-conceding as to duties, taxes, judgments, or other demands of the United States, or of the citizens of other States, that it would soon die of itself, and the medium of gold and silver be universally restored. This is what ought to be done. But it will not be done. *Carthago non delibitur*. The overbearing clamor of merchants, speculators, and projectors, will drive us before them with our eyes open, until, as in France, under the Mississippi bubble, our citizens will be overtaken by the crush of this baseless fabric, without other satisfaction than that of execrations on the heads of those functionaries, who, from ignorance, pusillanimity or corruption, have betrayed the fruits of their industry into the hands of projectors and swindlers.

When I speak comparatively of the paper emission of the old Congress and the present banks, let it not be imagined that I cover them under the same mantle. The object of the former was a holy one; for if ever there was a holy war, it was that which saved our liberties and gave us independence. The object of the latter, is to enrich swindlers at the expense of the honest and industrious part of the nation.

The sum of what has been said is, that pretermitting the constitutional question on the authority of Congress, and considering this application on the grounds of reason alone, it would be best that our medium should be so proportioned to our produce, as to be on a par with that of the countries with which we trade, and whose medium is in a sound state; that specie is the most perfect medium, because it will preserve its own level; because, having intrinsic and universal value, it can never die in our hands, and it is the surest resource of reliance in time of war; that the trifling econ-

omy of paper, as a cheaper medium, or its convenience for
transmission, weighs nothing in opposition to the advantages of the precious metals; that it is liable to be abused,
has been, is, and forever will be abused, in every country in
which it is permitted; that it is already at a term of abuse
in these States, which has never been reached by any other
nation, France excepted, whose dreadful catastrophe should
be a warning against the instrument which produced it;
that we are already at ten or twenty times the due quantity
of medium; insomuch, that no man knows what his property
is now worth, because it is bloating while he is calculating;
and still less what it will be worth when the medium shall
be relieved from its present dropsical state; and that it is a
palpable falsehood to say we can have specie for our paper
whenever demanded. Instead, then, of yielding to the cries
of scarcity of medium set up by speculators, projectors and
commercial gamblers, no endeavors should be spared to begin the work of reducing it by such gradual means as may
give time to private fortunes to preserve their poise, and
settle down with the subsiding medium; and that, for this
purpose, the States should be urged to concede to the General Government, with a saving of chartered rights, the
exclusive power of establishing banks of discount for paper.

To the existence of banks of *discount* for *cash*, as on the
continent of Europe, there can be no objection, because
there can be no danger of abuse, and they are a convenience
both to merchants and individuals. I think they should even
be encouraged, by allowing them a larger than legal interest
on short discounts, and tapering thence, in proportion as the
term of discount is lengthened, down to legal interest on
those of a year or more. Even banks of *deposit*, where cash
should be lodged, and a paper acknowledgment taken out as
its representative, entitled to a return of the cash on demand, would be convenient for remittances, travelling persons, &c. But, liable as its cash would be to be pilfered and
robbed, and its paper to be fraudulently re-issued, or issued
without deposit, it would require skilful and strict regula-

tion. This would differ from the bank of Amsterdam, in the circumstance that the cash could be redeemed on returning the note.

When I commenced this letter to you, my dear Sir, on Mr. Law's memorial, I expected a short one would have answered that. But as I advanced, the subject branched itself before me into so many collateral questions, that even the rapid views I have taken of each have swelled the volume of my letter beyond my expectations, and, I fear, beyond your patience. Yet on a revisal of it, I find no part which has not so much bearing on the subject as to be worth merely the time of perusal. I leave it then as it is; and will add only the assurances of my constant and affectionate esteem and respect.

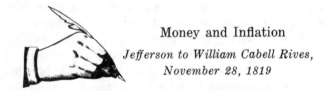

Money and Inflation
Jefferson to William Cabell Rives,
November 28, 1819

The Panic of 1819 revived Jefferson's distrust of paper money and he proposed some rather drastic remedies.

DEAR SIR: The distresses of our country, produced first by the flood, then the ebb of bank paper, are such as cannot fail to engage the interposition of the legislature. Many propositions will, of course, be offered, from all of which something may probably be culled to make a good whole. I explained to you my project, when I had the pleasure of possessing you here; and I now send its outline in writing, as I believe I promised you. Although preferable things will I hope be offered, yet some twig of this may perhaps be thought worthy of being engrafted on a better stock. But I send it with no particular object or request, but to use it as you please. Suppress it, suggest it, sound opinions, or anything else, at will, only keeping my name unmentioned, for which purpose it is copied in another hand, being ever solicitous to avoid all offence which is heavily felt, when retired from the bustle and contentions of the world. If we suffer the moral of the present lesson to pass away without improvement by the eternal suppression of bank *paper*, then indeed is the condition of our country desperate, until the slow advance of public instruction shall give to our functionaries the wisdom of their station. . . .

The plethory of circulating medium which raised the prices of everything to several times their ordinary and standard value, in which state of things many and heavy debts were contracted; and the sudden withdrawing too great a proportion of that medium, and reduction of prices far below that standard, constitute the disease under which we are now laboring, and which must end in a general revolution of property, if some remedy is not applied. That remedy is clearly a gradual reduction of the medium to its standard level, that is to say, to the level which a metallic medium will always find for itself, so as to be in equilibrio with that of the nations with which we have commerce.

To effect this,

Let the whole of the present paper medium be suspended in its circulation after a certain and not distant day.

Ascertain by proper inquiry the greatest sum of it which has at any one time been in actual circulation.

Take a certain term of years for its gradual reduction, suppose it to be five years; then let the solvent banks issue 5/6ths of that amount in new notes, to be attested by a public officer, as a security that neither more or less is issued, and to be given out in exchange for the suspended notes, and the surplus in discount.

Let 1/5th of these notes bear on their face that the bank will discharge them with specie at the end of one year; another 5th at the end of two years; a third 5th at the end of three years; and so of the 4th and 5th. They will be sure to be brought in at their respective periods of redemption.

Make it a high offence to receive or pass within this State a note of any other.

There is little doubt that our banks will agree readily to this operation; if they refuse, declare their charters forfeited by their former irregularities, and give summary process against them for the suspended notes.

The Bank of the United States will probably concur also; if not, shut their doors and join the other States in respectful, but firm applications to Congress, to concur in constituting a tribunal (a special convention, *e.g.*) for settling amicably the question of their right to institute a bank and that also of the States to do the same.

A stay-law for the suspension of executions, and their discharge at five annual instalments, should be accommodated to these measures.

Interdict forever, to both the State and national governments, the power of establishing any paper bank; for without this interdiction, we shall have the same ebbs and flows of medium, and the same revolutions of property to go through every twenty or thirty years.

In this way the value of property, keeping pace nearly with the sum of circulating medium, will descend gradually to its proper level, at the rate of about 1/5th every year, the sacrifices of what shall be sold for payment of the first instalments of debts will be moderate, and time will be given for economy and industry to come in aid of those subsequent. Certainly no nation ever abandoned to the avarice and jugglings of private individuals to regulate, according to their own interests, the quantum of circulating medium for the nation, to inflate, by deluges of paper, the nominal prices of property, and then to buy up that property at 1*s*. in the pound, having first withdrawn the floating medium which might endanger a competition in purchase. Yet this is what has been done, and will be done, unless stayed by the protecting hand of the legislature. The evil has been

produced by the error of their sanction of this ruinous
machinery of banks; and justice, wisdom, duty all require
that they should interpose and arrest it before the schemes
of plunder and spoilation desolate the country. It is believed
that harpies are already hoarding their money to commerce
these scenes on the separation of the legislature; and we
know that lands have been already sold under the hammer
for less than a year's rent.

5 ★ ★ ★ ★

JEFFERSON AND THE

PRESIDENCY

It is very easy to see Jefferson the President as the philosophical theorist brought to judgment by the realities of political necessity. John Randolph of Roanoke became completely disillusioned with his cousin, remarking that during his first term Jefferson had done little more than spell Federalism backward, "and now [1805] he is spelling it forward." The advocate of limited government had flouted constitutional authority in the course of purchasing Louisiana; the enemy of that most Hamiltonian of all institutions, the Bank of the United States, had silently acquiesced in its continuance; the relentless critic of executive power now wielded executive power as great as either of his two predecessors.

The charges have a good deal of substance. However, it must be borne in mind that Jefferson never lost his capacity to distinguish ends from means. If he urged Congress to approve the great purchase and ignore constitutional scruples, it was because they were "doing for them [the people] unauthorized what we know they would have done for themselves."

Perhaps Jefferson's greatness was in daring to bring a philosophy into the arena of practical politics without allowing himself to be hamstrung by its theoretical dogma. Dumas Malone suggested that part of Jefferson's greatness lay in his ability to have one foot guided by the political rail and the other by the philosophical without ever allowing the rails to cross.

The Jeffersonian legacy for the twentieth century is that he remained faithful to the credo that institutions exist to serve men, not the other way around. If his methods were anachronistic for the material world of the twentieth century, his firm

141

conviction that man could govern himself is a continuing reminder that the bulwark of freedom is mankind's faith in itself.

The Office of President

Jefferson to James Madison,
January 26, 1811

When our present government was first established, we had many doubts on this question [the preference of a plural over a singular executive], and many leanings towards a supreme executive counsel. It happened that at that time the experiment of such an one was commenced in France, while the single executive was under trial here. We watched the motions and effects of these two rival plans, with an interest and anxiety proportioned to the importance of a choice between them. The experiment in France failed after a short course, and not from any circumstance peculiar to the times or nation, but from those internal jealousies and dissensions in the Director, which will ever arise among men equal in power, without a principal to decide and control their differences. We had tried a similar experiment in 1784, by establishing a committee of the States, composed of member from every State, then thirteen, to exercise the executive functions during the recess of Congress. They fell immediately into schisms and dissensions, which became at length so inveterate as to render all co-operation among them impracticable; they dissolved themselves, abandoning the helm of government, and it continued without a head, until Congress met the ensuing winter. This was then imputed to the temper of two or three individuals; but the wise ascribed it to the nature of man.

The failure of the French Directory, and from the same cause, seems to have authorized a belief that the form of a plurality, however promising in theory, is impracticable with men constituted with the ordinary passions. While the tranquil and steady tenor of our single executive, during a course of twenty-two years of the most tempestuous times the history of the world has ever presented, gives a rational hope that this important problem is at length solved. Aided by the counsels of a cabinet of heads of departments, originally four, but now five, with whom the President consults, either singly or altogether, he has the benefit of their wisdom and information, brings their views to one centre, and produces an unity of action and direction in all the branches of the government.

The excellence of this construction of the executive power has already manifested itself here under very opposite circumstances. During the administration of our first President, his cabinet of four members was equally divided by as marked an opposition of principle as monarchism and republicanism could bring into conflict. Had that cabinet been a directory, like positive and negative quantities in algebra, the opposing wills would have balanced each other and produced a state of absolute inaction. But the President heard with calmness the opinions and reasons of each, decided the course to be pursued, and kept the government steadily in it, unaffected by the agitation. The public knew well the dissensions of the cabinet, but never had an uneasy thought on their account, because they knew also they had provided a regulating power which would keep the machine in steady movement. I speak with an intimate knowledge of these scenes, *quorum pars fui*; as I may of others of a character entirely opposite.

The third administration, which was of eight years, presented an example of harmony in a cabinet of six persons, to which perhaps history has furnished no parallel. There never arose, during the whole time, an instance of an unpleasant thought or word between the members. We sometimes met under differences of opinion, but scarcely ever failed, by conversing and reasoning, so to modify each other's ideas, as to produce an unanimous result. Yet, able and amicable as these members were, I am not certain this would have been the case, had each possessed equal and

independent powers. Illdefined limits of their respective departments, jealousies, trifling at first, but nourished and
strengthened by repetition of occasions, intrigues without
doors of designing persons to build an importance to themselves on the divisions of others, might, from small beginnings, have produced persevering oppositions. But the
power of decision in the President left no object for internal
dissension, and external intrigue was stifled in embryo by
the knowledge which incendiaries possessed, that no division they could foment would change the course of the executive power. I am not conscious that my participations in
executive authority have produced any bias in favor of
the single executive; because the parts I have acted have
been in the subordinate, as well as superior stations, and
because, if I know myself, what I have felt, and what I have
wished, I know that I have never been so well pleased as
when I could shift power from my own, on the shoulders
of others; nor have I ever been able to conceive how any
rational being could propose happiness to himself from the
exercise of power over others.

I am still, however, sensible of the solidity of your principle, that, to insure the safety of the public liberty, its
depository should be subject to be changed with the greatest
ease possible, and without suspending or disturbing for a
moment the movements of the machine of government. You
apprehend that a single executive, with eminence of talent,
and destitution of principle, equal to the object, might, by
usurpation, render his powers hereditary. Yet I think history furnishes as many examples of a single usurper arising
out of a government by a plurality, as of temporary trusts
of power in a single hand rendered permanent by usurpation. I do not believe, therefore, that this danger is lessened
in the hands of a plural executive. Perhaps it is greatly
increased, by the state of inefficiency to which they are
liable from feuds and divisions among themselves. The conservative body you propose might be so constituted, as,
while it would be an admirable sedative in a variety of

smaller cases, might also be a valuable sentinel and check on the liberticide views of an ambitious individual. I am friendly to this idea.

But the true barriers of our liberty in this country are our State governments; and the wisest conservative power ever contrived by man, is that of which our Revolution and present government found us possessed. Seventeen distinct States, amalgamated into one as to their foreign concerns, but single and independent as to their internal administration, regularly organized with a legislature and governor resting on the choice of the people, and enlightened by a free press, can never be so fascinated by the arts of one man, as to submit voluntarily to his usurpation. Nor can they be constrained to it by any force he can possess. While that may paralyze the single State in which it happens to be encamped, sixteen others, spread over a country of two thousand miles diameter, rise up on every side, ready organized for deliberation by a constitutional legislature, and for action by their governor, constitutionally the commander of the militia of the State, that is to say, of every man in it able to bear arms; and that militia, too, regularly formed into regiments and battalions, into infantry, cavalry and artillery, trained under officers general and subordinate, legally appointed, always in readiness, and to whom they are already in habits of obedience. The republican government of France was lost without a struggle, because the party of *"un et indivisible"* had prevailed; no provincial organizations existed to which the people might rally under authority of the laws, the seats of the directory were virtually vacant, and a small force sufficed to turn the legislature out of their chamber, and to salute its leader chief of the nation. But with us, sixteen out of seventeen States rising in mass, under regular organization, and legal commanders, united in object and action by their Congress, or, if that be in *duresse*, by a special convention, present such obstacles to an usurper as forever to stifle ambition in the first conception of that object.

The President and Diplomacy

Memorandum, April 24, 1790

Although the point at issue was a minor one, Jefferson took the occasion to state his belief in the sweeping authority of the executive branch in foreign affairs.

The constitution having declared that the President shall *nominate* and, by and with the advice and consent of the Senate, shall *appoint* ambassadors, other public ministers, and consuls, the President desired my opinion whether the Senate has a right to negative the *grade* he may think it expedient to use in a foreign mission as well as the *person* to be appointed.

I think the Senate has no right to negative the *grade*.

The constitution has divided the powers of government into three branches, Legislative, Executive and Judiciary, lodging each with a distinct magistracy. The Legislative it has given completely to the Senate and House of Representatives. It has declared that the Executive powers shall be vested in the President, submitting special articles of it to a negative by the Senate, and it has vested the Judiciary power in the courts of justice, with certain exceptions also in favor of the Senate.

The transaction of business with foreign nations is Executive altogether. It belongs, then, to the head of that department, except as to such portions of it as are specially submitted to the Senate. Exceptions are to be construed strictly.

The constitution itself indeed has taken care to circumscribe this one within very strict limits; for it gives the *nomination* of the foreign agents to the President, the *appointments* to him and the Senate jointly, and the *commissioning* to the President.

This analysis calls our attention to the strict import of

each term. To *nominate* must be to *propose*. *Appointment*
seems that act of the will which constitutes or makes the
agent, and the *commission* is the public evidence of it. But
there are still other acts previous to these not specially
enumerated in the constitution, to wit: 1st. The destination
of a mission to the particular country where the public
service calls for it, and second the character or grade to be
employed in it. The natural order of all these is first, destination; second, grade; third, nomination; fourth, appointment; fifth, commission. If *appointment* does not comprehend the neighboring acts of *nomination* or *commission*,
(and the constitution says it shall not, by giving them exclusively to the President,) still less can it pretend to comprehend those previous and more remote, of *destination* and
grade.

The constitution, analysing the three last, shows they do
not comprehend the two first. The fourth is the only one it
submits to the Senate, shaping it into a right to say that
"A or B is unfit to be appointed." Now, this cannot comprehend a right to say that "A or B is indeed fit to be appointed," but the grade fixed on is not the fit one to employ,
or, "our connections with the country of his destination are
not such as to call for any mission."

The Senate is not supposed by the constitution to be
acquainted with the concerns of the Executive department.
It was not intended that these should be communicated to
them, nor can they therefore be qualified to judge of the
necessity which calls for a mission to any particular place,
or of the particular grade, more or less marked, which special and secret circumstances may call for. All this is left
to the President. They are only to see that no unfit person
be employed.

It may be objected that the Senate may by continual neg-
atives on the *person*, do what amounts to a negative on the
grade, and so, indirectly, defeat this right of the President.
But this would be a breach of trust; an abuse of power confided to the Senate, of which that body cannot be supposed

capable. So the President has a power to convoke the Legislature, and the Senate might defeat that power by refusing
to come. This equally amounts to a negative on the power of
convoking. Yet nobody will say they possess such a negative,
or would be capable of usurping it by such oblique means.
If the constitution had meant to give the Senate a negative
on the grade or destination, as well as the person, it would
have said so in direct terms, and not left it to be effected by
a sidewing. It could never mean to give them the use of one
power through the abuse of another.

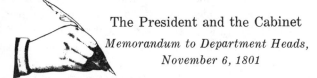

The President and the Cabinet

Memorandum to Department Heads,
November 6, 1801

Jefferson attempted to set up an administrative structure
which would preserve the balance between departmental initiative
and responsibility while insuring that the President was in firm
control.

DEAR SIR: Coming all of us into executive office, new,
and unfamiliar with the course of business previously practised, it was not to be expected we should, in the first outset,
adopt in every part a line of proceeding so perfect as to
admit no amendment. The mode and degrees of communication, particularly between the Presidents and heads of departments, have not been practised exactly on the same
scale in all of them. Yet it would certainly be more safe and
satisfactory for ourselves as well as the public, that not
only the best, but also an uniform course of proceeding as
to manner and degree, should be observed. Having been a
member of the first administration under Gen. Washington,
I can state with exactness what our course then was. Letters
of business came addressed sometimes to the President, but
most frequently to the heads of departments. If addressed
to himself, he referred them to the proper department to be

acted on: if to one of the secretaries, the letter, if it required no answer, was communicated to the President,
simply for his information. If an answer was requisite, the
secretary of the department communicated the letter and
his proposed answer to the President. Generally they were
simply sent back after perusal, which signified his approbation. Sometimes he returned them with an informal note,
suggesting an alteration or a query. If a doubt of any importance arose, he reserved it for conference. By this means,
he was always in accurate possession of all facts and proceedings in every part of the Union, and to whatsoever
department they related; he formed a central point for the
different branches; preserved an unity of object and action
among them; exercised that participation in the suggestion
of affairs which his office made incumbent on him; and met
himself the due responsibility for whatever was done. During Mr. Adams' administration, his long and habitual absences from the seat of government, rendered this kind of
communication impracticable, removed him from any share
in the transaction of affairs, and parcelled out the government in fact, among four independent heads, drawing sometimes in opposite directions. That the former is preferable
to the latter course, cannot be doubted. It gave, indeed, to
the heads of departments the trouble of making up, once a
day, a packet of all their communications for the perusal of
the President; it commonly also retarded one day their dis-
patches by mail. But in pressing cases, this injury was
prevented by presenting that case singly for immediate
attention; and it produced us in return the benefit of his
sanction for every act we did. Whether any change of circumstances may render a change in this procedure necessary, a little experience will show us. But I cannot withhold
recommending to heads of departments, that we should
adopt this course for the present, leaving any necessary
modification of it to time and trial. I am sure my conduct
must have proved, better than a thousand declarations
would, that my confidence in those whom I am so happy

as to have associated with me, is unlimited, unqualified and unabated. I am well satisfied that everything goes on with a wisdom and rectitude which I could not improve. If I had the universe to choose from, I could not change one of my associates to my better satisfaction. My sole motives are these before expressed, as governing the first administration in chalking out the rules of their proceeding; adding to them only a sense of obligation imposed on me by the public will, to meet personally the duties to which they have appointed me. If this mode of proceeding shall meet the approbation of the heads of departments, it may go into execution without giving them the trouble of an answer; if any other can be suggested which would answer our views and add less to their labors, that will be a sufficient reason for my preferring it to my own proposition, to the substance of which only, and not the form, I attach any importance.

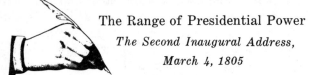

The Range of Presidential Power

The Second Inaugural Address,
March 4, 1805

Here Jefferson gave an accounting of his first administration. Although he is careful to credit Congress for the "merit of the measures," there is ample evidence that it is the President's hand which guides the ship of state. Note his attitude toward the press, despite the fact that he himself was the target for some outrageous attacks.

Proceeding, fellow citizens, to that qualification which the constitution requires, before my entrance on the charge again conferred upon me, it is my duty to express the deep sense I entertain of this new proof of confidence from my fellow citizens at large, and the zeal with which it inspires me, so to conduct myself as may best satisfy their just expectations.

On taking this station on a former occasion, I declared

the principles on which I believed it my duty to administer the affairs of our commonwealth. My conscience tells me that I have, on every occasion, acted up to that declaration, according to its obvious import, and to the understanding of every candid mind.

In the transaction of your foreign affairs, we have endeavored to cultivate the friendship of all nations, and especially of those with which we have the most important relations. We have done them justice on all occasions, favored where favor was lawful, and cherished mutual interests and intercourse on fair and equal terms. We are firmly convinced, and we act on that conviction, that with nations, as with individuals, our interests soundly calculated, will ever be found inseparable from our moral duties; and history bears witness to the fact, that a just nation is taken on its word, when recourse is had to armaments and wars to bridle others.

At home, fellow citizens, you best know whether we have done well or ill. The suppression of unnecessary offices, of useless establishments and expenses, enabled us to discontinue our internal taxes. These covering our land with officers, and opening our doors to their institutions, had already begun that process of domiciliary vexation which, once entered, is scarcely to be restrained from reaching successively every article of produce and property. If among these taxes some minor ones fell which had not been inconvenient, it was because their amount would not have paid the officers who collected them, and because, if they had any merit, the state authorities might adopt them, instead of others less approved.

The remaining revenue on the consumption of foreign articles, is paid cheerfully by those who can afford to add foreign luxuries to domestic comforts, being collected on our seaboards and frontiers only, and incorporated with the transactions of our mercantile citizens, it may be the pleasure and pride of an American to ask, what farmer, what mechanic, what laborer, ever sees a tax-gatherer of the

United States? These contributions enable us to support the current expenses of the government, to fulfill contracts with foreign nations, to extinguish the native right of soil within our limits, to extend those limits, and to apply such a surplus to our public debts, as places at a short day their final redemption, and that redemption once effected, the revenue thereby liberated may, by a just repartition among the states, and a corresponding amendment of the constitution, be applied, *in time of peace*, to rivers, canals, roads, arts, manufactures, education, and other great objects within each state. *In time of war*, if injustice, by our selves or others, must sometimes produce war, increased as the same revenue will be increased by population and consumption, and aided by other resources reserved for that crisis, it may meet within the year all the expenses of the year, without encroaching on the rights of future generations, by burdening them with the debts of the past. War will then be but a suspension of useful works, and a return to a state of peace, a return to the progress of improvement.

I have said, fellow citizens, that the income reserved had enabled us to extend our limits; but that extension may possibly pay for itself before we are called on, and in the meantime, may keep down the accruing interest; in all events, it will repay the advances we have made. I know the acquisition of Louisiana has been disapproved by some, from a candid apprehension that the enlargement of our territory would endanger its union. But who can limit the extent to which the federative principle may operate effectively? The larger our association, the less will it be shaken by local passions; and in any view, is it not better that the opposite bank of the Mississippi should be settled by our own brethren and children, than by strangers of another family? With which shall we be most likely to live in harmony and friendly intercourse?

In matters of religion, I have considered that its free exercise is placed by the constitution independent of the

powers of the general government. I have therefore undertaken, on no occasion, to prescribe the religious exercises
suited to it; but have left them, as the constitution found
them, under the direction and discipline of state or church
authorities acknowledged by the several religious societies.

The aboriginal inhabitants of these countries I have regarded with the commiseration their history inspires. Endowed with the faculties and the rights of men, breathing
an ardent love of liberty and independence, and occupying
a country which left them no desire but to be undisturbed,
the stream of overflowing population from other regions
directed itself on these shores; without power to divert, or
habits to contend against, they have been overwhelmed by
the current, or driven before it; now reduced within limits
too narrow for the hunter's state, humanity enjoins us to
teach them agriculture and the domestic arts; to encourage
them to that industry which alone can enable them to maintain their place in existence, and to prepare them in time
for that state of society, which to bodily comforts adds the
improvement of the mind and morals. We have therefore
liberally furnished them with the implements of husbandry
and household use; we have placed among them instructors
in the arts of first necessity; and they are covered with the
aegis of the law against aggressors from among ourselves.

But the endeavors to enlighten them on the fate which
awaits their present course of life, to induce them to exercise their reason, follow its dictates, and change of circumstances, have powerful obstacles to encounter; they are
combated by the habits of their bodies, prejudice of their
minds, ignorance, pride, and the influence of interested and
crafty individuals among them, who feel themselves something in the present order of things, and fear to become
nothing in any other. These persons inculcate a sanctimonious reverence for the customs of their ancestors; that
whatsoever they did, must be done through all time; that
reason is a false guide, and to advance under its counsel, in

their physical, moral, or political condition, is perilous innovation; that their duty is to remain as their Creator made them, ignorance being safety, and knowledge full of danger; in short, my friends, among them is seen the action and counteraction of good sense and bigotry; they, too, have their anti-philosophers, who find an interest in keeping things in their present state, who dread reformation, and exert all their faculties to maintain the ascendency of habit over the duty of improving our reason, and obeying its mandates.

In giving these outlines, I do not mean, fellow citizens, to arrogate to myself the merit of the measures; that is due, in the first place, to the reflecting character of our citizens at large, who, by the weight of public opinion, influence and strengthen the public measures; it is due to the sound discretion with which they select from among themselves those to whom they confide the legislative duties; it is due to the zeal and wisdom of the characters thus selected, who lay the foundations of public happiness in wholesome laws, the execution of which alone remains for others; and it is due to the able and faithful auxiliaries, whose patriotism has associated with me in the executive functions.

During this course of administration, and in order to disturb it, the artillery of the press has been levelled against us, charged with whatsoever its licentiousness could devise or dare. These abuses of an institution so important to freedom and science, are deeply to be regretted, inasmuch as they tend to lessen its usefulness, and to sap its safety; they might, indeed, have been corrected by the wholesome punishments reserved and provided by the laws of the several States against falsehood and defamation; but public duties more urgent press on the time of the public servants, and the offenders have therefore been left to find their punishment in the public indignation.

Nor was it uninteresting to the world, that an experiment should be fairly and fully made, whether freedom of discus-

sion, unaided by power, is not sufficient for the propagation
and protection of truth—whether a government, conducting
itself in the true spirit of its constitution, with zeal and
purity, and doing no act which it would be unwilling the
whole world should witness, can be written down by falsehood and defamation. The experiment has been tried; you
have witnessed the scene; our fellow citizens have looked on,
cool and collected; they saw the latent source from which
these outrages proceeded; they gathered around their public functionaries, and when the constitution called them to
the decision by suffrage, they pronounced their verdict,
honorable to those who had served them, and consolatory to
the friend of man, who believes he may be intrusted with
his own affairs.

No inference is here intended, that the laws, provided by
the State against false and defamatory publications, should
not be enforced; he who has time, renders a service to public morals and public tranquillity, in reforming these abuses
by the salutary coercions of the law; but the experiment is
noted, to prove that, since truth and reason have maintained
their ground against false opinions in league with false
facts, the press, confined to truth, needs no other legal restraint; the public judgment will correct false reasoning
and opinions, on a full hearing of all parties; and no other
definite line can be drawn between the inestimable liberty
of the press and its demoralizing licentiousness. If there be
still improprieties which this rule would not restrain, its
supplement must be sought in the censorship of public
opinion.

Contemplating the union of sentiment now manifested so
generally, as auguring harmony and happiness to our future
course, I offer to our country sincere congratulations. With
those, too, not yet rallied to the same point, the disposition
to do so is gaining strength; facts are piercing through the
veil drawn over them; and our doubting brethren will at
length see, that the mass of their fellow citizens, with whom

they cannot yet resolve to act, as to principles and measures, think as they think, and desire what they desire; that our wish, as well as theirs, is, that the public efforts may be directed honestly to the public good, that peace be cultivated, civil and religious liberty unassailed, law and order preserved, equality of rights maintained, and that state of property, equal or unequal, which results to every man from his own industry, or that of his fathers. When satisfied of these views, it is not in human nature that they should not approve and support them; in the meantime, let us cherish them with patient affection; let us do them justice, and more than justice, in all competitions of interest; and we need not doubt that truth, reason, and their own interests, will at length prevail, will gather them into the fold of their country, and will complete their entire union of opinion, which gives to a nation the blessing of harmony, and the benefit of all its strength.

I shall now enter on the duties to which my fellow citizens have again called me, and shall proceed in the spirit of those principles which they have approved. I fear not that any motives of interest may lead me astray; I am sensible of no passion which could seduce me knowingly from the path of justice; but the weakness of human nature, and the limits of my own understanding, will produce errors of judgment sometimes injurious to your interests. I shall need, therefore, all the indulgence I have heretofore experienced—the want of it will certainly not lessen with increasing years. I shall need, too, the favor of that Being in whose hands we are, who led our forefathers, as Israel of old, from their native land, and planted them in a country flowing with all the necessaries and comforts of life; who has covered our infancy with his providence, and our riper years with his wisdom and power; and to whose goodness I ask you to join with me in supplications, that he will so enlighten the minds of your servants, guide their councils, and prosper their measures, that whatsoever they do, shall result in your good, and shall secure to you the peace, friendship, and approbation of all nations.

Appointments to Office

Jefferson to Elias Simpson and Others,
July 12, 1801

Should the party faithful be rewarded by appointment to public office? Should a good public servant be ousted if he were an active member of the opposition party? Between claims of the victors for spoils and charges of political vindictiveness toward the Federalists, Jefferson satisfied no one—probably not even himself.

GENTLEMEN,—I have received the remonstrance you were pleased to address to me, on the appointment of Samuel Bishop to the office of collector of New Haven, lately vacated by the death of David Austin. The right of our fellow-citizens to represent to the public functionaries their opinion on proceedings interesting to them, is unquestionably a constitutional right, often useful, sometimes necessary, and will always be respectfully acknowledged by me.

Of the various executive duties, no one excites more anxious concern that that of placing the interests of our fellow citizens in the hands of honest men, with understandings sufficient for their stations. No duty, at the same time, is more difficult to fulfill. The knowledge of characters possessed by a single individual is, of necessity, limited. To seek out the best through the whole Union, we must resort to other information, which, from the best of men, acting disinterestedly and with the purest motives, is sometimes incorrect. In the case of Samuel Bishop, however, the subject of your remonstrance, time was taken, information was sought, and such obtained as could leave no room for doubt

of his fitness. From private sources it was learned that his
understanding was sound, his integrity pure, his character
unstained. And the offices confided to him within his own
State, are public evidences of the estimation in which he is
held by the State in general, and the city and township
particularly in which he lives. He is said to be the town
clerk, a justice of the peace, mayor of the city of New
Haven, an office held at the will of the legislature, chief
judge of the court of common pleas for New Haven county,
a court of high criminal and civil jurisdiction wherein most
causes are decided without the right of appeal or review,
and sole judge of the court of probates, wherein he singly
decides all questions of wills, settlement of estates, testate
and intestate, appoints guardians, settles their accounts,
and in fact has under his jurisdiction and care all the property real and personal of persons dying. The last two offices,
in the annual gift of the legislature, were given to him in
May last. Is it possible that the man to whom the legislature
of Connecticut has so recently committed trusts of such
difficulty and magnitude, is "unfit to be the collector of the
district of New Haven" though acknowledged in the same
writing, to have obtained all this confidence "by a long life
of usefulness?" It is objected, indeed, in the remonstrance,
that he is seventy-seven years of age; but at a much more
advanced age, our Franklin was the ornament of human
nature. He may not be able to perform in person, all the
details of his office; but if he gives us the benefit of his
understanding, his integrity, his watchfulness, and takes
care that all the details are well performed by himself or
his necessary assistants, all public purposes will be answered. The remonstrance, indeed, does not allege that the
office *has been* illy conducted, but only apprehends that it
will be so. Should this happen in event, be assured I will do
in it what shall be just and necessary for the public service.
In the meantime, he should be tried without being pre-
judged.

The removal, as it is called, of Mr. Goodrich, forms an-

other subject of complaint. Declarations by myself in favor
of *political tolerance*, exhortations to *harmony* and affection
in social intercourse, and to respect for the *equal rights* of
the minority, have, on certain occasions, been quoted and
misconstrued into assurances that the tenure of offices was
to be undisturbed. But could candor apply such a construction? It is not indeed in the remonstrance that we find it;
but it leads to the explanations which that calls for. When
it is considered, that during the late administration, those
who were not of a particular sect of politics were excluded
from all office; when, by a steady pursuit of this measure,
nearly the whole offices of the United States were monopo-
lized by that sect; when the public sentiment at length
declared itself, and burst open the doors of honor and confidence to those whose opinions they more approved, was it
to be imagined that this monopoly of office was still to be
continued in the hands of the minority? Does it violate their
equal rights, to assert some rights in the majority also? Is it
political intolerance to claim a proportionate share in the
direction of the public affairs? Can they not *harmonize* in
society unless they have everything in their own hands? If
the will of the nation, manifested by their various elections,
calls for an administration of government according with
the opinions of those elected; if, for the fulfilment of that
will, displacements are necessary, with whom can they so
justly begin as with persons appointed in the last moments
of an administration, not for its own aid, but to begin a
career at the same time with their successors, by whom
they had never been approved, and who could scarcely expect from them a cordial co-operation. Mr. Goodrich was
one of these. Was it proper for him to place himself in office,
without knowing whether those whose agent he was to be
would have confidence in his agency? Can the preference of
another, as successor to Mr. Austin, be candidly called
a removal of Mr. Goodrich? If a due participation of office
is a matter of right, how are vacancies to be obtained?
Those by death are few; by resignation, none. Can any other

mode than that of removal be proposed? This is a painful
office; but it is made my duty, and I meet it as such. I proceed in the operation with deliberation and inquiry, that it
may injure the best men least, and effect the purposes of
justice and public utility with the least private distress;
that it may be thrown, as much as possible, on delinquency,
on oppression, on intolerance, on ante-revolutionary adherence to our enemies.

The remonstrance laments "that a change in the administration must produce a change in the subordinate officers;"
in other words, that it should be deemed necessary for all
officers to think with their principal? But on whom does
this imputation bear? On those who have excluded from
office every shade of opinion which was not theirs? Or on
those who have been so excluded? I lament sincerely that
unessential differences of opinion should ever have been
deemed sufficient to interdict half the society from the
rights and the blessings of self-government, to proscribe
them as unworthy of every trust. It would have been to me
a circumstance of great relief, had I found a moderate participation of office in the hands of the majority. I would
gladly have left to time and accident to raise them to their
just share. But their total exclusion calls for prompter cor-
rections. I shall correct the procedure; but that done, return
with joy to that state of things, when the only questions
concerning a candidate shall be, is he honest? Is he capable?
Is he faithful to the Constitution?

I tender you the homage of my high respect.

National Security

Special Message, January 22, 1807

Jefferson was criticized for the apparent vindictiveness with
which he pursued the conspirator, Aaron Burr. Yet, as President,

Portrait of Aaron Burr by John Vanderlyn
Yale University Art Gallery

one of his principal duties was the security of the nation. Were not stern measures necessary against those who plotted treason?

TO THE SENATE AND HOUSE OF REPRESENTATIVES OF THE UNITED STATES: Agreeably to the request of the House of Representatives, communicated in their resolution of the sixteenth instant, I proceed to state under the reserve therein expressed, information received touching an illegal combination of private individuals against the peace and safety of the Union, and a military expedition planned by them against the territories of a power in amity with the United States, with the measures I have pursued for suppressing the same. I had for some time been in the constant expectation of receiving such further information as would have enabled me to lay before the legislature the termination as well as the beginning and progress of this scene of depravity, so far as it has been acted on the Ohio and its waters. From this the state and safety of the lower country might have been estimated on probable grounds, and the delay was indulged the rather, because no circumstance had yet made it necessary to call in the aid of the legislative functions. Information now recently communicated has brought us nearly to the period contemplated. The mass of what I have received, in the course of these transactions, is voluminous, but little has been given under the sanction of an oath, so as to constitute formal and legal evidence. It is chiefly in the form of letters, often containing such a mixture of rumors, conjectures, and suspicions, as render it difficult to sift out the real facts, and unadvisable to hazard more than general outlines, strengthened by concurrent information, or the particular credibility of the relater. In this state of the evidence, delivered sometimes too under the restriction of private confidence, neither safety nor justice will permit the exposing names, except that of the principal actor, whose guilt is placed beyond question.

Some time in the latter part of September, I received intimations that designs were in agitation in the western

country, unlawful and unfriendly to the peace of the Union;
and that the prime mover in these was Aaron Burr, heretofore distinguished by the favor of his country. The grounds
of these intimations being inconclusive, the objects uncertain, and the fidelity of that country known to be firm, the
only measure taken was to urge the informants to use their
best endeavors to get further insight into the designs and
proceedings of the suspected persons, and to communicate
them to me.

It was not until the latter part of October, that the objects of the conspiracy began to be perceived, but still so
blended and involved in mystery that nothing distinct could
be singled out for pursuit. In this state of uncertainty as to
the crime contemplated, the acts done, and the legal course
to be pursued, I thought it best to send to the scene where
these things were principally in transaction, a person, in
whose integrity, understanding, and discretion, entire confidence could be reposed, with instructions to investigate
the plots going on, to enter into conference (for which he
had sufficient credentials) with the governors and all other
officers, civil and military, and with their aid to do on the
spot whatever should be necessary to discover the designs
of the conspirators, arrest their means, bring their persons
to punishment, and to call out the force of the country to
suppress any unlawful enterprise in which it should be
found they were engaged. By this time it was known that
many boats were under preparation, stores of provisions
collecting, and an unusual number of suspicious characters
in motion on the Ohio and its waters. Besides despatching
the confidential agent to that quarter, orders were at the
same time sent to the governors of the Orleans and Mississippi territories, and to the commanders of the land and
naval forces there, to be on their guard against surprise,
and in constant readiness to resist any enterprise which
might be attempted on the vessels, posts, or other objects
under their care; and on the 8th of November, instructions
were forwarded to General Wilkinson to hasten an accom-

modation with the Spanish commander on the Sabine, and as soon as that was effected, to fall back with his principal force to the hither bank of the Mississippi, for the defence of the intersecting points on that river. By a letter received from that officer on the 25th of November, but dated October 21st, we learn that a confidential agent of Aaron Burr had been deputed to him, with communications partly written in cipher and partly oral, explaining his designs, exaggerating his resources, and making such offers of emolument and command, to engage him and the army in his unlawful enterprise, as he had flattered himself would be successful. The general, with the honor of a soldier and fidelity of a good citizen, immediately despatched a trusty officer to me with information of what had passed, proceeding to establish such an understanding with the Spanish commandant on the Sabine as permitted him to withdraw his force across the Mississippi, and to enter on measures for opposing the projected enterprise.

The general's letter, which came to hand on the 25th of November, as has been mentioned, and some other information received a few days earlier, when brought together, developed Burr's general designs, different parts of which only had been revealed to different informants. It appeared that he contemplated two distinct objects, which might be carried on either jointly or separately, and either the one or the other first, as circumstances should direct. One of these was the severance of the Union of these States by the Alleghany mountains; the other, an attack on Mexico. A third object was provided, merely ostensible, to wit: the settlement of a pretended purchase of a tract of country on the Washita, claimed by a Baron Bastrop. This was to serve as the pretext for all his preparations, an allurement for such followers as really wished to acquire settlements in that country, and a cover under which to retreat in the event of final discomfiture of both branches of his real design.

He found at once that the attachment of the western country to the present Union was not to be shaken; that its dissolution could not be effected with the consent of its inhabitants, and that his resources were inadequate, as yet, to effect it by force. He took his course then at once, determined to seize on New Orleans, plunder the bank there, possess himself of the military and naval stores, and proceed on his expedition to Mexico; and to this object all his means and preparations were now directed. He collected from all the quarters where himself or his agents possessed influence, all the ardent, restless, desperate, and disaffected persons who were ready for any enterprise analogous to their characters. He seduced good and well-meaning citizens, some by assurances that he possessed the confidence of the government and was acting under its secret patronage, a pretence which obtained some credit from the state of our differences with Spain; and others by offers of land in Bastrop's claim on the Washita.

This was the state of my information of his proceedings about the last of November, at which time, therefore, it was first possible to take specific measures to meet them. The proclamation of November 27th, two days after the receipt of General Wilkinson's information, was now issued. Orders were despatched to every intersecting point on the Ohio and Mississippi, from Pittsburg to New Orleans, for the employment of such force either of the regulars or of the militia, and of such proceedings also of the civil authorities, as might enable them to seize on all the boats and stores provided for the enterprise, to arrest the persons concerned, and to suppress effectually the further progress of the enterprise. A little before the receipt of these orders in the State of Ohio, our confidential agent, who had been diligently employed in investigating the conspiracy, had acquired sufficient information to open himself to the governor of that State, and apply for the immediate exertion of the authority and power of the State to crush the combination.

Governor Tiffin and the legislature, with a promptitude, and energy, and patriotic zeal, which entitle them to a distinguished place in the affection of their sister States, effected the seizure of all the boats, provisions, and other preparations within their reach, and thus gave a first blow, materially disabling the enterprise in its outset.

In Kentucky, a premature attempt to bring Burr to justice, without sufficient evidence for his conviction, had produced a popular impression in his favor, and a general disbelief of his guilt. This gave him an unfortunate opportunity of hastening his equipments. The arrival of the proclamation and orders, and the application and information of our confidential agent, at length awakened the authorities of that State to the truth, and then produced the same promptitude and energy of which the neighboring State had set the example. Under an act of their legislature of December 23d, militia was instantly ordered to different important points, and measures taken for doing whatever could yet be done. Some boats (accounts vary from five to double or treble that number) and persons (differently estimated from one to three hundred) had in the meantime passed the falls of the Ohio, to rendezvous at the mouth of the Cumberland, with others expected down that river.

Not apprized, till very late, that any boats were building on Cumberland, the effect of the proclamation had been trusted to for some time in the State of Tennessee; but on the 19th of December, similar communications and instructions with those of the neighboring States were despatched by express to the governor, and a general officer of the western division of the State, and on the 23d of December our confidential agent left Frankfort for Nashville, to put into activity the means of that State also. But by information received yesterday, I learn that on the 22d of December, Mr. Burr descended the Cumberland with two boats merely of accommodation, carrying with him from that State no quota toward his unlawful enterprise. Whether after the arrival of the proclamation, of the orders, or of our agent, any exertion which could be made by that State, or the orders of the governor of Kentucky for calling out the militia at the mouth of Cumberland, would be in time to arrest these boats, and those from the falls of the Ohio, is still doubtful.

On the whole, the fugitives from Ohio, with their associates from Cumberland, or any other place in that quarter, cannot threaten serious danger to the city of New Orleans.

By the same express of December nineteenth, orders were sent to the governors of New Orleans and Mississippi, supplementary to those which had been given on the twenty-fifth of November, to hold the militia of their territories in readiness to co-operate for their defence, with the regular troops and armed vessels then under command of General Wilkinson. Great alarm, indeed, was excited at New Orleans by the exaggerated accounts of Mr. Burr, disseminated through his emissaries, of the armies and navies he was to assemble there. General Wilkinson had arrived there himself on the 24th of November, and had immediately put into activity the resources of the place for the purpose of its defence; and on the tenth of December he was joined by his troops from the Sabine. Great zeal was shown by the inhabitants generally, the merchants of the place readily agreeing to the most laudable exertions and sacrifices for manning the armed vessels with their seamen, and the other citizens manifesting unequivocal fidelity to the Union, and a spirit of determined resistance to their expected assailants.

Surmises have been hazarded that this enterprise is to receive aid from certain foreign powers. But these surmises are without proof or probability. The wisdom of the measures sanctioned by Congress at its last session had placed us in the paths of peace and justice with the only powers with whom we had any differences, and nothing has happened since which makes it either their interest or ours to pursue another course. No change of measures has taken place on our part; none ought to take place at this time. With the one, friendly arrangement was then proposed, and the law deemed necessary on the failure of that was suspended to give time for a fair trial of the issue. With the same power, negotiation is still preferred, and provisional measures only are necessary to meet the event of rupture. While, therefore, we do not deflect in the slightest degree from the course we then assumed, and are still pursuing, with mutual consent, to restore a good understanding, we are not to impute to them practices as irreconcilable to interest as to good faith, and changing necessarily the relations of peace and justice between us to those of war. These surmises are, therefore, to be imputed to the vauntings of the author of this enterprise, to multiply his partisans by magnifying the belief of his prospects and support.

By letters from General Wilkinson, of the 14th and 18th of September, which came to hand two days after date of the resolution of the House of Representatives, that is to say, on the morning of the 18th instant, I received the important affidavit, a copy of which I now communicate, with extracts of so much of the letters as come within the scope of the resolution. By these it will be seen that of three of the principal emissaries of Mr. Burr, whom the general had caused to be apprehended, one had been liberated by *habeas corpus*, and the two others, being those particularly employed in the endeavor to corrupt the general and army of the United States, have been embarked by him for our ports in the Atlantic States, probably on the consideration that an impartial trial could not be expected during the present agitations of New Orleans, and that that city was not as yet a safe place of confinement. As soon as these persons shall arrive, they will be delivered to the custody of the law, and left to such course of trial, both as to place and process, as its functionaries may direct. The presence of the highest judicial authorities, to be assembled at this place within a few days, the means of pursuing a sounder course of proceedings here than elsewhere, and the aid of the executive means, should the judges have occasion to use them, render it equally desirable for the criminals as for the public, that being already removed from the place where they were first apprehended, the first regular arrest should take place here, and the course of proceedings receive here its proper direction.

Presidential Papers

Memorandum to the National Archives, December 29, 1801

Do the letters and documents of the President belong to him or to the nation? Jefferson draws a distinction which few Presidents have observed.

SIR: Having no confidence that the office of the private secretary of the President of the U.S. will ever be a regular and safe deposit for public papers or that due attention will ever be paid on their transmission from one Secretary or President to another, I have, since I have been in office, sent every paper, which I deem merely public, and coming to my hands, to be deposited in one of the offices of the heads of departments; so that I shall never add a single paper to those constituting the records of the President's office; nor, should any accident happen to me, will there be any papers in my possession which ought to go into any public office. I make the selection regularly as I go along, retaining in my possession only my private papers, or such as, relating to public subjects, were meant still to be personally confidential for myself. Mr. Meredith the late treasurer, in obedience to the law which directs the Treasurer's accounts to be transmitted to and remain with the President, having transmitted his accounts, I send them to you to be deposited for safe keeping in the domestic branch of the office of Secretary of State, which I suppose to be the proper one. Accept assurances of my affectionate esteem and high respect.

Presidential Protocol

November, 1803

The Republican President was determined to do away with the "monarchist" pretensions of his predecessors. The only two formal occasions in the Executive Mansion were the Fourth of July and New Year's Day.

i.   In order to bring the members of society together in the first instance, the custom of the country has established that residents shall pay the first visit to strangers, and, among strangers, first comers to later comers, foreign and domestic; the character of stranger ceasing after the first visits. To this rule there is a single exception. Foreign ministers, from the necessity of making themselves known, pay the first visit to the ministers of the nation, which is returned.

ii.   When brought together in society, all are perfectly equal, whether foreign or domestic, titled or untitled, in or out of office.

All other observances are but exemplifications of these two principles.

I.   1st.   The families of foreign ministers, arriving at the seat of government, receive the first visit from those of the national ministers, as from all other residents.

2d.   Members of the Legislature and of the Judiciary, independent of their offices, have a right as strangers to receive the first visit.

II.   1st.   No title being admitted here, those of foreigners give no precedence.

2d.   Differences of grade among diplomatic members, give no precedence.

3d.   At public ceremonies, to which the government invites the presence of foreign ministers and their families, a convenient seat or station will be provided for them, with any other strangers invited and the families of the national ministers, each taking place as they arrive, and without any precedence.

4th. To maintain the principle of equality, or of pele mele, and prevent the growth of precedence out of courtesy, the members of the Executive will practice at their own houses, and recommend an adherence to the ancient usage of the country, of gentlemen in mass giving precedence to the ladies in mass, in passing from one apartment where they are assembled into another.

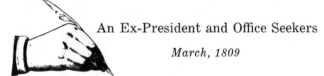

An Ex-President and Office Seekers

March, 1809

After his retirement, Jefferson received so many requests for recommendations that he had this answer printed for mailing replies.

The friendship which has long subsisted between the President of the United States and myself gave me reason to expect, on my retirement from office, that I might often receive applications to interpose with him on behalf of persons desiring appointments. Such an abuse of his dispositions towards me would necessarily lead to the loss of them, and to the transforming me from the character of a friend to that of an unreasonable and troublesome solicitor. It therefore became necessary for me to lay down as a law for my future conduct never to interpose in any case, either with him or the heads of departments (from whom it must go to him) in any application whatever for office. To this rule I must scrupulously adhere, for were I to depart from it in a single instance I could no longer plead it with truth to my friends in excuse for my not complying with their requests. I hope therefore that the declining it in the present, as in every other case, will be ascribed to its true cause, the obligation of this general law, and not to any disinclination existing in this particular case; and still less to an unwillingness to be useful to my friends on all occasions not forbidden by a special impropriety.

JEFFERSON AND THE ART OF DIPLOMACY

6
★
★
★
★

With the outbreak of war in Europe in 1792, American governmental leaders, including George Washington, Thomas Jefferson, and Alexander Hamilton, quickly concluded that the safety of the United States lay in a policy of neutrality. Since the United States was, at best, a second-rate power, this course involved a delicate and dangerous game which lasted for twenty years.

It was impossible for the United States to isolate herself in North America because its thriving commerce was necessary to the nation's economic life. Maintaining neutrality and continuing to trade with the warring powers of Europe inevitably brought the United States into diplomatic conflict with the two major antagonists, England and France. The numerous clashes between Jefferson's pro-French attitudes and Alexander Hamilton's tendency to take a pro-British view have often obscured the fact that both men were preeminently American and that it was the safety and security of the United States which was the overriding objective of their respective policies.

Louis Hacker in *Alexander Hamilton and the American Tradition* has written, "A Hamiltonian would be a realist in foreign affairs today as Hamilton was in the 1790's; a Jeffersonian would be an idealist." Hacker thus preserves the myth begun by Jefferson's contemporaries, and continued by historians since, that he was a woolly-minded dreamer whose head was perpetually surrounded by philosophical clouds.

What was remarkable about Jefferson was that, despite the fact that he was a philosopher who dealt with idealistic abstractions, he did not allow this to interfere with the realities of politics and diplomacy. He was fully capable of playing the game of *realpolitick*, of placing his moral abstractions on the shelf while he pursued the objective of national security. When the War of the French Revolution began, the United States was still party to treaties which dated back to the War of Independence when France had rendered indispensable aid to the cause of American freedom. Faced with possible conflicts between these obligations and the policy of neutrality, Jefferson's appraisal was coldly realistic.

The French Alliance

Memorandum, April 28, 1793

I proceed in compliance with the requisition of the President to give an opinion in writing on the general question, whether the United States have a right to renounce their treaties with France, or to hold them suspended til the government of that country shall be established?

In the consultation at the President's on the 19th inst., the Secretary of the Treasury took the following positions and consequences. France was a monarchy when we entered into treaties with it; but it has declared itself a republic, and is preparing a republican form of government. As it may issue in a republic or a military despotism, or something else which may possibly render our alliance with it dangerous to ourselves, we have a right of election to renounce the treaty altogether, or to declare it suspended till their government shall be settled in the form it is ultimately to take; and then we may judge whether we will call the treaties into operation again, or declare them forever null. Having that right of election, now, if we receive their minister without any qualifications, it will amount to an act of election to continue the treaties; and if the change they are undergoing should issue in a form which should bring danger on us, we shall not be then free to renounce them. To elect to continue them is equivalent to the making a new treaty, at this time, in the same form, that is to say, with a clause of guarantee, during a war, is a departure from neutrality, and would make us associates in the war. To renounce or suspend the treaties, therefore, is a necessary act of neutrality.

If I do not subscribe to the soundness of this reasoning, I do most fully to its ingenuity. I shall now lay down the principles which, according to my understanding, govern the case.

I consider the people who constitute a society or nation as the source of all authority in that nation; as free to transact their common concerns by any agents they think proper; to change these agents individually, or the organization of them in form or function whenever they please; that all the acts done by these agents under the authority of the nation, are the acts of the nation, are obligatory to them and enure to their use, and can in no wise be annulled or affected by any change in the form of the government, or of the persons administering it, consequently the treaties between the United States and France, were not treaties between the United States and Louis Capet, but between the two nations of America and France; and the nations remaining in existence, though both of them have since changed their forms of government, the treaties are not annulled by these changes. The law of nations, by which this question is to be determined, is composed of three branches. 1. The moral law of our nature. 2. The usages of nations. 3. Their special conventions. The first of these only concerns this question, that is to say the moral law to which man has been subjected by his creator, and of which his feelings or conscience, as it is sometimes called, are the evidence with which his creator has furnished him. The moral duties which exist between individual and individual in a state of nature, accompany them into a state of society, and the aggregate of the duties of all the individuals composing the society constitutes the duties of that society towards any other; so that between society and society the same moral duties exist as did between the individuals composing them,

while in an unassociated state, and their maker not having
released them from those duties on their forming themselves into a nation. Compacts then, between nation and
nation, are obligatory on them by the same moral law
which obliges individuals to observe their compacts. There
are circumstances, however, which sometimes excuse the
non-performance of contracts between man and man; so
are there also between nation and nation. When performance, for instance, becomes *impossible*, non-performance is
not immoral; so if performance becomes *self-destructive* to
the party, the law of self-preservation overrules the laws of
obligation in others. For the reality of these principles I
appeal to the true fountains of evidence, the head and heart
of every rational and honest man. It is there nature has
written her moral laws, and where every man may read
them for himself. He will never read there the permission
to annul his obligations for a time, or forever, whenever
they become dangerous, useless, or disagreeable; certainly
not when merely useless or disagreeable, as seems to be
said in an authority which has been quoted, (Vattel, p. 2,
197) and though he may, under certain degrees of danger,
yet the danger must be imminent, and the degree great. Of
these, it is true, that nations are to be judges for themselves; since no one nation has a right to sit in judgment
over another, but the tribunal of our consciences remains,
and that also of the opinion of the world. These will revise
the sentence we pass in our own case, and as we respect
these, we must see that in judging ourselves we have honestly done the part of impartial and rigorous judges.

But reason which gives this right of self-liberation from
a contract in certain cases, has subjected it to certain just
limitations.

The danger which absolves us must be great, inevitable
and imminent. Is such the character of that now apprehended from our treaties with France? What is that
danger?

1.   Is it that if their government issues in a military des-

potism, an alliance with them may taint us with despotic principles? But their government when we allied ourselves to it, was perfect despotism, civil, and military, yet the treaties were made in that very state of things, and, therefore, that danger can furnish no just cause.

2.   Is it that their government may issue in a republic, and too much strengthen our republican principles? But this is the hope of the great mass of our constituents, and not their dread. They do not look with longing to the happy mean of a limited monarchy.

3.   But, says the doctrine I am combatting, the change the French are undergoing, may possibly end in something we know not what, and may bring on us danger we know not whence. In short, it may end in a Rawhead and bloody bones in the dark. Very well—let Raw-head and bloody bones come. We shall be justified in making our peace with him by renouncing our ancient friends and his enemies; for observe, it is not the *possibility of danger* which absolves a party from his contract, for that possibility always exists, and in every case. It existed in the present one, at the moment of making the contract. If *possibilities* would void contracts, there never could be a valid contract, for possibilities hang over everything. Obligation is not suspended till the danger is become real, and the moment of it so imminent, that we can no longer avoid decision without forever losing the opportunity to do it. But can a danger which has not yet taken its shape, which does not yet exist, and never may exist which cannot therefore be defined—can such a danger, I ask, be so imminent that if we fail to pronounce on it in this moment, we can never have another opportunity of doing it?

4.   As to the danger apprehended, Is it that (the treaties remaining valid) the clause guaranteeing their West Indian lands will engage us in the war? But does the

guarantee engage us to enter into the war on any event? Are we to enter into it before we are called on by our allies?

Have we been called on by them? Shall we ever be called on?

Is it their interest to call on us?

Can they call on us before their islands are invaded, or immediately threatened?

If they can save themselves, have they a right to call on us?

Are we obliged to go to war at once, without trying peaceable negotiations with their enemy?

If all these questions are against us, there are still others left behind.

Are we in a condition to go to war?

Can we be expected to begin before we are in condition?

Will the islands be lost if we do not save them?

Have we the means of saving them?

If we cannot save them, are we bound to go to war for a desperate object?

Many, if not most of these questions offer grounds of doubt whether the clause of guarantee will draw us into the war. Consequently, if this be danger apprehended, it is not yet certain enough to authorize us in sound morality to declare, at this moment, the treaties null.

5.   Is danger apprehended from the 17th article of the treaty of commerce, which admits French ships of war and privateers to come and go freely, with prizes made on their enemies, while their enemies are not to have the same privilege with prizes made on the French? But Holland and Prussia have approved of this article in our treaty with France, by subscribing to an express salvo of it in our treaties with them. . . . And England, in her last treaty with France (Art. 40), has entered into the same stipulation verbatim,

and placed us in her ports on the same footing in which she is in ours, in case of a war of either of us with France. If we are engaged in such a war, England must receive prizes made on us by the French, and exclude those made on the French by us. Nay, further; in this very article of her treaty with France, is a salvo of any similar article in any anterior treaty of either party; and ours with France being anterior, this salvo confirms it expressly. Neither of these three powers, then, have a right to complain of this article in our treaty.

6. Is the danger apprehended from the 22d article of our treaty of commerce, which prohibits the enemies of France from fitting out privateers in our posts, or selling their prizes here; but we are free to refuse the same thing to France, there being no stipulation to the contrary; and we ought to refuse it on principles of fair neutrality.

7. But the reception of a minister from the republic of France, without qualifications, it is thought, will bring us into danger; because this, it is said, will determine the continuance of the treaty, and take from us the right of self-liberation, when at any time hereafter our safety would require us to use it. The reception of the minister at all (in favor of which Colonel Hamilton has given his opinion, though reluctantly, as he confessed), is an acknowledgment of the legitimacy of their government; and if the qualifications meditated are to deny that legitimacy, it will be a curious compound which is to admit and to deny the same thing. But I deny that the reception of a minister has anything to do with the treaties. There is not a word in either of them about sending ministers. This has been done between us under the common usage of nations, and can have no effect either to continue or annul the treaties.

But how can any act of election have the effect to continue

a treaty which is acknowledged to be going on still?—for it was not pretended the treaty was void, but only voidable if we choose to declare it so. To make it void, would require an act of election, but to let it go on, requires only that we should do nothing; and doing nothing can hardly be an infraction of peace or neutrality.

But I go further and deny that the most explicit declaration made at this moment that we acknowledge the obligation of the treaties, could take from us the right of noncompliance at any future time, when compliance would involve us in great and inevitable danger. . . .

[There follows a detailed examination of the principles of international law.]

. . . After evidence so copious and explicit of the respect of this author [Emmeric de Vattel] for the sanctity of treaties, we should hardly have expected that his authority would have been resorted to for a wanton invalidation of them whenever they should become merely *useless or disagreeable*. We should hardly have expected that, rejecting all the rest of his book, this scrap would have been culled and made the hook whereon to hang such a chain of immoral consequences. Had the passage accidentally met our eye, we should have imagined it had fallen from the author's pen under some momentary view, not sufficiently developed to found a conjecture what he meant, and we may certainly affirm that a fragment like this cannot weigh against the authority of all other writers; against the uniform and systematic doctrine of the very work from which it is torn; against the moral feelings and the reason of all honest men. If the terms of the fragment are not misunderstood, they are in full contradiction to all the written and unwritten evidences of morality. If they are misunderstood, they are no longer a foundation for the doctrines which have been built on them.

But even had this doctrine been as true as it is manifestly false, it would have been asked, to whom is it that the treaties with France have become *disagreeable*? How will it be proved that they are *useless*?

The conclusion of the sentence suggests a reflection too strong to be suppressed, "for the party may say with truth that it would not have allied itself with this nation if it had been under the present form of its government." The republic of the United States allied itself with France when under a despotic government. She changes her government, and declares it shall be a republic; prepares a form of republic extremely free, and in the meantime is governing herself as such. And it is proposed that America shall declare the treaties void, because it may say with truth that it would not have allied itself with that nation if it had been under the present form of its government. Who is the American who can say with truth that he would not have allied himself to France if she had been a republic? Or that a republic of any form would be as *disagreeable* as her ancient despotism?

Upon the whole I conclude, that the treaties are still binding, notwithstanding the change of government in France; that no part of them but the clause of guarantee holds up *danger*, even at a distance, and consequently that a liberation from no other part would be prepared in any case; that if that clause may ever bring *danger*, it is neither extreme nor imminent, nor even probable that the authority for renouncing a treaty, when *useless or disagreeable*, is either misunderstood or in opposition to itself, to all other writers, and to every moral feeling; that were it not so, these treaties are in fact neither useless or disagreeable; that the receiving a minister from France at this time is an act of no significance with respect to the treaties, amounting neither to an admission nor denial of them, forasmuch as he comes not under any stipulation in them; that were it an explicit admission, or were it an express declaration of their obligation now to be made, it would not take from us that right which exists at all times, of liberating ourselves when an adherence to the treaties would be *ruinous* or *destructive* to the society; and that the not renouncing the treaties now is so far from being a breach of neutrality, that the doing it would be the breach, by giving just cause of war to France.

Commerce and Diplomacy

Report to Congress,
December 16, 1793

Economic coercion became one of the basic concepts of Jeffersonian foreign policy.

. . . Our navigation involves still higher considerations. As a branch of industry, it is valuable, but as a resource of defence, essential.

Its value, as a branch of industry, is enhanced by the dependence of so many other branches on it. In times of general peace it multiplies competitors for employment in transportation, and so keeps that at its proper level; and in times of war, that is to say, when those nations who may be our principal carriers, shall be at war with each other, if we have not within ourselves the means of transportation, our produce must be exported in belligerent vessels, at the increased expense of war-freight and insurance, and the articles which will not bear that, must perish on our hands.

But it is as a resource of defence that our navigation will admit neither neglect nor forbearance. The position and circumstances of the United States leave them nothing to fear on their land-board, and nothing to desire beyond their present rights. But on their seaboard, they are open to injury, and they have there, too, a commerce which must be protected. This can only be done by possessing a respectable body of citizen-seamen, and of artists and establishments in readiness for ship-building.

Were the ocean, which is the common property of all, open to the industry of all, so that every person and vessel should be free to take employment wherever it could be found, the United States would certainly not set the example of appropriating to themselves, exclusively, any portion of the common stock of occupation. They would rely on the enterprise and activity of their citizens for a due participation of the benefits of the seafaring business, and for keeping the marine class of citizens equal to their object. But if particular nations grasp at undue shares, and, more especially, if they seize on the means of the United States, to convert them into aliment for their own strength, and withdraw them entirely from the support of those to whom they belong, defensive and protecting measures become necessary on the part of the nation whose marine resources are thus invaded; or it will be disarmed of its defence; its productions will lie at the mercy of the nation which has possessed itself exclusively of the means of carrying them, and its politics may be influenced by those who command its commerce. The carriage of our own commodities, if once established in another channel, cannot be resumed in the moment we may desire. If we lose the seamen and artists whom it now occupies, we lose the present means of marine defence, and time will be requisite to raise up others, when disgrace or losses shall bring home to our feelings the error of having abandoned them. The materials for maintaining our due share of navigation, are ours in abundance. And, as to the mode of using them, we have only to adopt the principles of those who put us on the defensive, or other equivalent and better fitted to our circumstances.

The following principles, being founded in reciprocity, appear perfectly just, and to offer no cause of complaint to any nation:

1. Where a nation imposes high duties on our productions, or prohibits them altogether, it may be proper for us to do the same by theirs; first burdening or excluding those productions which they bring here, in competition with our own of the same kind; selecting next, such manufactures as we take from them in greatest quantity,

and which, at the same time, we could the soonest furnish to ourselves, or obtain from other countries; imposing on them duties lighter at first, but heavier and heavier afterwards, as other channels of supply open. Such duties have the effect of indirect encouragement to domestic manufactures of the same kind, may induce the manufacturer to come himself into these States, where cheaper subsistence, equal laws, and a vent of his wares, free of duty, may ensure him the highest profits from his skill and industry. And here, it would be in the power of the State governments to co-operate essentially, by opening the resources of encouragement which are under their control, extending them liberally to artists in those particular branches of manufacture for which their soil, climate, population and other circumstances have matured them, and fostering the precious efforts and progress of *household* manufacture, by some patronage suited to the nature of its objects, guided by the local informations they possess, and guarded against abuse by their presence and attentions. The oppressions on our agriculture, in foreign ports, would thus be made the occasion of relieving it from a dependence on the councils and conduct of others, and of promoting arts, manufactures and population at home.

2. Where a nation refuses permission to our merchants and factors to reside within certain parts of their dominions, we may, if it should be thought expedient, refuse residence to theirs in any and every part of ours, or modify their transactions.

3. Where a nation refuses to receive in our vessels any productions but our own, we may refuse to receive, in theirs, any but their own productions. The first and second clauses of the bill reported by the committee, are well formed to effect this object.

4. Where a nation refuses to consider any vessel as ours which has not been built within our territories, we

should refuse to consider as theirs, any vessel not built within their territories.

5. Where a nation refuses to our vessels the carriage even of our own productions, to certain countries under their domination, we might refuse to theirs of every description, the carriage of the same productions to the same countries. But as justice and good neighborhood would dictate that those who have no part in imposing the restriction on us, should not be the victims of measures adopted to defeat its effect, it may be proper to confine the restriction to vessels owned or navigated by any subjects of the same dominant power, other than the inhabitants of the country to which the said productions are to be carried. And to prevent all inconvenience to the said inhabitants, and to our own, by too sudden a check on the means of transportation, we may continue to admit the vessels marked for future exclusion, on an advanced tonnage, and for such length of time only, as may be supposed necessary to provide against that inconvenience.

The establishment of some of these principles by Great Britain, alone, has already lost us in our commerce with that country and its possessions, between eight and nine hundred vessels of near 40,000 tons burden, according to statements from official materials, in which they have confidence. This involves a proportional loss of seamen, shipwrights, and ship-building, and is too serious a loss to admit forbearance of some effectual remedy.

It is true we must expect some inconvenience in practice from the establishment of discriminating duties. But in this, as in so many other cases, we are left to choose between two evils. These inconveniences are nothing when weighed against the loss of wealth and loss of force, which will follow our perseverance in the plan of indiscrimination. When once it shall be perceived that we are either in the system or in the habit of giving equal advantages to those who ex-

tinguish our commerce and navigation by duties and prohibitions, as to those who treat both with liberality and
justice, liberality and justice will be converted by all into
duties and prohibitions. It is not to the moderation and
justice of others we are to trust for faith and equal access
to market with our productions, or for our due share in the
transportation of them; but to our own means of independence, and the firm will to use them. Nor do the inconveniences of discrimination merit consideration. Not one of the
nations before mentioned, perhaps not a commercial nation
on earth, is without them. In our case one distinction alone
will suffice: that is to say, between nations who favor our
productions and navigation, and those who do not favor
them. One set of moderate duties, say the present duties, for
the first, and a fixed advance on these as to some articles,
and prohibitions as to others, for the last.

Still, it must be repeated that friendly arrangements are
preferable with all who will come into them; and that we
should carry into such arrangements all the liberality and
spirit of accommodation which the nature of the case will
admit.

France has, of her own accord, proposed negotiations for
improving, by a new treaty on fair and equal principles, the
commercial relations of the two countries. But her internal
disturbances have hitherto prevented the prosecution of
them to effect, though we have had repeated assurances of
a continuance of the disposition.

Proposals of friendly arrangement have been made on
our part, by the present government, to that of Great
Britain, as the message states; but, being already on as
good a footing in law, and a better in fact, than the most
favored nation, they have not, as yet, discovered any disposition to have it meddled with.

We have no reason to conclude that friendly arrangements would be declined by the other nations, with whom
we have such commercial intercourse as may render them
important. In the meanwhile, it would rest with the wisdom

of Congress to determine whether, as to those nations, they will not surcease *ex parte* regulations, on the reasonable presumption that they will concur in doing whatever justice and moderation dictate should be done.

"Free Ships Make Free Goods"
Memorandum, December 20, 1793

The right of neutrals to trade in time of war was laid down by the American Congress in 1776. President Woodrow Wilson was still insisting on this right in 1917.

A doubt being entertained whether the use of word *modern*, as applied to the *law of nations* in the President's proclamation, be not inconsistent with ground afterwards taken in a letter to Genet, I will state the matter while it is fresh in my mind—beginning it from an early period.

It cannot be denied that according to the general law of nations, the goods of an enemy are lawful prize in the bottom of a friend, and the goods of a friend privileged in the bottom of an enemy; or in other words, that *the goods follow the owner*. The inconvenience of this principle in subjecting neutral vessels to vexatious searches at sea, has for more than a century rendered it usual for nations to substitute a *conventional* principle *that the goods shall follow the bottom*, instead of the *natural* one before mentioned. France has done it in all her treaties; so I believe had Spain, before the American Revolution. Britain had not done it. When that war had involved those powers, Russia, foreseeing that her commerce would be much harassed by the British ships, engaged Denmark, Sweden, and Portugal to arm, and to declare that the conventional principle should be observed by the powers at war, towards neutrals, and that they would make common cause against the party who should violate it; declaring expressly, at the same time, that that Convention should be in force only during the war then existing. Holland acceded to the Convention, and Britain instantly attacked her. But the other neutral powers did not think proper to comply with their stipulation of making common cause. France declared at once that she would conform to the conventional principle. This in fact imposed no new obligation on her, for she was already bound by her treaties with all those powers to observe that principle. Spain made the same declaration. Congress gave similar orders to their vessels; but Congress afterwards gave instructions to their ministers abroad not to engage them in any future combination of powers for the general enforcement of the conventional principle that goods should follow the bottom, as this might at some time or other engage them in a war for other nations; but to introduce the principle separately with every nation by the treaties they were authorized to make with each. It has been already done with France and Holland, and it was afterwards done with Prussia, and made a regular part in every treaty they proposed to others. After the war, Great Britain established it between herself and France. When she engaged in the present war with France, it was thought extremely desirable for us to get this principle admitted by her, and hoping that as she had acceded to it in one instance, she might be induced to admit it as a principle now settled by the common consent of nations (for every nation, belligerent or neutral, had stipulated it on one or more occasions), that she might be induced to consider it as now become a *conventional* law of nations, I proposed to insert the word *modern* in the proclamation, to open upon her the idea that we should require the acquiescence in that principle as the condition of our remaining in peace. It was thought desirable by the other gentlemen; but having no expectation of any effect from it, they acquiesced in the insertion of the word, merely to gratify me. I had another view, which I did not mention to them, because I apprehended it would occasion the loss of the word.

By the ancient law of nations, e.g., in the time of the

Romans, the furnishing a limited aid of troops, though stipulated, was deemed a cause of war. This is one of the improvements in the law of nations. I thought we might conclude, by parity of reasoning, that the guaranteeing a limited portion of territory, in a stipulated case, might not, by the modern law of nations, be a cause of war. I therefore meant by the introduction of that word, to lay the foundation of the execution of our guarantee, by way of negotiation with England. The word was, therefore, introduced, and a strong letter was written to Mr. Pinckney to observe to Great Britain that we were bound by our treaties with the other belligerent powers to observe the same principles during this war: that we were willing to observe the same principles towards her; and indeed, that we considered it as essential to proceed by the same rule to all, and to propose to her to select those articles concerning our conduct in a case of our neutrality from any one of our treaties which she pleased; or that we would take those from her own treaty with France, and make a temporary Convention of them for the term of the present war; and he was instructed to press this strongly. I told Genet that we had done this; but instead of giving us time to work our principles into effect by negotiation, he immediately took occasion in a letter, to threaten that if we did not resent the conduct of the British in taking French property in American bottoms, and protect their goods by *effectual measures* (meaning by arms), he would give direction that the principle of our treaty of goods following the bottom, should be disregarded. He was, at the same time, in the habit of keeping our goods taken in British bottoms; so that they were to take the gaining alternative of each principle, and give us the losing one. It became necessary to oppose this in the answer to his letter, and it was impossible to do it soundly, but by placing it on its true ground, to wit: that the law of nations established as a general rule that *goods should follow the owner*, and that the making them *follow the vessel* was an exception depending on special conventions only in those cases

where the Convention had been made: that the exception
had been established by us in our treaties with France,
Holland, and Prussia, and that we should endeavor to
extend it to England, Spain, and other powers; but that till
it was done, we had no right to make war for the enforcement of it. He thus obliged us to abandon in the first moment the ground we were endeavoring to gain, that is to
say, his ground against England and Spain, and to take the
very ground of England and Spain against him. This was
my private reason for proposing the term *modern* in the
proclamation; that it might reserve us a ground to obtain
the very things he wanted. But the world, who knew nothing
of these private reasons, were to understand by the expression the *modern law of nations*, that law with all the improvements and mollifications of it which an advancement
of civilization in *modern* times had introduced. It does not
mean strictly anything which is not a part of the *law of
nations* in *modern times*, and therefore could not be inconsistent with the ground taken in the letter to Genet, which
was that of the *law of nations*, and by no means could be
equivalent to a declaration by the President of the specific
principle, that *goods should follow the bottom*.

The Waste of War
From Notes on Virginia,
Query XXII, 1785

Jefferson was philosophically opposed to war, but here he points
out the simple fact of war as an economic waste.

. . . If when cleared of the present contest, and of the
debts with which that will charge us, we come to measure
force hereafter with any European power. Such events are
devoutly to be deprecated. Young as we are, and with such
a country before us to fill with people and with happiness,
we should point in that direction the whole generative force

of nature, wasting none of it in efforts of mutual destruction. It should be our endeavor to cultivate the peace and friendship of every nation, even of that which has injured us most, when we shall have carried our point against her. Our interest will be to throw open the doors of commerce, and to knock off all its shackles, giving perfect freedom to all persons for the vent of whatever they may chuse to bring into our ports, and asking the same in theirs. Never was so much false arithmetic employed on any subject, as that which has been employed to persuade nations that it is their interest to go to war. Were the money which it has cost to gain, at the close of a long war, a little town, or a little territory, the right to cut wood here, or to catch fish there, expended in improving what they already possess, in making roads, opening rivers, building ports, improving the arts, and finding employment for their idle poor, it would render them much stronger, much wealthier and happier. This I hope will be our wisdom. And, perhaps, to remove as much as possible the occasions of making war, it might be better for us to abandon the ocean altogether, that being the element whereon we shall be principally exposed to jostle with other nations; to leave to others to bring what we shall want, and to carry what we can spare. This would make us invulnerable to Europe, by offering none of our property to their prize, and would turn all our citizens to the cultivation of the earth; and, I repeat it again, cultivators of the earth are the most virtuous and independent citizens. It might be time enough to seek employment for them at sea, when the land no longer offers it. But the actual habits of our countrymen attach them to commerce. They will exercise it for themselves. Wars then must sometimes be our lot; and all the wise can do, will be to avoid that half of them which would be produced by our follies and our own acts of injustice; and to make for the other half the best preparations we can. Of what nature should these be? A land army would be useless for offence, and not the best nor safest instrument of defence. For either of these purposes, the sea is the field on which we should meet an European enemy. On that element it is necessary we should possess some power. To aim at such a navy as the greater nations of Europe possess, would be a foolish and wicked waste of the energies of our countrymen. It would be to pull on our own heads that load of military expense which makes the European laborer go supperless to bed, and moistens his bread with the sweat of his brows. It will be enough if we enable ourselves to prevent insults from those nations of Europe which are weak on the sea, because circumstances exist, which render even the stronger ones weak as to us. Providence has placed their richest and most defenceless possessions at our door; has obliged their most precious commerce to pass, as it were, in review before us. To protect this, or to assail, a small part only of their naval force will ever be risked across the Atlantic. The dangers to which the elements expose them here are too well known, and the greater dangers to which they would be exposed at home were any general calamity to involve their whole fleet. They can attack us by detachment only; and it will suffice to make ourselves equal to what they may detach. Even a smaller force than they may detach will be rendered equal or superior by the quickness with which any check may be repaired with us, while losses with them will be irreparable till too late. A small naval force then is sufficient for us, and a small one is necessary. What this should be, I will not undertake to say. I will only say, it should by no means be so great as we are able to make it. Suppose the million of dollars, or three hundred thousand pounds, which Virginia could annually spare without distress, to be applied to the creating a navy. A single year's contribution would build, equip, man, and send to sea a force which should carry three hundred guns. The rest of the confederacy, exerting themselves in the same proportion, would equip in the same time fifteen hundred guns more. So that one year's contributions would set up a navy of eighteen hundred guns. The British ships of the line average seventy-six guns; their frigates thirty-eight. Eighteen hundred guns then would form a fleet of thirty ships, eighteen of which might be of the line, and twelve frigates. Allowing eight men, the British average, for every gun, their annual expense, including subsistence, clothing, pay, and ordinary repairs, would be about $1,280 for every gun, or $2,304,000 for the whole. I state this only as one year's possible exertion, without deciding whether more or less than a year's exertion should be thus applied.

The value of our lands and slaves, taken conjunctly, doubles in about twenty years. This arises from the multiplication of our slaves, from the extension of culture, and increased demand for lands. The amount of what may be raised will of course rise in the same proportion.

Jefferson as Machiavelli
Jefferson to Robert Livingston,
April 18, 1802

Jefferson gave this letter to Dupont de Nemours to deliver to Livingston in Paris when the latter was negotiating for the purchase of Louisiana. Jefferson invited Dupont to read the letter, certain that he would circulate its contents among his business and political acquaintances in Paris. Whether Jefferson really meant his threatening words or not, it should be remembered that poker is an American game.

. . . The cession of Louisiana and the Floridas by Spain to France, works most sorely on the United States. On this subject the Secretary of State has written to you fully, yet I cannot forbear recurring to it personally, so deep is the impression it makes on my mind. It completely reverses all the political relations of the United States, and will form a new epoch in our political course. Of all nations of any consideration, France is the one which, hitherto, has offered the fewest points on which we could have any conflict of right, and the most points of a communion of interests. From these causes, we have ever looked to her as our *natural friend,* as one with which we never could have an occasion of difference. Her growth, therefore, we viewed as our own, her misfortunes ours. There is on the globe one single spot, the possessor which is our natural and habitual enemy. It is New Orleans, through which the produce of three-eighths of our territory must pass to market, and from its fertility it will ere long yield more than half of our whole produce, and contain more than half of our inhabitants. France, placing herself in that door, assumes to us the attitude of defiance. Spain might have retained it quietly for years. Her pacific dispositions, her feeble state, would induce her to increase our facilities there, so that her possession of the place would be hardly felt by us, and it would not, perhaps, be very long before some circumstances might arise, which might make the cession of it to us the price of something of more worth to her. Not so can it ever be in the hands of France: the impetuosity of her temper, the energy and restlessness of her character, placed in a point of eternal friction with us, and our character, which, though quiet and loving peace and the pursuit of wealth, is high-minded, despising wealth in competition with insult or injury, enterprising and energetic as any nation on earth; these circumstances render it impossible that France and the United States can continue long friends, when they meet in so irritable a position. They, as well as we, must be blind if they do not see this; and we must be very improvident if we do not begin to make arrangements on that hypothesis. The day that France takes possession of New Orleans, fixes the sentence which is to restrain her forever within her low-water mark. It seals the union of two nations, who, in conjunction, can maintain exclusive possession of the ocean. From that moment, we must marry ourselves to the British fleet and nation. We must turn all our attention to a maritime force, for which our resources place us on very high ground; and having

formed and connected together a power which may render
reinforcement of her settlements here impossible to France,
make the first cannon which shall be fired in Europe the
signal for the tearing up any settlement she may have made,
and for holding the two continents of America in sequestra-
tion for the common purposes of the United British and
American nations. This is not a state of things we seek or
desire. It is one which this measure, if adopted by France,
forces on us as necessarily, as any other cause, by the laws
of nature, brings on its necessary effect. It is not from a
fear of France that we deprecate this measure proposed by
her. For however greater her force is than ours, compared
in the abstract, it is nothing in comparison of ours, when
to be exerted on our soil. But it is from a sincere love of
peace, and a firm persuasion, that bound to France by the
interests and the strong sympathies still existing in the
minds of our citizens, and holding relative positions which
insure their continuance, we are secure of a long course of
peace. Whereas, the change of friends, which will be rendered necessary if France changes that position, embarks us
necessarily as a belligerent power in the first war of
Europe. In that case, France will have held possession of
New Orleans during the interval of a peace, long or short,
at the end of which it will be wrested from her. Will this
short-lived possession have been an equivalent to her for the
transfer of such a weight into the scale of her enemy? Will
not the amalgamation of a young, thriving nation, continue
to that enemy the health and force which are at present so
evidently on the decline? And will a few years' possession of
New Orleans add equally to the strength of France? She
may say she needs Louisiana for the supply of her West
Indies. She does not need it in time of peace, and in war she
could not depend on them, because they would be so easily
intercepted. I should suppose that all these considerations
might in some proper form, be brought into view of the
government of France. Though stated by us, it ought not to
give offence; because we do not bring them forward as a

menace, but as consequences not controllable by us, but inevitable from the course of things. We mention them, not as things which we desire by any means, but as things we deprecate; and we beseech a friend to look forward to and prevent them for our common interest.

If France considers Louisiana, however, as indispensable for her views, she might perhaps be willing to look about for arrangements which might reconcile it to our interests. If anything could do this, it would be the ceding to us the island of New Orleans and the Floridas. This would certainly, in a great degree, remove the causes of jarring and irritation between us, and perhaps for such a length of time, as might produce other means of making the measure permanently conciliatory to our interests and friendships. It would, at any rate, relieve us from the necessity of taking immediate measures for countervailing such an operation by arrangements in another quarter. But still we should consider New Orleans and the Floridas as no equivalent for the risk of a quarrel with France, produced by her vicinage.

I have no doubt you have urged these considerations, on every proper occasion, with the government where you are. They are such as must have effect, if you can find means of producing thorough reflection on them by that government. The idea here is, that the troops sent to St. Domingo, were to proceed to Louisiana after finishing their work in that island. If this were the arrangement, it will give you time to return again and again to the charge. For the conquest of St. Domingo will not be a short work. It will take considerable time, and wear down a great number of soldiers. Every eye in the United States is now fixed on the affairs of Louisiana. Perhaps nothing since the revolutionary war, has produced more uneasy sensations through the body of the nation. Notwithstanding temporary bickerings have taken place with France, she has still a strong hold on the affections of our citizens generally. I have thought it not amiss, by way of supplement to the letters of the Secretary of

State, to write to you this private one, to impress you with the importance we affix to this transaction. I pray you to cherish Dupont. He has the best disposition for the continuance of friendship between the two nations, and perhaps you may be able to make a good use of him.

Accept assurances of my affectionate esteem and high consideration.

War Resumes in Europe
Message to Congress, October 17, 1803

The truce between England and France (1801–1803) had ended, and Jefferson urges the nation to be neutral in opinion as well as in policy.

. . . We have seen with sincere concern the flames of war lighted up again in Europe, and nations with which we have the most friendly and useful relations engaged in mutual destruction. While we regret the miseries in which we see others involved let us bow with gratitude to that kind Providence which, inspiring with wisdom and moderation our late legislative councils while placed under the urgency of the greatest wrongs, guarded us from hastily entering into the sanguinary contest, and left us only to look on and to pity its ravages. These will be heaviest on those immediately engaged. Yet the nations pursuing peace will not be exempt from all evil. In the course of this conflict, let it be our endeavor, as it is our interest and desire, to cultivate the friendship of the belligerent nations by every act of justice and of incessant kindness; to receive their armed vessels with hospitality from the distresses of the sea, but to administer the means of annoyance to none; to establish in our harbors such a police as may maintain law and order; to restrain our citizens from embarking individually in a war in which their country takes no part; to punish severely those persons, citizen or alien, who shall usurp the cover of our flag for vessels not entitled to it, infecting thereby with suspicion those of real Americans, and committing us into controversies for the redress of wrongs not our own; to exact from every nation the observance, toward our vessels and citizens, of those principles and practices which all civilized people acknowledge; to merit the character of a just nation, and maintain that of an independent one, preferring every consequence to insult and habitual wrong. Congress will consider whether the existing laws enable us efficaciously to maintain this course with our citizens in all places, and with others while within the limits of our jurisdiction, and will give them the new modifications necessary for these objects.

Some contraventions of right have already taken place, both within our jurisdictional limits and on the high seas. The friendly disposition of the governments from whose agents they have proceeded, as well as their wisdom and regard for justice, leave us in reasonable expectation that they will be rectified and prevented in future; and that no act will be countenanced by them which threatens to disturb our friendly intercourse. Separated by a wide ocean from the nations of Europe, and from the political interests which entangle them together, with productions and wants which render our commerce and friendship useful to them and theirs to us, it cannot be the interest of any to assail us, nor ours to disturb them. We should be most unwise, indeed, were we to cast away the singular blessings of the position in which nature has placed us, the opportunity she has endowed us with of pursuing, at a distance from foreign contentions, the paths of industry, peace, and happiness; of cultivating general friendship, and of bringing collisions of interest to the umpirage of reason rather than of force. How desirable then must it be in a government like ours, to see its citizens adopt individually the views, the interests, and the conduct which their country should pursue, divesting themselves of those passions and partialities which tend to lessen useful friendships, and to embarrass and embroil us in the calamitous scenes of Europe. Confident, fellow citizens, that you will duly estimate the importance of neutral dispositions toward the observance of neutral conduct, that you will be sensible how much it is our duty to look on the bloody arena spread before us with commiseration indeed, but with no other wish than to see it closed, I am persuaded you will cordially cherish these dispositions in all discussions among yourselves, and in all communications with your constituents; and I anticipate with satisfaction the measures of wisdom which the great interests now committed to *you* will give you an opportunity of providing, and *myself* that of approving and carrying into execution with the fidelity I owe to my country.

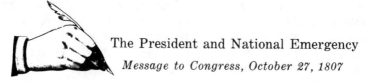

The President and National Emergency
Message to Congress, October 27, 1807

Many people considered *HMS Leopard's* attack on the *USS Chesapeake* in June, 1807, as an act of war, and if Jefferson had so desired, he probably could have gotten a declaration of war from Congress. Instead, he took what measures he felt the commander in chief should take and then asked Congress for the ultimate economic weapon, an embargo.

Circumstances, fellow citizens, which seriously threatened the peace of our country, have made it a duty to convene you at an earlier period than usual. The love of peace, so much cherished in the bosoms of our councils, and induced forbearance under so many wrongs, may not insure our continuance in the quiet pursuits of industry. The many injuries and depredations committed on our commerce and navigation upon the high seas for years past, the successive innovations on those principles of public law which have been established by the reason and usage of nations as the rule of their intercourse, and the umpire and security of their rights and peace, and all the circumstances which induced the extraordinary mission to London, are already known to you. The instructions given to our ministers [James Monroe and William Pinkney] were framed in the sincerest spirit of amity and moderation. They accordingly proceeded, in conformity therewith, to propose arrangements which might embrace and settle all the points in difference between us, which might bring us to a mutual understanding on our neutral and national rights, and provide for a commercial intercourse on conditions of some equality. After long and fruitless endeavors to effect the purposes of their mission, and to obtain arrangements within the limits of their instructions, they concluded to sign such as could be obtained, and to send them for consideration, candidly declaring to the other negotiators, at the same time, that they were acting against their instructions, and that their government, therefore, could not be pledged for ratification. Some of the articles proposed might have been admitted on a principle of compromise, but others were too highly disadvantageous, and no sufficient provision was made against the principal source of the irritations and collisions which were constantly endangering the peace of the two nations. The question, therefore, whether a treaty should be accepted in that form could have admitted but of one decision, even had no declarations of the other party impaired our confidence in it. Still anxious not to close the door against friendly adjustment, new modifications were framed, and further concessions authorized than could before have been supposed necessary; and our ministers were instructed to resume their negotiations on these grounds. On this new reference to amicable discussion, we were reposing in confidence, when on the 22d day of June last, by

a formal order from the British admiral, the frigate Chesapeake, leaving her port for distant service, was attacked by
one of those vessels which had been lying in our harbors
under the indulgences of hospitality, was disabled from proceeding, had several of her crew killed, and four taken
away. On this outrage, no commentaries are necessary. Its
character has been pronounced by the indignant voice of
our citizens with an emphasis and unanimity never ex-
ceeded. I immediately, by proclamation, interdicted our
harbors and waters to all British armed vessels, forbade
intercourse with them, and uncertain how far hostilities
were intended, and the town of Norfolk, indeed, being
threatened with immediate attack, a sufficient force was
ordered for the protection of that place, and such other
preparations commenced and pursued as the prospect rendered proper. An armed vessel of the United States was
despatched with instructions to our ministers at London
to call on that government for the satisfaction and security
required by the outrage. A very short interval ought now
to bring the answer, which shall be communicated to you
as soon as received; then also, or as soon after as the public
interests shall be found to admit, the unratified treaty, and
the proceedings relative to it, shall be made known to you.

The aggression thus begun has been continued on the
part of the British commanders, by remaining within our
waters, in defiance of the authority of the country, by habitual violations of its jurisdiction, and at length by putting
to death one of the persons whom they had forcibly taken
from on board the Chesapeake. These aggravations necessarily lead to the policy either of never admitting an armed
vessel into our harbors, or of maintaining in every harbor
such an armed force as may constrain obedience to the laws,
and protect the lives and property of our citizens, against
their armed guests. But the expense of such a standing
force, and its inconsistence with our principles, dispense
with those courtesies which would necessarily call for it,

and leave us equally free to exclude the navy, as we are the army, of a foreign power, from entering our limits.

To former violations of maritime rights, another is now added of very extensive effect. The government of that nation has issued an order interdicting all trade by neutrals between ports not in amity with them; and being now at war with nearly every nation on the Atlantic and Mediterranean seas, our vessels are required to sacrifice their cargoes at the first port they touch, or to return home without the benefit of going to any other market. Under this new law of the ocean, our trade on the Mediterranean has been swept away by seizures and condemnations, and that in other seas is threatened with the same fate. . . .

The appropriations of the last session, for the defence of our seaport towns and harbors, were made under expectation that a continuance of our peace would permit us to proceed in that work according to our convenience. It has been thought better to apply the sums then given, toward the defence of New York, Charleston, and New Orleans chiefly, as most open and most likely first to need protection; and to leave places less immediately in danger to the provisions of the present session.

The gun-boats, too, already provided, have on a like principle been chiefly assigned to New York, New Orleans, and the Chesapeake. Whether our movable force on the water, so material in aid of the defensive works on the land, should be augmented in this or any other form, is left to the wisdom of the legislature. For the purpose of manning these vessels in sudden attacks on our harbors, it is a matter for consideration, whether the seamen of the United States may not justly be formed into a special militia, to be called on for tours of duty in defence of the harbors where they shall happen to be; the ordinary militia of the place furnishing that portion which may consist of landsmen.

The moment our peace was threatened, I deemed it indispensable to secure a greater provision of those articles of

military stores with which our magazines were not sufficiently furnished. To have awaited a previous and special
sanction by law would have lost occasions which might not
be retrieved. I did not hesitate, therefore, to authorize engagements for such supplements to our existing stock as
would render it adequate to the emergencies threatening us;
and I trust that the legislature, feeling the same anxiety for
the safety of our country, so materially advanced by this
precaution, will approve, when done, what they would have
seen so important to be done if then assembled. Expenses,
also unprovided for, arose out of the necessity of calling all
our gunboats into actual service for the defence of our harbors; of all which accounts will be laid before you.

Whether a regular army is to be raised, and to what extent, must depend on the information so shortly expected.
In the meantime, I have called on the States for quotas of
militia, to be in readiness for present defence; and have,
moreover, encouraged the acceptance of volunteers; and I
am happy to inform you that these have offered themselves
with great alacrity in every part of the Union. They are
ordered to be organized, and ready at a moment's warning
to proceed on any service to which they may be called, and
every preparation within the executive powers has been
made to insure us the benefit of early exertions. . . .

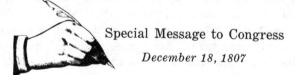

Special Message to Congress

December 18, 1807

The communications now made, showing the great and
increasing dangers with which our vessels, our seamen, and
merchandise, are threatened on the high seas and elsewhere,
from the belligerent powers of Europe, and it being a great
importance to keep in safety these essential resources, I
deem it my duty to recommend the subject to the considera-

tion of Congress, who will doubtless perceive all the advantages which may be expected from the inhibition of the departure of our vessels from the ports of the United States.

Congress and Foreign Policy
Jefferson to Thomas Mann Randolph,
February 7, 1809

Jefferson ascribed the failure of the embargo, not to the threat of New England secession, as is so often alleged, but to political cowardice in his own Republican party.

DEAR SIR, — I thought Congress had taken their ground firmly for continuing their embargo till June, and then war. But a sudden and unaccountable revolution of opinion took place the last week, chiefly among the New England and New York members, and in a kind of panic they voted the 4th of March for removing the embargo, and by such a majority as gave all reason to believe they would not agree either to war or non-intercourse. This, too, was after we had become satisfied that the Essex Junto had found their expectation desperate, of inducing the people there to either separation or forcible opposition. The majority of Congress, however, has now rallied to the removing the embargo on the 4th of March, non-intercourse with *France* and *Great Britain*, trade everywhere else, and continuing war preparations. The further details are not yet settled, but I believe it is perfectly certain that the embargo will be taken off the 4th of March. Present my warmest affections to my dearest Martha, and the young ones, and accept the assurances of them to yourself.

Jefferson to Gen. Henry Dearborn,
July 16, 1810

DEAR GENERAL AND FRIEND,—Your favor of May the 31st

was duly received, and I join in congratulations with you on the resurrection of republican principles in Massachusetts and New Hampshire, and the hope that the professors of these principles will not again easily be driven off their ground. The federalists, during their short-lived ascendency, have nevertheless, by forcing us from the embargo, inflicted a wound on our interests which can never be cured, and on our affections which will require time to cicatrize. I ascribe all this to one pseudo-republican, [Joseph] Story. He came on (in place of [Benjamin] Crowninshield, I believe) and staid only a few days; long enough, however, to get complete hold of [Ezekiel] Bacon, who giving in to his representations, became panicstruck, and communicated his panic to his colleagues, and they to a majority of the sound members of Congress. They believed in the alternative of repeal or civil war, and produced the fatal measure of repeal. This is the immediate parent of all our present evils, and has reduced us to a low standing in the eyes of the world. I should think that even the federalists themselves must now be made, by their feelings, sensible of their error. The wealth which the embargo brought home safely, has now been thrown back into the laps of our enemies, and our navigation completely crushed, and by the unwise and unpatriotic conduct of those engaged in it. Should the orders prove genuine, which are said to have been given against our fisheries, they too are gone; and if not true as yet, they will be true on the first breeze of success which England shall feel, for it has now been some years that I am perfectly satisfed her intentions have been to claim the ocean as her conquest, and prohibit any vessel from navigating it, but on such a tribute as may enable her to dominion over it. She has hauled in, or let herself out, been bold or hesitating, according to occurrences, but has in no situation done anything which might amount to a relinquishment of her intentions. I have ever been anxious to avoid a war with England, unless forced by a situation more losing than war itself. But I did believe we could coerce her to justice by peaceable

means, and the embargo, evaded as it was, proved it would
have coerced her had it been honestly executed. The proof
she exhibited on that occasion, that she can exercise such an
influence in this country as to control the will of its government and three-fourths of its people, and oblige the three
fourths to submit to one-fourth, is to me the most mortify-
ing circumstance which has occurred since the establishment of our government. The only prospect I see of lessening
that influence, is in her own conduct, and not from anything
in our power. Radically hostile to our navigation and commerce useless, at least, if not injurious to herself in the end,
and perhaps salutary to us as removing out of our way the
chief causes and provocations to war.

But these are views which concern the present and future
generation, among neither of which I count myself. You
may live to see the change in our pursuits, and chiefly in
those of your own State, which England will effect. I am not
certain that the change on Massachusetts, by driving her to
agriculture, manufactures and emigration, will lessen her
happiness. But once more to be done with politics. How does
Mrs. Dearborn do? How do you both like your situation?
Do you amuse yourself with a garden, a farm or what? That
your pursuits, whatever they be, may make you both easy,
healthy and happy, is the prayer of your sincere friend.

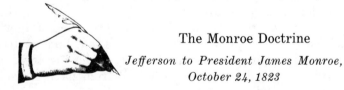

The Monroe Doctrine

*Jefferson to President James Monroe,
October 24, 1823*

The Monroe Doctrine originated from a proposal by England
that the United States join with her in a declaration supporting
the newly independent nations of Latin America. Monroe and
John Quincy Adams, fearing that Great Britain might use such
an agreement to intrude into the affairs of the Western Hemi-

sphere, finally rejected the offer in favor of a unilateral declaration by the United States.

DEAR SIR: The question presented by the letters you have sent me, is the most momentous which has ever been offered to my contemplation since that of Independence. That made us a nation, this sets our compass and points the course which we are to steer through the ocean of time opening on us. And never could we embark on it under circumstances more auspicious. Our first and fundamental maxim should be, never to entangle ourselves in the broils of Europe. Our second, never to suffer Europe to intermeddle with cis-Atlantic affairs. America, North and South, has a set of interests distinct from those of Europe, and peculiarly her own, separate and apart from that of Europe. While the last is laboring to become the domicil of despotism, our endeavor should surely be, to make our hemisphere that of freedom. One nation, most of all, could disturb us in this pursuit; she now offers to lead, aid, and accompany us in it. By acceding to her proposition, we detach her from the bands, bring her mighty weight into the scale of free government, and emancipate a continent at one stroke, which might otherwise linger long in doubt and difficulty. Great Britain is the nation which can do us the most harm of anyone, or all on earth; and with her on our side we need not fear the whole world. With her then, we should most sedulously cherish a cordial friendship; and nothing would tend more to knit our affections than to be fighting once more, side by side, in the same cause. Not that I would purchase amity at the price of taking part in her wars. But the war in which the present proposition might engage us, should that be its consequence, is not her war, but ours. Its object to introduce and establish the American system, of keeping out of our land all foreign powers, of never permitting those of Europe to intermeddle with the affairs of our nations. It is to maintain our own principle, not to depart from it. And if, to facilitate this, we can effect a division in the body of the European powers, and draw over to our side its most powerful member, surely we should do it. But I am clearly of Mr. Canning's opinion, that it will prevent instead of provoking war. With Great Britain withdrawn from their scale and shifted into that of our two continents, all Europe combined would not undertake such a war. For how would they propose to get at either enemy without superior fleets? Nor is the occasion to be slighted which this proposition offers, of declaring our protest against the atrocious violations of the rights of nations, by the interference of anyone in the internal affairs of another, so flagitiously begun by Bonaparte, and now continued by the equally lawless Alliance, calling itself Holy.

But we have first to ask ourselves a question. Do we wish to acquire to our own confederacy any one or more of the Spanish provinces? I candidly confess, that I have ever looked on Cuba as the most interesting addition which could ever be made to our system of States. The control which, with Florida Point, this island would give us over the Gulf of Mexico, and the countries and isthmus bordering on it, as well as all those whose waters flow into it, would fill up the measure of our political well-being. Yet, as I am sensible that this can never be obtained, even with her own consent, but by war; and its independence, which is our second interest (and especially its independence of England), can be secured without it, I have no hesitation in abandoning my first wish to future chances, and accepting its independence, with peace and the friendship of England, rather than its association, at the expense of war and her enmity.

I could honestly, therefore, join in the declaration proposed, that we aim not at the acquisition of any of those possessions, that we will not stand in the way of any amicable arrangement between them and the mother country; but that we will oppose, with all our means, the forcible interposition of any other power, as auxiliary, stipendiary, or under any other form or pretext, and most especially, their transfer to any power by conquest, cession, or acquisition in any other way. I should think it, therefore, advisable, that the Executive should encourage the British government to a continuance in the dispositions expressed in these letters, by an assurance of his concurrence with them as far as his authority goes; and that as it may lead to war, the declaration of which requires an act of Congress, the case shall be laid before them for consideration at their first meeting, and under the reasonable aspect in which it is seen by himself.

I have been so long weaned from political subjects, and have so long ceased to take any interest in them, that I am sensible I am not qualified to offer opinions on them worthy of any attention. But the question now proposed involves consequences so lasting, and effects so decisive of our future destinies, as to rekindle all the interest I have heretofore felt on such occasions, and to induce me to hazard of opinions, which will prove only my wish to contribute still my mite towards anything which may be useful to our country. And praying you to accept it at only what it is worth, I add the assurance of my constant and affectionate friendship and respect.

JEFFERSON AND EDUCATION

7 ★
★
★

Aspiring candidates for political office seldom lose an opportunity to let loose floods of oratory in support of public education. The same was true in the eighteenth century and then, as now, any resemblance between campaign promises and concrete legislative action is often purely coincidental. Except in New England, colonial and state legislatures passed an occasional law declaring a general intention to establish or support a public school system, but when it came to financial appropriations, there was either no action or the buck was passed to the local governments in the counties and towns. Even in New England "free schools" did not mean universal education at public expense, but a system which was supported by the payment of student fees and the admission of a limited number of children of poor families free of charge. To send one's children to such schools without payment of fees was to admit publicly that one was a pauper.

Jefferson was convinced that universal education was a necessary ingredient to the cultivation of American democracy. He accepted the Enlightenment dictum that mankind was by and large imperfect and selfish, but he was equally convinced that the education of the body politic would produce a workable system of self-government. As the chronology of the documents which follow indicates, Jefferson's concern was not a sometime thing. After serving in the Congress which adopted the Declaration of Independence, his first major government service was his appointment to a commission to revise and encode the statutes of the new state of Virginia. He used the occasion to draw up a comprehensive plan for public education which included every phase from elementary schools to a state university. The final accomplishment of his long career was building the University of Virginia.

Yet, for Jefferson, education was not confined to systems and

institutions. It was a process by which every man acquired a
mastery of the knowledge which would enable him to guide his
own destiny. As with all institutions, he regarded schools as a
means, the end of which was simply an efficient way of dispensing
knowledge on a large scale. He himself had very little formal
schooling before he went to William and Mary, and he seems to
have had no very high opinion of his alma mater then or later.
He believed, in fact, that a man's education is never complete, and
he remained an avid and eager student to the end of his days.

A Bill for the More General
Diffusion of Knowledge
Proposed to the Virginia Assembly, 1779

Whereas it appeareth that however certain forms of government are better calculated than others to protect individuals in the free exercise of their natural rights, and are
at the same time themselves better guarded against degeneracy, yet experience hath shewn, that even under the best
forms, those entrusted with power have, in time, and by
slow operations, perverted it into tyranny; and it is believed
that the most effectual means of preventing this would be,
to illuminate, as far as practicable, the minds of the people
at large, and more especially to give them knowledge of
those facts, which history exhibiteth, that, possessed thereby of the experience of other ages and countries, they may
be enabled to know ambition under all its shapes, and
prompt to exert their natural powers to defeat its purposes;
and whereas it is generally true that that people will be happiest whose laws are best, and are best administered, in
proportion as those who form and administer them are wise
and honest; whence it becomes expedient for promoting the
publick happiness that those persons, whom nature hath
endowed with genius and virtue, should be rendered by liberal education worthy to receive, and able to guard the
sacred deposit of the rights and liberties of their fellow

citizens, and that they should be called to that charge without regard to wealth, birth or other accidental condition or circumstance; but the indigence of the greater number disabling them from so educating, at their own expence, those of their children whom nature hath fitly formed and disposed to become useful instruments for the public, it is better that such should be sought for and educated at the common expence of all, that that the happiness of all should be confided to the weak or wicked:

Be it therefore enacted by the General Assembly, that in every county within this commonwealth, there shall be chosen annually, by the electors qualified to vote for Delegates, three of the most honest and able men of their county to be called the Aldermen of the county; and that the election of the said Alderman shall be held at the same time and place, before the same persons, and notified and conducted in the same manner as by law is directed for the annual election of Delegates for the county.

The person before whom such election is holden shall certify to the court of the said county the names of the Aldermen chosen, in order that the same may be entered of record, and shall give notice of their election to the said Aldermen within a fortnight after such election.

The said Aldermen on the first Monday in October, if it be fair, and if not, then on the next fair day, excluding Sunday, shall meet at the court-house of their county, and proceed to divide their said county into hundreds, bounding the same by water courses, mountains, or limits, to be run and marked, if they think necessary, by the county surveyor, and at the county expence, regulating the size of the said hundreds, according to the best of their discretion, so as that they may contain a convenient number of children to make up a school, and be of such convenient size that all the children within each hundred may daily attend the school to be established therein, distinguishing each hundred by a particular name; which division, with the names of the several hundreds, shall be returned to the court of the county and be entered of record, and shall remain unaltered until the increase or decrease of inhabitants shall render an alteration necessary, in the opinion of any succeeding Aldermen, and also in the opinion of the court of the county.

The electors aforesaid residing within every hundred shall meet on the third Monday in October after the first election of Aldermen, at such place, within their hundred, as the said Aldermen shall direct, notice thereof being previously given to them by such person residing within the hundred as the said Aldermen shall require who is hereby enjoined to obey such requisition, on pain of being punished by amercement and imprisonment. The electors being so assembled shall choose the most convenient place within their hundred for building a school-house. If two or more places, having a greater number of votes than any others, shall be equal among themselves, the Aldermen, or such of them as are not of the same hundred, on information thereof, shall decide between them. The said Aldermen shall forthwith proceed to have a school-house built at the said place, and shall see that the same be kept in repair, and, when necessary, that it be rebuilt; but whenever they shall think necessary that it be rebuilt, they shall give notice as before directed, to the electors of the hundred to meet at the said school-house, on such day as they shall appoint, to determine by vote, in the manner before directed, whether it shall be rebuilt at the same, or what other place in the hundred.

At every of these schools shall be taught reading, writing, and common arithmetick, and the books which shall be used therein for instructing the children to read shall be such as will at the same time make them acquainted with Graecian, Roman, English, and American history. At these schools all of the free children, male and female, resident within the respective hundred, shall be intitled to receive tuition gratis, for the term of three years, and as much longer, at their private expence, as their parents, guardians or friends, shall think proper.

Over every ten of these schools (or such other number nearest thereto, as the number of hundreds in the county will admit, without fractional divisions) an overseer shall be appointed annually by the Aldermen at their first meeting, eminent for his learning, integrity, and fidelity to the commonwealth, whose business and duty it shall be, from time to time, to appoint a teacher to each school, who shall give assurance of fidelity to the commonwealth, and to remove him as he shall see cause; to visit every school once in every half year at the least; to examine the schollars; see that any general plan of reading and instruction recommended by the visiters of William and Mary College shall be observed; and to superintend the conduct of the teacher in every thing relative to his school.

Every teacher shall receive a salary of _____ by the year, which, with the expences of building and repairing the schoolhouses, shall be provided in such manner as other county expences are by law directed to be provided and shall also have his diet, lodging, and washing found him, to be levied in like manner, save only that such levy shall be on the inhabitants of each hundred for the board of their own teacher only.

And in order that grammar schools may be rendered convenient to the youth in every part of the commonwealth, Be it farther enacted, that on the first Monday in November, after the first appointment of overseers for the hundred schools, if fair, and if not, then on the next fair day, excluding Sunday, after the hour of one in the afternoon, the said overseers appointed for the schools in the counties of Princess Ann, Norfolk, Nansemond and Isle-of-Wight, shall meet at Nansemond court-house; those for the counties of Southampton, Sussex, Surry and Prince George, shall meet at Sussex court-house; those for the counties of Brunswick, Mecklenburg and Lunenburg, shall meet at Lunenburg court-house; those for the counties of Dinwiddie, Amelia and Chesterfield, shall meet at Chesterfield court-house; those for the counties of Powhatan, Cumberland, Goochland,

Mid-eighteenth century engraving of the College of
William and Mary
Library of Congress

Henrico and Hanover, shall meet at Henrico court-house;
those for the counties of Prince Edward, Charlotte and
Halifax, shall meet at Charlotte court-house; those for the
counties of Henry, Pittsylvania and Bedford, shall meet at
Pittsylvania court-house; those for the counties of Bucking-
ham, Amherst, Albemarle and Fluvanna, shall meet at
Albemarle court-house; those for the counties of Botetourt,
Rockbridge, Montgomery, Washington and Kentucky, shall
meet at Botetourt court-house; those for the counties of
Augusta, Rockingham and Greenbrier, shall meet at Augusta court-house; those for the counties of Accomack and
Northampton, shall meet at Accomack court-house; those
for the counties of Elizabeth City, Warwick, York, Glou-
cester, James City, Charles City and New-Kent, shall meet
at James City court-house; those for the counties of Lan-
caster, Northumberland, Richmond and Westmoreland, shall
meet at Richmond court-house; those for the counties of
King George, Stafford, Spotsylvania, Prince William and
Fairfax, shall meet at Spotsylvania court-house; those
for the counties of Loudoun and Fauquier, shall meet at
Loudoun court-house; those for the counties of Culpeper,
Orange and Louisa, shall meet at Orange court-house;
those for the counties of Shenandoah and Frederick, shall
meet at Frederick court-house; those for the counties of
Hampshire and Berkeley, shall meet at Berkeley court-
house; and those for the counties of Yohogania, Monongalia
and Ohio, shall meet at Monongalia court-house; and shall
fix on such place in some one of the counties in their district
as shall be most proper for situating a grammar school-
house, endeavouring that the situation be as central as may
be to the inhabitants of the said counties, that it be furnished with good water, convenient to plentiful supplies of
provision and fuel, and more than all things that it be
healthy. And if a majority of the overseers present should
not concur in their choice of any one place proposed, the
method of determining shall be as follows: If two places
only were proposed, and the votes be divided, they shall

decide between them by fair and equal lot; if more than two places were proposed, the question shall be put on those two which on the first division had the greater number of votes; or if no two places had a greater number of votes than the others, as where the votes shall have been equal between one or both of them and some other or others, then it shall be decided by fair and equal lot (unless it can be agreed by a majority of votes) which of the places having equal numbers shall be thrown out of the competition, so that the question shall be put on the remaining two, and if on this ultimate question the votes shall be equally divided, it shall then be decided finally by lot.

The said overseers having determined the place at which the grammar school for their district shall be built, shall forthwith (unless they can otherwise agree with the proprietors of the circumjacent lands as to location and price) make application to the clerk of the county in which the said house is to be situated, who shall thereupon issue a writ, in the nature of a writ of ad quod damnum, directed to the sheriff of the said county commanding him to summon and impannel twelve fit persons to meet at the place, so destined for the grammar school house, on a certain day, to be named in the said writ, not less than five, nor more than ten, days from the date thereof; and also to give notice of the same to the proprietors and tenants of the lands to be viewed, if they be to be found within the county, and if not, then to their agents therein if any they have. Which freeholders shall be charged by the said sheriff impartially, and to the best of their skill and judgment to view the lands round about the said place, and to locate and circumscribe, by certain metes and bounds, one hundred acres thereof, having regard therein principally to the benefit and convenience of the said school, but respecting in some measure also the convenience of the said proprietors, and to value and appraise the same in so many several and distinct parcels as shall be owned or held by several and distinct owners or tenants, and according to their respective interests and estates therein. And after such location and apraisement so made, the said sheriff shall forthwith return the same under the hands and seals of the said jurors, together with the writ, to the clerk's office of the said county and the right and property of the said proprietors and tenants in the said lands so circumscribed shall be immediately devested and be transferred to the commonwealth for the use of the said grammar school, in full and absolute dominion, any want of consent or disability to consent in the said owners or tenants notwithstanding. But it shall not be lawful for the said overseers so to situate the said grammar school-house, nor to the said jurors so to locate the said lands, as to include the mansion-house of the proprietor of the lands, nor the offices, curtilage, or garden, thereunto immediately belonging.

The said overseers shall forthwith proceed to have a house of brick or stone, for the said grammar school, with necessary offices, built on the said lands, which grammar school-house shall contain a room for the school, a hall to dine in, four rooms for a master and usher, and ten or twelve lodging rooms for the scholars.

To each of the said grammar schools shall be allowed out of the public treasury, the sum of pounds, out of which shall be paid by the Treasurer, on warrant from the Auditors, to the proprietors or tenants of the lands located, the value of their several interests as fixed by the jury, and the balance thereof shall be delivered to the said overseers to defray the expence of the said buildings.

In these grammar schools shall be taught the Latin and Greek languages, English grammar, geography, and the higher part of numerical arithmetick, to wit, vulgar and decimal fractions, and the extraction of the square and cube roots.

A visiter from each county constituting the district shall be appointed, by the overseers, for the county, in the month of October annually, either from their own body or from their county at large, which visiters or the greater part of them, meeting together at the said grammar school on the first Monday in November, if fair, and if not, then on the next fair day, excluding Sunday, shall have power to choose their own Rector, who shall call and preside at future meetings, to employ from time to time a master, and if necessary, an usher, for the said school, to remove them at their will, and to settle the price of tuition to be paid by the scholars. They shall also visit the school twice in every year at the least, either together or separately at their discretion, examine the scholars, and see that any general plan of instruction recommended by the visiters of William and Mary College shall be observed. The said masters and ushers, before they enter on the execution of their office, shall give assurance of fidelity to the commonwealth.

A steward shall be employed and removed at will by the master, on such wages as the visiters shall direct; which steward shall see to the procuring provisions, fuel, servants for cooking, waiting, house cleaning, washing, mending, and gardening on the most reasonable terms; the expence of which, together with the steward's wages, shall be divided equally among all the scholars boarding either on the public or private expence, and also the price of their tuitions due to the master or usher, shall be paid quarterly by the respective scholars, their parents, or guardians, and shall be recoverable, if withheld, together with costs, on motion in any Court of Record, ten days notice thereof being previously given to the party, and a jury impannelled to try the issue joined, or enquire of the damages. The said steward shall also, under the direction of the visiters, see that the houses be kept in repair, and necessary enclosures be made and repaired, the accounts for which, shall, from time to time, be submitted to the Auditors, and on their warrant paid by the Treasurer.

Every overseer of the hundred schools shall, in the month of September annually, after the most diligent and impartial examination and enquiry, appoint from among the boys who shall have been two years at the least at some one of

the schools under his superintendance, and whose parents
are too poor to give them farther education, some one of the
best and most promising genius and disposition, to proceed
to the grammar school of his district; which appointment
shall be made in the court-house of the county, on the court
day for that month if fair, and if not, then on the next fair
day, excluding Sunday, in the presence of the Aldermen, or
two of them at the least, assembled on the bench for that
purpose, the said overseer being previously sworn by them
to make such appointment, without favor or affection, according to the best of his skill and judgment, and being
interrogated by the said Aldermen, either on their own motion, or on suggestions from the parents, guardians, friends,
or teachers of the children, competitors for such appointment; which teachers shall attend for the information of
the Aldermen. On which interregatories the said Aldermen,
if they be not satisfied with the appointment proposed, shall
have right to negative it; whereupon the said visiter may
proceed to make a new appointment, and the said Aldermen
again to interrogate and negative, and so toties quoties until an appointment be approved.

Every boy so appointed shall be authorised to proceed to
the grammar school of his district, there to be educated and
boarded during such time as is hereafter limited; and his
quota of the expences of the house together with a compensation to the master or usher for his tuition, at the rate of
twenty dollars by the year, shall be paid by the Treasurer
quarterly on warrant from the Auditors.

A visitation shall be held, for the purpose of probation,
annually at the said grammar school on the last Monday in
September, if fair, and if not, then on the next fair day,
excluding Sunday, at which one third of the boys sent
hither by appointment of the said overseers, and who shall
have been there one year only, shall be discontinued as public foundationers, being those who, on the most diligent
examination and enquiry, shall be thought to be of the least
promising genius and disposition; and of those who shall

have been there two years, all shall be discontinued, save one only the best in genius and disposition, who shall be at liberty to continue there four years longer on the public foundation, and shall thence forward be deemed a senior.

The visiters for the district which, or any part of which, be southward and westward of James river, as known by that name, or by the names of Fluvanna and Jackson's river, in every other year, to wit, at the probation meetings held in the years, distinguished in the Christian computation by odd numbers, and the visiters for all the other districts at their said meetings to be held in those years, distinguished by even numbers, after diligent examination and enquiry as before directed, shall chuse one among the said seniors, of the best learning and most hopeful genius and disposition, who shall be authorised by them to proceed to William and Mary College, there to be educated, boarded, and clothed, three years; the expence of which annually shall be paid by the Treasurer on warrant from the Auditors.

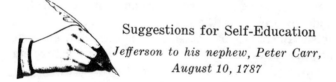

Suggestions for Self-Education
Jefferson to his nephew, Peter Carr,
August 10, 1787

Notice that, although Jefferson gives his young nephew a detailed plan of study, he carefully refrains from telling him what to conclude from his study, only that "you are to judge . . . by your own reason."

Dear Peter

I have received your two letters of Decemb. 30. and April 18. and am very happy to find by them, as well as by letters from Mr. Wythe, that you have been so fortunate as to attract his notice and good will: I am sure you will find this to have been one of the most fortunate events of your life, as I have ever been sensible it was of mine. I inclose you a sketch of the sciences to which I would wish you to apply in such order as Mr. Wythe shall advise: I mention also the books in them worth your reading, which submit to his correction. [Jefferson enclosed a bibliography which contained categories of ancient and modern history, poetry, religion, politics and law, science, agriculture, and mathematics; the authors ranged from Thucydides and Ovid through Shakespeare to Voltaire and Hume.] Many of these are among your father's books, which you should have brought to you. As I do not recollect those of them not in his library, you must write to me for them, making out a catalogue of such as you think you shall have occasion for in 18 months from the date of your letter, and consulting Mr. Wythe on the subject. To this sketch I will add a few particular observations.

1. Italian. I fear the learning this language will confound your French and Spanish. Being all of them degenerated dialects of the Latin, they are apt to mix in conversation. I have never seen a person speaking the three languages who did not mix them. It is a delightful language, but late events having rendered the Spanish more useful, lay it aside to prosecute that.

2. Spanish. Bestow great attention on this, and endeavor to acquire an accurate knowledge of it. Our future connections with Spain and Spanish America will render that language a valuable acquisition. The antient history of a great part of America too is written in that language. I send you a dictionary.

3. Moral philosophy. I think it lost time to attend lectures in this branch. He who made us would have been a pitiful bungler if he had made the rules of our moral conduct a matter of science. For one man of science, there are thousands who are not. What would have become of thetm? Man was destined for society. His morality therefore was to be formed to this object. He was endowed with a sense of right and wrong merely relative to this. This sense is as much a part of his nature as the

sense of hearing, seeing, feeling; it is the true foundation of morality, and not the truth, &c., as fanciful writers have imagined. The moral sense, or conscience, is as
much a part of man as his leg or arm. It is given to all
human beings in a stronger or weaker degree, as force
of members is given them in a greater or less degree. It
may be strengthened by exercise, as may any particular limb of the body. This sense is submitted indeed in
some degree to the guidance of reason; but it is a small
stock which is required for this: even a less one than
what we call Common sense. State a moral case to a
ploughman and a professor. The former will decide it as
well, and often better than the latter, because he has not
been led astray by artificial rules. In this branch therefore read good books because they will encourage as well
as direct your feelings. The writings of Sterne particularly form the best course of morality that ever was
written. Besides these read the books mentioned in the
inclosed paper; and above all things lose no occasion of
exercising your dispositions to be grateful, to be generous, to be charitable, to be humane, to be true, just,
firm, orderly, couragious &c. Consider every act of this
kind as an exercise which will strengthen your moral
faculties, and increase your worth.

4. Religion. Your reason is now mature enough to receive
this object. In the first place divest yourself of all bias
in favour of novelty and singularity of opinion. Indulge
them in any other subject rather than that of religion.
It is too important, and the consequences of error may
be too serious. On the other hand shake off all the fears
and servile prejudices under which weak minds are
servilely crouched. Fix reason firmly in her seat, and
call to her tribunal every fact, every opinion. Question
with boldness even the existence of a god; because, if
there be one, he must more approve the homage of reason, than that of blindfolded fear. You will naturally

examine first the religion of your own country. Read
the bible then, as you would read Livy or Tacitus. The
facts which are within the ordinary course of nature
you will believe on the authority of the writer, as you
do those of the same kind in Livy and Tacitus. The testimony of the writer weighs in their favor in one scale,
and their not being against the laws of nature does not
weigh against them. But those facts in the bible which
contradict the laws of nature, must be examined with
more care, and under a variety of faces. Here you must
recur to the pretensions of the writer to inspiration from
god. Examine upon what evidence his pretensions are
founded, and whether that evidence is so strong as that
it's falshood would be more improbable than a change
of the laws of nature in the case he relates. For example
in the book of Joshua we are told the sun stood still several hours. Were we to read that fact in Livy or Tacitus
we should class it with their showers of blood, speaking
of statues, beasts &c., but it is said that the writer of
that book was inspired. Examine therefore candidly
what evidence there is of his having been inspired. The
pretension is entitled to your enquiry, because millions
believe it. On the other hand you are Astronomer
enough to know how contrary it is to the law of nature
that a body revolving on it's axis, as the earth does,
should have stopped, should not by that sudden stoppage
have prostrated animals, trees, buildings, and should
after a certain time have resumed it's revolution, and
that without a second general prostration. Is this arrest
of the earth's motion, or the evidence which affirms it,
most within the law of probabilities? You will next read
the new testament. It is the history of a personage
called Jesus. Keep in your eye the opposite pretensions.
1. Of those who say he was begotten by god, born of a
virgin, suspended and reversed the laws of nature at
will, and ascended bodily into heaven: and 2. of those

who say he was a man, of illegitimate birth, of a benevolent heart, enthusiastic mind, who set out without pretensions to divinity, ended in believing them, and was
punished capitally for sedition by being gibbeted according to the Roman law which punished the first commission of that offence by whipping, and the second by
exile or death *in furca*. See this law in the Digest Lib.
48. tit. 19 § 28. 3. and Lipsius Lib. 2. de cruce. cap. 2.
These questions are examined in the books I have mentioned under the head of religion, and several others.
They will assist you in your enquiries, but keep your
reason firmly on the watch in reading them all. Do not
be frightened from this enquiry by any fear of it's consequences. If it ends in a belief that there is no god, you
will find incitements to virtue in the comfort and pleas-
antness you feel in it's exercise, and the love of others
which it will procure you. If you find reason to believe
there is a god, a consciousness that you are acting under
his eye, and that he approves you, will be a vast additional incitement. If that there be a future state, the
hope of a happy existence in that increases the appetite
to deserve it; if that Jesus was also a god, you will be
comforted by a belief of his aid and love. In fine, I
repeat that you must lay aside all prejudice on both
sides, and neither believe nor reject any thing because
any other person, or description of persons have rejected or believed it. Your own reason is the only oracle
given you by heaven, and you are answerable not for
the rightness but uprightness of the decision.—I forgot
to observe when speaking of the New testament that
you should read all the histories of Christ, as well of
those whom a council of ecclesiastics have decided for
us to be Pseudo-evangelists, as those they named Evangelists, because these Pseudo-evangelists pretended to
inspiration as much as the others, and you are to judge
their pretensions by your own reason, and not by the

reason of those ecclesiastics. Most of these are lost. There are some however still extant, collected by Fabricius which I will endeavor to get and send you.

5. Travelling. This makes men wiser, but less happy. When men of sober age travel, they gather knowledge which they may apply usefully for their country, but they are subject ever after to recollections mixed with regret, their affections are weakened by being extended over more objects, and they learn new habits which cannot be gratified when they return home. Young men who travel are exposed to all these inconveniences in a higher degree, to others still more serious, and do not acquire that wisdom for which a previous foundation is requisite by repeated and just observations at home. The glare of pomp and pleasure is analogous to the motion of their blood, it absorbs all their affection and attention, they are torn from it as from the only good in this world, and return to their home as to a place of exile and condemnation. Their eyes are for ever turned back to the object they have lost, and it's recollection poisons the residue of their lives. Their first and most delicate passions are hackneyed on unworthy objects here, and they carry home only the dregs, insufficient to make themselves or any body else happy. Add to this that a habit of idleness, an inability to apply themselves to business is acquired and renders them useless to themselves and their country. These observations are founded in experience. There is no place where your pursuit of knowledge will be so little obstructed by foreign objects as in your own country, nor any wherein the virtues of the heart will be less exposed to be weakened. Be good, be learned, and be industrious, and you will not want the aid of travelling to render you precious to your country, dear to your friends, happy within yourself. I repeat my advice to take a great deal of exercise, and on foot. Health is the first requisite after morality. Write to me often and be assured of the interest I take in your success, as well as

of the warmth of those sentiments of attachment with
which I am, dear Peter, your affectionate friend.

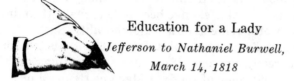

Education for a Lady
Jefferson to Nathaniel Burwell,
March 14, 1818

Although the reader will find Jefferson somewhat condescend-
ing toward women, most men of his time concluded that women
could not and should not be especially well educated. Jefferson
had a great deal of respect for intelligent women and enjoyed
their company.

A plan of female education has never been a subject of
systematic contemplation with me. It has occupied my attention so far only as the education of my own daughters
occasionally required. Considering that they would be placed
in a country situation where little aid could be obtained
from abroad, I thought it essential to give them a solid
education, which might enable them, when become mothers,
to educate their own daughters, and even to direct the
course for sons, should their fathers be lost, or incapable, or
inattentive. My surviving daughter accordingly, the mother
of many daughters as well as sons, has made their education
the object of her life, and being a better judge of the practical part than myself, it is with her air and that of one of
her *élèves*, that I shall subjoin a catalogue of the books for
such a course of reading as we have practised.

A great obstacle to good education is the inordinate passion prevalent for novels, and the time lost in that reading
which should be instructively employed. When this poison
infects the mind, it destroys its tone and revolts it against
wholesome reading. Reason and fact, plain and unadorned,
are rejected. Nothing can engage attention unless dressed in
all the figments of fancy, and nothing so bedecked comes
amiss. The result is a bloated imagination, sickly judgment,

and disgust towards all the real businesses of life. This mass of trash, however, is not without some distinction; some few modeling their narratives, although fictitious, on the incidents of real life, have been able to make them interesting and useful vehicles of a sound morality. Such, I think, are Marmontel's new moral tales, but not his old ones, which are really immoral. Such are the writings of· Miss Edgeworth, and some of those of Madame Genlis. For a like reason, too, much poetry should not be indulged. Some is useful for forming style and taste. Pope, Dryden, Thomson, Shakespeare, and of the French, Moliere, Racine, the Corneilles, may be read with pleasure and improvement.

The French language, become that of the general intercourse of nations, and from their extraordinary advances, now the depository of all science, is an indispensable part of education for both sexes. In the subjoined catalogue, therefore, I have placed the books of both languages indifferently, according as the one or the other offers what is best. [This catalog is not available.]

The ornaments, too, and the amusements of life, are entitled to their portion of attention. These, for a female, are dancing, drawing, and music. The first is a healthy exercise, elegant, and very attractive for young people. Every affectionate parent would be pleased to see his daughter qualified to participate with her companions and without awkwardness at least, in the circles of festivity, of which she occasionally becomes a part. It is a necessary accomplishment, therefore, although of short use; for the French rule is wise, that no lady dances after marriage. This is founded in solid physical reasons, gestation and nursing leaving little time to a married lady when this exercise can be either safe or innocent. Drawing is thought less of in this country than in Europe. It is an innocent and engaging amusement, often useful, and a qualification not to be neglected in one who is to become a mother and an instructor. Music is invaluable where a person has an ear. Where they have not, it should not be attempted. It furnishes a delightful recreation for

Martha Jefferson Randolph, oldest daughter of Thomas Jefferson
Thomas Jefferson Memorial Foundation

the hours of respite from the cares of the day, and lasts us through life. The taste of this country, too, calls for this accomplishment more strongly than for either of the others.

I need say nothing of household economy, in which the mothers of our country are generally skilled, and generally careful to instruct their daughters. We all know its value, and that diligence and dexterity in all its processes are inestimable treasures. The order and economy of a house are as honorable to the mistress as those of the farm to the master, and if either be neglected, ruin follows, and children destitute of the means of living.

This sir, is offered as a summary sketch on a subject on which I have not thought much. It probably contains nothing but what has already occurred to yourself, and claims your acceptance on no other ground than as a testimony of my respect for your wishes, and of my great esteem and respect.

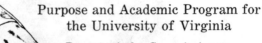

Purpose and Academic Program for the University of Virginia

Report of the Commissioners,
August 1–4, 1818

It is properly called "Mr. Jefferson's University." He selected the site, used his matchless political guile to get state support for it, drew the architectural plans (including the landscaping and gardens), acted as building contractor, and selected the faculty. Here he lays out the blueprint for its academic program.

In proceeding to the third and fourth duties prescribed by the Legislature, of reporting "the branches of learning, which should be taught in the University, and the number and description of the professorships they will require," the Commissioners were first to consider at what point it was understood that university education should commence. Certainly not with the alphabet, for reasons of expediency and impracticability, as well from the obvious sense of the Legislature, who, in the same act, make other provision for the primary instruction of the poor children, expecting, doubtless, that in other cases it would be provided by the parent, or become, perhaps, subject of future and further attention of the Legislature. The objects of this primary education determine its character and limits. The objects would be,

To give to every citizen the information he needs for the transaction of his own business;

To enable him to calculate for himself, and to express and preserve his ideas, his contracts and accounts, in writing;

To improve, by reading, his morals and faculties;

To understand his duties to his neighbors and country, and to discharge with competence the functions confided to him by either;

To know his rights; to exercise with order and justice

those he retains; to choose with discretion the fiduciary of those he delegates; and to notice their conduct with diligence, with candor, and judgment;

And, in general, to observe with intelligence and faithfulness all the social relations under which he shall be placed.

To instruct the mass of our citizens in these, their rights, interests and duties, as men and citizens, being then the objects of education in the primary schools, whether private or public, in them should be taught reading, writing and numerical arithmetic, the elements of mensuration (useful in so many callings), and the outlines of geography and history. And this brings us to the point at which are to commence the higher branches of education, of which the Legislature require the development; those, for example, which are,

To form the statesmen, legislators and judges, on whom public prosperity and individual happiness are so much to depend;

To expound the principles and structure of government, the laws which regulate the intercourse of nations, those formed municipally for our own government, and a sound spirit of legislation, which, banishing all arbitrary and unnecessary restraint on individual action, shall leave us free to do whatever does violate the equal rights of another;

To harmonize and promote the interests of agriculture, manufactures and commerce, and by well informed views of political economy to give a free scope to the public industry;

To develop the reasoning faculties of our youth, enlarge their minds, cultivate their morals, and instill into them the precepts of virtue and order;

To enlighten them with mathematical and physical sciences, which advance the arts, and administer to the health, the subsistence, and comforts of human life;

And, generally, to form them to habits of reflection and correct action, rendering them examples of virtue to others, and of happiness within themselves.

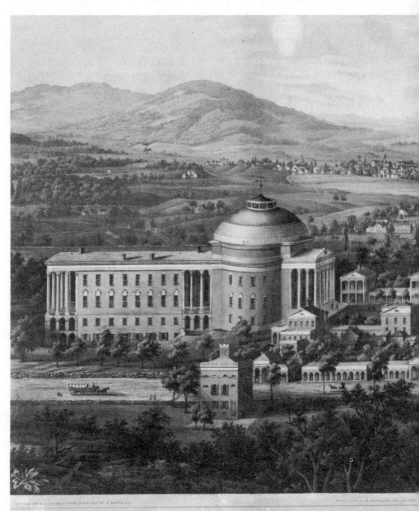

VIEW OF THE UNIV
CHARLOTTESVI
TAKEN FRO

Academical Village of the University of Virginia
Department of Graphics, University of Virginia

ITY OF VIRGINIA

MONTICELLO

UNTAIN

These are the objects of that higher grade of education, the benefits and blessings of which the Legislature now propose to provide for the good and ornament of their country, the gratification and happiness of their fellow-citizens, of ·the parent especially, and his progeny, on which all his affections are concentrated.

In entering on this field, the Commissioners are aware that they have to encounter much difference of opinion as to the extent which it is expedient that this institution should occupy. Some good men, and even of respectable information, consider the learned sciences as useless acquirements; some think they do not better the condition of man; and others that education, like private and individual concerns, should be left to private individual effort; not reflecting that an establishment embracing all the sciences which may be useful and even necessary in the various vocations of life, with the buildings and aparatus belonging to each, are far beyond the reach of individual means, and must either derive existence from public patronage, or not exist at all. This would leave us, then, without those callings which depend on education, or send us to other countries to seek the instruction they require. But the Commissioners are happy in considering the statute under which they are assembled as proof that the Legislature is far from the abandonment of objects so interesting. They are sensible that the advantages of well-directed education, moral, political and economical, are truly above all estimate. Education generates habits of application, of order, and the love of virtue; and controls, by the force of habit, any innate obliquities in our moral organization. We should be far, too, from the discouraging persuasion that man is fixed, by the law of his nature, at a given point; that his improvement is a chimera, and the hope delusive of rendering ourselves wiser, happier or better than our forefathers were. As well might it be urged that the wild and uncultivated tree, hitherto yielding sour and bitter fruit only, can never be made to yield better;

yet we know that the grafting art implants a new tree on
the savage stock, producing what is most estimable both in
kind and degree. Education, in like manner, engrafts a new
man on the native stock, and improves what in his nature
was vicious and perverse into qualities of virtue and social
worth. And it cannot be but that each generation succeeding
to the knowledge acquired by all those who preceded it,
adding to it their own acquisitions and discoveries, and
handing the mass down for successive and constant accumu-
lation, must advance the knowledge and well-being of mankind, not *infinitely*, as some have said, but *indefinitely*, and
to a term which no one can fix and foresee. Indeed, we need
look back half a century, to times which many now living
remember well, and see the wonderful advances in the
sciences and arts which have been made within that period.
Some of these have rendered the elements themselves sub-
servient to the purposes of man, have harnessed them to the
yoke of his labors, and effected the great blessings of mod-
erating his own, of accomplishing what was beyond his
feeble force, and extending the comforts of life to a much
enlarged circle, to those who had before known its necessaries only. That these are not the vain dreams of sanguine
hope, we have before our eyes real and living examples.
What, but education, has advanced us beyond the condition
of our indigenous neighbors? And what chains them to their
present state of barbarism and wretchedness, but a bigoted
veneration for the supposed superlative wisdom of their fathers, and the preposterous idea that they are to look backward for better things, and not forward, longing, as it
should seem, to return to the days of eating acorns and
roots, rather than indulge in the degeneracies of civilization?
And how much more encouraging to the achievements of
science and improvement is this, than the desponding view
that the condition of man cannot be ameliorated, that what
has been must ever be, and that to secure ourselves where
we are, we must tread with awful reverence in the footsteps

of our fathers. This doctrine is the genuine fruit of the alliance between Church and State; the tenants of which, finding themselves but too well in their present condition, oppose all advances which might unmask their usurpations, and monopolies of honors, wealth, and power, and fear every change, as endangering the comforts they now hold. Nor must we omit to mention, among the benefits of education, the incalculable advantage of training up able counsellors to administer the affairs of our country in all its departments, legislative, executive and judiciary, and to bear their proper share in the councils of our national government; nothing more than education advancing the prosperity, the power, and the happiness of a nation.

Encouraged, therefore, by the sentiments of the Legislature, manifested in this statute, we present the following tabular statement of the branches of learning which we think should be taught in the University, forming them into groups, each of which are within the powers of a single professor:

    I. Languages
        ancient: Latin
                Greek
                Hebrew

   II. Languages
        modern: French
                Spanish
                Italian
                German
                Anglo-Saxon

  III. Mathematics
        pure: Algebra
             Fluxions
             Geometry
                 Elementary
                 Transcendental

       Architecture
       Military
       Naval

IV. Physico-Mathematics:
       Mechanics
       Statics
       Dynamics
       Pneumatics
       Acoustics
       Optics
       Astronomy
       Geography

V. Physics
    or Natural Philosophy: Chemistry
                            Mineralogy

VI. Botany
      Zoology

VII. Anatomy
      Medicine

VIII. Government
       Political Economy
       Law of Nature and Nations
       History, being interwoven with Politics and Law

IX. Law, municipal

X. Ideology
       General Grammar
       Ethics
       Rhetoric
       Belles Lettres and the fine arts

Some of the terms used in this table being subject to a difference of acceptation, it is proper to define the meaning and comprehension intended to be given them here:

Geometry, Elementary, is that of straight lines and of the circle. Transcendental, is that of all other curves; it includes, of course, *Projectiles*, a leading branch of military art.

Military Architecture includes Fortification, another branch of that art.

Statics respect matter generally, in a state of rest, and include Hydrostatics, or the laws of fluids particularly, at rest or in equilibrio.

Dynamics, used as a general term, include Dynamics proper, or the laws of *solids* in motion; and Hydrodynamics, or Hydraulics, those of fluids in motion.

Pneumatics teach the theory of air, its weight, motion, condensation, rarefaction, &c.

Acoustics, or Phonics, the theory of sound.

Optics, the laws of light and vision.

Physics, or Physiology, in a general sense, mean the doctrine of the physical objects of our senses.

Chemistry is meant, with its other usual branches, to comprehend the theory of agriculture.

Mineralogy, in addition to its peculiar subjects, is here understood to embrace what is real in geology.

Ideology is the doctrine of thought.

General Grammar explains the construction of language.

Some articles in this distribution of sciences will need observation. A professor is proposed for ancient languages, the Latin, Greek, and Hebrew, particularly; but these languages being the foundation common to all the sciences, it is difficult to foresee what may be the extent of this school. At the same time, no greater obstruction to industrious study could be proposed than the presence, the intrusions and the noisy turbulence of a multitude of small boys; and if they are to be placed here for the rudiments of the languages, they may be so numerous that its character and value as an University will be merged in those of a Grammar school. It is, therefore, greatly to be wished, that preliminary schools, either on private or public establishment, could be distributed in districts through the State, as preparatory to the entrance of students into the University. The tender age at which this part of education commences, generally about the tenth year, would weigh heavily with parents in sending their sons to a school so distant as the central establishment would be from most of them. Districts of such extent as that every parent should be within a day's journey of his son at school, would be desirable in cases of sickness, and convenient for supplying their ordinary wants, and might be made to lessen sensibly the expense of this part of their education. And where a sparse population would not, within such a compass, furnish subjects sufficient to maintain a school, a competent enlargement of district must, of necessity be submitted to. At these district schools or colleges, boys should be rendered able to read the easier authors, Latin and Greek. This would be useful and sufficient for many not intended for an University education. At these, too, might be taught English grammar, the higher branches of numerical arithmetic, the geometry of straight lines and of the circle, the elements of navigation, and geography to a sufficient degree, and thus afford to greater numbers the means of being qualified for the various vocations of life, needing more instruction than merely menial or praedial labor, and the same advantages to youths whose education may have been neglected until too late to lay a foundation in the learned languages. These institutions, intermediate between the primary schools and University, might then be the passage of entrance for youths into the University, where their classical learning might be critically completed, by a study of the authors of highest degree; and it is at this stage only that they should be received at the University. Giving then a portion of their time to a finished knowledge of the Latin and Greek, the rest might be appropriated to the modern languages, or to the commencement of the course of science for which they should be destined. This would generally be about the fifteenth year of their age, when they might go with more safety and contentment to that distance from their parents. Until this preparatory provision shall be made, either the University will be overwhelmed with the grammar school, or a separate establishment, under one or more ushers, for its lower classes, will be advisable, at a mile or two distant from the general one; where, too, may be exercised the stricter government necessary for young boys, but unsuitable for youths arrived at years of discretion.

The considerations which have governed the specification of languages to be taught by the professor of modern languages were, that the French is the language of general intercourse among nations, and as a depository of human science, is unsurpassed by any other language, living or dead; that the Spanish is highly interesting to us, as the language spoken by so great a portion of the inhabitants of our continents, with whom we shall probably have great intercourse ere long, and is that also in which is written the greater part of the earlier history of America. The Italian abounds with works of very superior order, valuable for their matter, and still more distinguished as models of the finest taste in style and composition. And the German now stands in a line with that of the most learned nations in richness and erudition and advance in the sciences. It is too of common descent with the language of our own country, a branch of the same original Gothic stock, and furnishes valuable illustrations for us. But in this point of view, the Anglo-Saxon is of peculiar value. We have placed it among the modern languages, because it is in fact that which we speak, in the earliest form in which we have knowledge of it. It has been undergoing, with time, those gradual changes which all languages, ancient and modern, have experienced; and even now needs only to be printed in the modern character and orthography to be intelligible, in a considerable degree, to an English reader. It has this value, too, above the Greek and Latin, that while it gives the radix of the mass of our language, they explain its innovations only. Obvious proofs of this have been presented to the modern reader in the disquisitions of Horn Tooke; and Fortescue Aland has well explained the great instruction which may be derived from it to a full understanding of our ancient common law, on which, as a stock, our whole system of law is engrafted. It will form the first link in the chain of an historical review of our language through all its successive changes to the present day, will constitute the foundation of that critical instruction in it which ought to be found in a seminary of general learning, and thus reward amply the few weeks of attention which would alone be requisite for its attainment; a language already fraught with all the eminent science of our parent country, the future vehicle of whatever we may ourselves achieve, and destined to occupy so much space on the globe, claims distinguished attention in American education.

Medicine, where fully taught, is usually subdivided into several professorships, but this cannot well be without the accessory of an hospital, where the student can have the benefit of attending clinical lectures, and of assisting at operations of surgery. With this accessory, the seat of our University is not yet prepared, either by its population or by the numbers of poor who would leave their own houses, and accept of the charities of an hospital. For the present, therefore, we propose but a single professor for both medicine and anatomy. By him the medical science may be taught, with a history and explanations of all its successive theories from Hippocrates to the present day; and anatomy fully treated. Vegetable pharmacy will make a part of the botanical course, and mineral and chemical pharmacy of those of mineralogy and chemistry. This degree of medical information is such as the mass of scientific students would wish to possess, as enabling them in their course through

life, to estimate with satisfaction the extent and limits of
the aid to human life and health, which they may understandingly expect from that art; and it constitutes such a
foundation for those intended for the profession, that the
finishing course of practice at the bedsides of the sick, and
at the operations of surgery in a hospital, can neither be
long nor expensive. To seek this finishing elsewhere, must
therefore be submitted to for a while.

In conformity with the principles of our Constitution,
which places all sects of religion on an equal footing, with
the jealousies of the different sects in guarding that equality from encroachment and surprise, and with the sentiments of the Legislature in favor of freedom of religion,
manifested on former occasions, we have proposed no professor of divinity; and the rather as the proofs of the being
of a God, the creator, preserver, and supreme ruler of the
universe, the author of all the relations of morality, and of
the laws and obligations these infer, will be within the
province of the professor of ethics; to which adding the
developments of these moral obligations, of those in which
all sects agree, with a knowledge of the languages, Hebrew,
Greek, and Latin, a basis will be formed common to all
sects. Proceeding thus far without offence to the Constitution, we have thought it proper at this point to leave every
sect to provide, as they think fittest, the means of further
instruction in their own peculiar tenets.

We are further of opinion, that after declaring by law
that certain sciences shall be taught in the University, fixing the number of professors they require, which we think
should, at present, be ten, limiting (except as to the professors who shall be first engaged in each branch) a maximum
for their salaries (which should be a certain but moderate
subsistence, to be made up by liberal tuition fees, as an
excitement to assiduity), it will be best to leave to the discretion of the visitors, the grouping of these sciences together, according to the accidental qualifications of the
professors; and the introduction also of other branches of

science, when enabled by private donations, or by public provision, and called for by the increase of population, or other change of circumstances; to establish beginnings, in short, to be developed by time, as those who come after us shall find expedient. They will be more advanced than we are in science and in useful arts, and will know best what will suit the circumstances of their day.

We have proposed no formal provision for the gymnastics of the school, although a proper object of attention for every institution of youth. These exercises with ancient nations, constituted the principle part of the education of their youth. Their arms and mode of warfare rendered them severe in the extreme; ours, on the same correct principle, should be adapted to our arms and warfare; and the manual exercise, military manoeuvres, and tactics generally, should be the frequent exercises of the students, in their hours of recreation. It is at that age of aptness, docility, and emulation of the practices of manhood, that such things are soonest learnt and longest remembered. The use of tools too in the manual arts is worthy of encouragement, by facilitating to such as choose it, an admission into the neighboring workshops. To these should be added the arts which embellish life, dancing, music, and drawing; the last more especially, as an important part of military education. These innocent arts furnish amusement and happiness to those who, having time on their hands, might less inoffensively employ it. Needing, at the same time, no regular incorporation with the institution, they may be left to accessory teachers, who will be paid by the individuals employing them, the University only providing proper apartments for their exercise.

The fifth duty prescribed to the Commissioners, is to propose such general provisions as may be properly enacted by the Legislature, for the better organizing and governing the University.

In the education of youth, provision is to be made for, 1, tuition; 2, diet; 3, lodgings; 4, government; and 5, honorary excitements. The first of these constitutes the proper functions of the professors; 2, the dieting of the students should be left to private boarding houses of their own choice, and at their own expense; to be regulated by the Visitors from time to time, the house only being provided by the University within its own precincts, and thereby of course subjected to the general regimen, moral or sumptuary, which they shall prescribe. 3. They should be lodged in dormitories, making a part of the general system of buildings. 4. The best mode of government for youth, in large collections, is certainly a desideratum not yet attained with us. It may be well questioned whether *fear* after a certain age, is a motive to which we should have ordinary recourse. The human character is susceptible of other incitements to correct conduct, more worthy of employ, and of better effect. Pride of character, laudable ambition, and moral dispositions are innate correctives of the indiscretions of that lively age; and when strengthened by habitual appeal and exercise, have a happier effect on future character than the degrading motive of fear. Hardening them to disgrace, to corporal punishments, and servile humiliations cannot be the best process for producing erect character. The affectionate deportment between father and son, offers in truth the best example for that of tutor and pupil; and the experience and practice of other countries, in this respect, may be worthy of enquiry and consideration with us. It will then be for the wisdom and discretion of the Visitors to devise and perfect a proper system of government, which, if it be founded in reason and comity, will be more likely to nourish in the minds of our youth the combined spirit of order and self-respect, so congenial with our political institutions, and so important to be woven into the American character.

Disciplinary Problems

Resolutions of the Board to the Faculty
of the University of Virginia,
October 3 and 5, 1825

Obviously college students created as many headaches for the administration a century and a half ago as they do today.

October 3, 1825

Resolved, that it be communicated to the Faculty of the professors of the University, as the earnest request and recommendation of the rector and Visitors, that so far as can be effected by their exertions, they cause the statutes and rules enacted for the government of the University, to be exactly and strictly observed; that the roll of each school particularly be punctually called at the hour at which its students should attend; that the absent and the tardy, without reasonable cause, be noted, and a copy of these notations be communicated by mail or otherwise to the parent or guardian of each student respectively, on the first days of every month during the term (instead of the days prescribed in a former statute for such communications).

That it is requested of them to make known to the students that it is with great regret that some breaches of order, committed by the unworthy few who lurk among them unknown, render necessary the extension to all of processes afflicting to the feelings of those who are conscious of their own correctness, and who are above all participation in these vicious irregularities. While the offenders continue unknown the tarnish of their faults spreads itself over the worthy also, and confounds all in a common censure. But that it is in their power to relieve themselves from the imputations and painful proceedings to which they are thereby subjected, by lending their aid to the faculty, on all occasions towards detecting the real guilty. The Visitors are aware that a prejudice prevails too extensively among the young that it is dishonorable to bear witness one against another. While this prevails, and under the form of a matter of conscience, they have been unwilling to authorize constraint, and have therefore, in their regulations on this subject, indulged the error, however unfounded in reason or morality. But this loose principle in the ethics of school-boy combinations, is unworthy of mature and regulated minds, and is accordingly condemned by the laws of their country, which, in offences within their cognisance, compel those who have knowledge of a fact, to declare it for the purposes of justice, and of the general good and safety of society. And certainly, where wrong has been done, he who knows and conceals the doer of it, makes himself an accomplice, and justly censurable as such. It becomes then but an act of justice to themselves, that the innocent and the worthy should throw off with disdain all communion of character with such offenders, should determine no longer to screen the irregular and the vicious under the respect of their cloak, and to notify them, even by a solemn association for the purpose, that they will cooperate with the faculty in future, for preservation of order, the vindication of their own character, and the reputation and usefulness of an institution which their country has so liberally established for their improvement, and to place within their reach those acquirements in knowledge on which their future happiness and fortunes depend. Let the good and the virtuous of the alumni of the University do this, and the disorderly will then be singled out for observation, and deterred by punishment, or disabled by expulsion, from infecting with their inconsideration the institution itself, and the sound mass of those which it is preparing for virtue and usefulness.

Although nocturnal absences from their chambers occasionally happening are not entirely forbidden, yet if frequent, habitual, or without excusable cause, they should be also noted and reported, with other special delinquencies, to the parent or guardian.

October 5, 1825

Resolved that the 47th enactment be amended, by inserting after the word "chewing" the words "or smoking." No student shall appear out of his dormitory masked or disguised in any manner whatever, which may render the recognition of his person more difficult, on pain of suspension or expulsion by the faculty of professors.

Intoxication shall, for the first offence, be liable to any of the minor punishments, and any repetition of the offence to any of the major punishments.

Lawn and Rotunda of University of Virginia
U. Va. Photography Division

Resolved, that the 40th enactment be amended, by inserting after the word "dissipation," the words "of profane swearing."

No person who has been a student at any other incorporated seminary of learning shall be received at this University, but on producing a certificate from such seminary or other satisfactory evidence to the faculty with respect to his general good conduct.

The professors being charged with the execution of the laws of the University, it becomes their duty to pursue proper means to discover and prevent offences. Respect from the student to the professor being at all times due, it is more especially so when the professor is engaged in his duty. Such respect, therefore, is solemnly enjoined on every student, and it is declared and enacted, that if any student refuse his name to a professor, or being required by him to stop, shall fail to do so, or shall be guilty of any other disrespect to a professor, he shall be liable to any of the punishments, minor or major.

JEFFERSON THE SCIENTIST

In the world of Thomas Jefferson the words "philosopher" and "doctor" had broader meanings than in the twentieth century. Medical doctors today are specialists in surgery or obstetrics or neurology. Doctors of philosophy are historians or physicists or linguists. The philosophers of the eighteenth century took all knowledge to be their province. Doctor Benjamin Franklin's title was an acknowledgment of the universal man, a tribute to his attainments as scientist, statesman, and man of letters.

There was a unity of thought, a belief in an ordered universe, which lay at the heart of Jeffersonian philosophy. Thus, the discovery by modern scientists of a food chain running from man to the tiny plankton of the oceans would have come as no surprise to the children of the Age of Reason.

The center of the American intellectual community was the American Philosophical Society, and its leading men in the years after the Revolution included David Rittenhouse, a mathematician; Benjamin Rush, a physician; Joseph Priestley, a chemist; and Benjamin Smith Barton, a botanist. In 1796 Jefferson was elected president of the Society and reelected annually for the next twenty years. Although he was clearly not the equal of Rittenhouse in mathematics, or Rush in medicine, or Barton in botany, Jefferson more nearly represented their ideal of the "philosopher" whose mind had an inquisitive range which theirs did not; for he insisted that there was a direct and intimate relationship between science and the affairs of mankind.

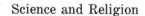

Science and Religion

Jefferson to John Adams, August 15, 1820

Jefferson struggles to reconcile scientific materialism and a philosopher's belief in God.

. . . let me turn to your puzzling letter of May the 12th, on matter, spirit, motion, etc. Its crowd of scepticisms kept me from sleep. I read it, and laid it down; read it, and laid it down, again and again; and to give rest to my mind, I was obliged to recur ultimately to my habitual anodyne, "I feel, therefore I exist." I feel bodies which are not myself: there are other existences then. I call them *matter*. I feel them changing place. This gives me *motion*. Where there is an absence of matter, I call it *void*, or *nothing*, or *immaterial space*. On the basis of sensation, or matter and motion, we may erect the fabric of all the certainties we can have or need. I can conceive *thought* to be an action of a particular organization of matter, formed for that purpose by its Creator, as well as that *attraction* is an action of matter, or *magnetism* of loadstone. When he who denies to the Creator the power of endowing matter with the mode of action called *thinking*, shall show how He could endow the sun with the mode of action called *attraction*, which reins the planets in the track of their orbits, or how an absence of matter can have a will, and by that will put matter into motion, then the Materialist may be lawfully required to explain the process by which matter exercises the faculty of thinking. When once we quit the basis of sensation, all is in the wind. To talk of *immaterial existences*, is to talk of *nothings*. To say that the human soul, angels, God, are immaterial, is to say, they are *nothings*, or that there is no God, no angels, no soul. I cannot reason otherwise: but I believe I am supported in my creed of materialism by the Lockes, the Tracys and the Stewarts. At what age of the Christian Church this heresy of *immaterialism*, or masked atheism, crept in, I do not exactly know. But a heresy it certainly is. Jesus taught nothing of it. He told us, indeed, that "God is a Spirit," but He has not defined what a spirit is, nor said that it is not *matter*. And the ancient fathers generally, of the three first centuries, held it to be matter, light and thin indeed, an etherial gas; but still matter. . . .

Rejecting all organs of information, therefore, but my senses, I rid myself of the pyrrhonisms with which an indulgence in speculations hyperphysical, so uselessly occupy and disquiet the mind. A single sense may indeed be sometimes deceived, but rarely; and never all our senses together, with their faculty of reasoning. They evidence realities, and there are enough of these for all the purposes of life, without plunging into the fathomless abyss of dreams and phantasms. I am satisfied, and sufficiently occupied with the things which are, without tormenting or troubling myself about those which may indeed be, but of which I have no evidence. I am sure that I really know many, many things, and none more surely than that I love you with all my heart, and pray for the continuance of your life until you shall be tired of it yourself.

Medical Science
Jefferson to Dr. Caspar Wistar,
June 21, 1807

Jefferson once observed that a gathering of as many as three doctors usually attracted buzzards.

. . . We know, from what we see and feel, that the animal body is in its organs and functions subject to derangement, inducing pain, and tending to its destruction. In this disordered state, we observe nature providing for the re-establishment of order, by exciting some salutary evacuation of the morbific matter, or by some other operation which escapes our imperfect senses and researches. She brings on a crisis, by stools, vomiting, sweat, urine, expectoration, bleeding, &c., which, for the most part, ends in the restoration of healthy action. Experience has taught us, also that there are certain substances, by which, applied to the living body, internally or externally, we can at will produce these same evacuations, and thus do, in a short time, what nature would do but slowly, and do effectually, what perhaps she would not have strength to accomplish. Where, then, we have seen a disease, characterized by specific signs or phenomena, and relieved by a certain natural evacuation or process, whenever that disease recurs under the same appearances, we may reasonably count on producing a solution of it by the use of such substances as we have found produce the same evacuation or movement. Thus, fulness of the stomach we can relieve by emetics; diseases of the bowels, by purgatives; inflammatory cases, by bleeding; intermittents, by the Peruvian bark; syphilis, by mercury; watchfulness, by opium; &c. So far, I bow to the utility of medicine. It goes to the well defined forms of disease, and happily, to those the most frequent. But the disorders of the animal body, and the symptoms indicating them, are as various as the elements of which the body is composed. The combinations, too, of these symptoms are so infinitely diversified, that many associations of them appear too rarely to establish a definite disease; and to an unknown disease, there cannot be a known remedy. Here then, the judicious, the moral, the humane physician should stop. Having been so often a witness to the salutary efforts which nature makes to re-establish the disordered functions, he should rather trust to their action, then hazard the interruption of that, and a greater derangement of the system, by conjectural experiments on a machine so complicated and so unknown as the human body, and a subject so sacred as human life. Or, if the appearance of doing something be necessary to keep alive the hope and spirit of the patient, it should be of the most innocent character. One of the most successful physicians I have ever known, has assured me, that he used more bread pills, drops of colored water, and powders of hickory ashes, than of all other medicines put together. It was certainly a pious fraud. But the adventurous physician goes on, and substitutes presumption for knowledge. From the scanty field of what is known, he launches into the boundless region of what is unknown. He establishes for his guide some fanciful theory of corpuscular attraction, of chemical agency, of mechanical powers, of stimuli, of irritability accumulated or exhausted, or depletion by the lancet and repletion by mercury, or some other ingenious dream, which lets him into all nature's secrets at short hand. On the principle which he thus assumes, he forms his table of nosology, arrays his diseases into families, and extends his curative treatment, by analogy, to all the cases he has thus arbitrarily marshalled together. I have lived myself to see the disciples of Hoffman, Boerhaave, Stahl, Cullen, Brown, succeed one another like the shifting figures of a magic lantern, and their fancies, like the dresses of the annual doll-babies from Paris, becoming, from their novelty, the vogue of the day, and yielding to the next novelty their ephemeral favor. The patient, treated on the fashionable theory, sometimes gets well in spite of the medicine. The medicine therefore restored him, and the young doctor receives new courage to proceed in his bold experiments on the lives of his fellow creatures. I believe we may safely affirm, that the inexperienced and presumptuous band of medical tyros let loose upon the world, destroys more of human life in one year, than all the Robin hoods, Cartouches, and Macheaths do in a century. It is in this part of medicine that I wish to see a reform, an abandonment of hypothesis for sober facts, the first degree of value set on clinical observation, and the lowest on visionary theories. I would wish the young practitioner, especially, to have deeply impressed on his mind, the real limits of his art, and that when the state of his patient gets beyond these, his office is to be a watchful, but quiet spectator of the operations of nature, giving them fair play by a well-regulated regimen, and by all the aid they can derive from the excitement of good spirits and hope in the patient. I have no doubt, that some diseases not yet understood may in time be transferred to the table of those known. But, were I a physician, I would rather leave the transfer to the slow hand of accident, than hasten it by guilty experiments on those who put their lives into my hands. The only foundations of medicine are, an intimate knowledge of the human body, and observation on the effects of medicinal substances on that. The anatomical and clinical schools, therefore, are those in which the young physician should be formed. If he enters innocence that of the theory of medicine, it is scarcely possible that he should come out untainted with error. His mind must be strong indeed, if, rising above juvenile credulity, it can maintain a wise infidelity against the authority of his instructors, and the bewitching delusions of their theories. You see that I estimate justly that portion of instruction which our medical students derive from your labors; and, associating with it one of the chairs which my old and able friend, Doctor Rush, so honorably fills, I consider them as the two fundamental pillars of the edifice. Indeed, I have such an opinion of the talents of the professors in the other branches which constitute the school of medicine with you, as to hope and believe, that it is from this side of the Atlantic, that Europe, which has taught us so many other things, will at length be led into sound principles in this branch of science, the most important of all others, being that to which we commit the care of health and life.

I dare say, that by the time, you are sufficiently sensible that old heads as well as young, may sometimes be charged with ignorance and presumption. The natural course of the human mind is certainly from credulity to scepticism; and this is perhaps the most favorable apology I can make for venturing so far out of my depth, and to one too, to whom the strong as well as the weak points of this science are so familiar. But having stumbled on the subject in my way, I wished to give a confession of my faith to a friend; and the rather, as I had perhaps, at times, to him as well as others, expressed my scepticism in medicine, without defining its extent or foundation. At any rate, it has permitted me, for a moment, to abstract myself from the cry and dreary waste of politics, into' which I have been impressed by the times on which I happened, and to indulge in the rich fields of nature, where alone I should have served as a volunteer, if left to my natural inclinations and partialities.

I salute you at all times with affection and respect.

A Modern Census

Memorial to Congress, January 10, 1808

Scholars would know a great deal more about the world of Thomas Jefferson if this proposal had been adopted. Not until 1850 did census takers do much more than count heads. "Th. Jefferson" was in 1808 "President" of both the Philosophical Society and of the United States.

The Memorial of the American Philosophical Society, Respectfully Sheweth

That this Society, instituted for the promotion of useful knowledge, understanding that the Legislature of the Union have under their consideration a bill for taking a new census of the inhabitants of the United States, consider it as offering an occasion of great value, and not otherwise to be obtained, of ascertaining sundry facts highly interesting and important to Society. Under this impression they beg leave respectfully to submit to the wisdom of the Legislature, the expediency of requiring from their Officers, in addition to the table in the former Act for the same purpose, others presenting a more detailed View of the inhabitants of the United States, under several different aspects.

They consider it as important to determine the effect of the soil and climate of the United States on the inhabitants thereof; and, for this purpose, dividing life into certain epochs, to ascertain the existing numbers within each epoch, from whence may be calculated the ordinary duration of life in these States, the chances of life for every epoch thereof, and the ratio of the increase of their population: firmly believing that the result will be sensibly different from what is presented by the tables of other countries, by which we are, from necessity, in the habit of estimating the probabilities of life here. And they humbly suggest, as proper for these purposes, the intervals between the following epochs, to wit:—birth, two, five, ten, sixteen, twenty one, and twenty five years of age, and every term of five years from thence to one hundred.

For the purpose also of more exactly distinguishing the increase of population by birth, and by immigration, they propose that another table shall present, in separate columns, the respective numbers of native citizens, citizens of foreign birth, and of Aliens.

In order to ascertain more compleatly the causes which influence life and health, and to furnish a curious and useful document of the distribution of society in these States, and of the conditions and vocations of our fellow citizens, they propose, that still another table shall be formed, specifying, in different columns, the number of free male inhabitants of all ages engaged in business, under the following or such other descriptions as the greater wisdom of the Legislature shall approve, to wit: 1. men of the learned professions, including clergymen, lawyers, physicians, those employed in the fine arts, teachers and scribes, in general. 2. Merchants and traders, including bankers, insurers, brokers and dealers of every kind. 3. Mariners. 4. handy craftsmen. 5. Labourers in agriculture. 6. Labourers of other descriptions. 7. domestic servants. 8. paupers. 9. persons of no particular calling living on their income: care being to be taken, that every person be noted but once in this table, and that under the description to which he principally belongs.

They flatter themselves, that from these data, truths will result very satisfactory to our citizens; that under the joint

Portrait of Jefferson by Mather Brown, 1786
Charles Francis Adams, Boston

The Comte de Buffon
Picture Collection, New York Public Library

influence of soil, climate and occupation, the duration of human life in this portion of the earth, will be found at least equal to what it is in any other; and that its population increases with a rapidity unequalled in all others.

What other views may be advantageously taken, they submit with those above suggested, to the superior wisdom of Congress, in whose decision they will acquiesce with unqualified respect.

By order of the society.

TH. JEFFERSON, *President*

Zoology and Paleontology

From Notes on Virginia, Query VI, 1785

European scientists, and especially the Comte de Buffon, contended that American mammals (including man) were physically smaller and therefore inferior to the European species. When Jefferson was in France, he met Buffon, and soon thereafter General John Sullivan of New Hampshire was the startled recipient of a request for the carcass of a moose. He complied and Jefferson triumphantly presented it to Buffon.

. . . Our quadrupeds have been mostly described by Linnaeus and Mons. de Buffon. Of these the mammoth, or big buffalo, as called by the Indians, must certainly have been the largest. Their tradition is, that he was carnivorous, and still exists in the northern parts of America. A delegation of warriors from the Delaware tribe having visited the Governor of Virginia, during the revolution, on matters of business, after these had been discussed and settled in council, the Governor asked them some questions relative to their country, and among others, what they knew or had heard of the animal whose bones were found at the Saltlicks on the Ohio. Their chief speaker immediately put himself into an attitude of oratory, and with a pomp suited to what he conceived the elevation of his subject, informed him that it was a tradition handed down from their fathers, "That in ancient times a herd of these tremendous animals came to the Big-bone licks, and began an universal destruction of the bear, deer, elks, buffaloes, and other animals which had been created for the use of the Indians; that the Great Man above, looking down and seeing this, was so enraged that he seized his lightning, descended on the earth, seated himself on a neighboring mountain, on a rock of which his seat and the print of his feet are still to be seen, and hurled his bolts among them till the whole were slaughtered, except the big bull, who presenting his forehead to the shafts, shook them off as they fell; but missing one at length, it wounded him in the side; whereon, springing round, he bounded over the Ohio, over the Wabash, the Illinois, and finally over the great lakes, where he is living at this day." It is well known, that on the Ohio, and in many parts of America further north, tusks, grinders, and skeletons of unparalleled magnitude, are found in great numbers, some lying on the surface of the earth, and some a little below it. A Mr. Stanley, taken prisoner near the mouth of the Tennessee, relates, that after being transferred through several tribes, from one to another, he was at length carried over the mountains west of the Missouri to a river which runs westwardly; that these bones abounded there, and that the natives described to him the animal to which they belonged as still existing in the northern parts of their country; from which description he judged it to be an elephant. Bones of the same kind have been lately found, some feet below the surface of the earth, in salines opened on the North Holston, a branch of the Tennessee, about the latitude of $36\frac{1}{2}°$ north. From the accounts published in Europe, I suppose it to be decided that these are of the same kind with those found in Siberia. Instances are mentioned of like animal remains found in the more southern climates of both hemispheres; but they are either so loosely mentioned as to leave a doubt of the fact, so inaccurately described as not

to authorize the classing them with the great northern
bones, or so rare as to found a suspicion that they have been
carried thither as curiosities from the northern regions. So
that, on the whole, there seem to be no certain vestiges of
the existence of this animal farther south than the salines
just mentioned. It is remarkable that the tusks and skeletons have been ascribed by the naturalists of Europe to the
elephant, while the grinders have been given to the hippopotamus, or river horse. Yet it is acknowledged, that the
tusks and skeletons are much larger than those of the elephant, and the grinders many times greater than those of
the hippopotamus, and essentially different in form. Wherever these grinders are found, there also we find the tusks
and skeleton; but no skeleton of the hippopotamus nor
grinders of the elephant. It will not be said that the hippopotamus and elephant came always to the same spot, the
former to deposit his grinders, and the latter his tusks and
skeleton. For what became of the parts not deposited there?
We must agree then, that these remains belong to each
other, that they are of one and the same animal, that this
was not a hippopotamus, because the hippopotamus had no
tusks, nor such a frame, and because the grinders differ in
their size as well as in the number and form of their points.
That this was not an elephant, I think ascertained by proofs
equally decisive. I will not avail myself of the authority of
the celebrated anatomist, who, from an examination of the
form and structure of the tusks, has declared they were
essentially different from those of the elephant; because
another anatomist, equally celebrated, has declared, on a
like examination, that they are precisely the same. Between
two such authorities I will suppose this circumstance equi-
vocal. But, 1. The skeleton of the mammoth (for so the
incognitum has been called) bespeaks an animal of five or
six times the cubic volume of the elephant, as Mons. de
Buffon has admitted. 2. The grinders are five times as large,
are square, and the grinding surface studded with four or
five rows of blunt points; whereas those of the elephant are

broad and thin, and their grinding surface flat. 3. I have
never heard an instance, and suppose there has been none,
of the grinder of an elephant being found in America. 4.
From the known temperature and constitution of the elephant, he could never have existed in those regions where
the remains of the mammoth have been found. The elephant
is a native only of the torrid zone and its vicinities; if, with
the assistance of warm apartments and warm clothing, he
has been preserved in the temperate climates of Europe, it
has only been for a small portion of what would have been
his natural period, and no instance of his multiplication in
them has ever been known. But no bones of the mammoth,
as I have before observed, have been ever found further
south than the salines of Holston, and they have been found
as far north as the Arctic circle. Those, therefore, who are
of opinion that the elephant and mammoth are the same,
must believe, 1. That the elephant known to us can exist
and multiply in the frozen zone; or, 2. That an eternal fire
may once have warmed those regions, and since abandoned
them, of which, however, the globe exhibits no unequivocal
indications; or, 3. That the obliquity of the ecliptic, when
these elephants lived, was so great as to include within the
tropics all those regions in which the bones are found; the
tropics being, as is before observed, the natural limits of
habitation for the elephant. But if it be admitted that this
obliquity has really decreased, and we adopt the highest rate
of decrease yet pretended, that is, of one minute in a century, to transfer the northern tropic to the Arctic circle,
would carry the existence of these supposed elephants two
hundred and fifty thousand years back; a period far beyond
our conception of the duration of animal bones less exposed
to the open air than these are in many instances. Besides,
though these regions would then be supposed within the
tropics, yet their winters would have been too severe for
the sensibility of the elephant. They would have had, too,
but one day and one night in the year, a circumstance to
which we have no reason to suppose the nature of the ele-

phant fitted. However, it has been demonstrated, that if a variation of obliquity in the ecliptic takes place at all, it is vibratory, and never exceeds the limits of nine degrees, which is not sufficient to bring these bones within the tropics. One of these hypotheses, or some other equally voluntary and inadmissible to cautious philosophy, must be adopted to support the opinion that these are the bones of the elephant. For my own part, I find it easier to believe that an animal may have existed, resembling the elephant in his tusks, and general anatomy, while his nature was in other respects extremely different. From the 30th degree of south latitude to the 30th degree of north, are nearly the limits which nature has fixed for the existence and multiplication of the elephant known to us. Proceeding thence northwardly to 36½ degrees, we enter those assigned to the mammoth. The farther we advance north, the more their vestiges multiply as far as the earth has been explored in that direction; and it is as probable as otherwise, that this progression continues to the pole itself, if land extends so far. The centre of the frozen zone, then, may be the acme of their vigor, as that of the torrid is of the elephant. This nature seems to have drawn a belt of separation between these two tremendous animals, whose breadth, indeed, is not precisely known, though at present we may suppose it about 6½ degrees of latitude; to have assigned to the elephant the regions south of these confines, and those north to the mammoth, founding the constitution of the one in her extreme of heat, and that of the other in the extreme of cold. When the Creator has therefore separated their nature as far as the extent of the scale of animal life allowed to this planet would permit, it seems perverse to declare it the same, from a partial resemblance of their tusks and bones. But to whatever animal we ascribe these remains, it is certain such a one has existed in America, and that it has been the largest of all terrestrial beings. It should have sufficed to have rescued the earth it inhabited, and the atmosphere it breathed, from the imputation of impotence in the conception and nourishment of animal life on a large scale; to have stifled, in its birth, the opinion of a writer, the most learned, too, of all others in the science of animal history, that in the new world, . . . that nature is less active, less energetic on one side of the globe than she is on the other. As if both sides were not warmed by the same genial sun; as if a soil of the same chemical composition was less capable of elaboration into animal nutriment; as if the fruits and grains from that soil and sun yielded a less rich chyle, gave less extension to the solids and fluids of the body, or produced sooner in the cartilages, membranes, and fibres, that rigidity which restrains all further extension, and terminates animal growth. The truth is, that a pigmy and a Patagonian, a mouse and a mammoth, derive their dimensions from the same nutritive juices. The difference of increment depends on circumstances unsearchable to beings with our capacities. Every race of animals seems to have received from their Maker certain laws of extension at the time of their formation. Their elaborate organs were formed to produce this, while proper obstacles were opposed to its further progress. Below these limits they cannot fall, nor rise above them. What intermediate station they shall take may depend on soil, on climate, on food, on a careful choice of breeders. But all the manna of heaven would never raise the mouse to the bulk of the mammoth.

The opinion advanced by the Count de Buffon, is 1. That the animals common both to the old and new world are smaller in the latter. 2. That those peculiar to the new are on a smaller scale. 3. That those which have been domesticated in both have degenerated in America; and 4. That on the whole it exhibits fewer species. And the reason he thinks is, that the heats of America are less; that more waters are spread over its surface by nature, and fewer of these drained off by the hand of man. In other words, that *heat* is friendly, and *moisture* adverse to the production and development of large quadrupeds. I will not meet this hypothesis on its first doubtful ground, whether the climate of

America be comparatively more humid? Because we are not furnished with observations sufficient to decide this question. And though, till it be decided, we are as free to deny as others are to affirm the fact, yet for a moment let it be supposed. The hypothesis, after this supposition, proceeds to another; that *moisture* is unfriendly to animal growth. The truth of this is inscrutable to us by reasoning *à priori*. Nature has hidden from us her *modus agendi*. Our only appeal on such questions is to experience; and I think that experience is against the supposition. It is by the assistance of *heat* and *moisture* that vegetables are elaborated from the elements of earth, air, water, and fire. We accordingly see the more humid climates produce the greater quantity of vegetables. Vegetables are mediately or immediately the food of every animal; and in proportion to the quantity of food, we see animals not only multiplied in their numbers, but improved in their bulk, as far as the laws of their nature will admit. Of this opinion is the Count de Buffon himself in another part of his work; . . . Here then a race of animals, and one of the largest too, has been increased in its dimensions by *cold* and *moisture*, in direct opposition to the hypothesis, which supposes that these two circumstances diminish animal bulk, and that it is their contraries *heat* and *dryness* which enlarge it. But when we appeal to experience we are not to rest satisfied with a single fact. Let us, therefore, try our question on more general ground. Let us take two portions of the earth, Europe and America for instance, sufficiently extensive to give operation to general causes; let us consider the circumstances peculiar to each, and observe their effect on animal nature. America, running through the torrid as well as temperate zone, has more *heat* collectively taken, than Europe. But Europe, according to our hypothesis, is the *dryest*. They are equally adapted then to animal productions; each being endowed with one of those causes which befriend animal growth, and with one which opposes it. If it be thought unequal to compare Europe with America, which is so much larger, I answer, not

Mr. Jefferson's polygraph

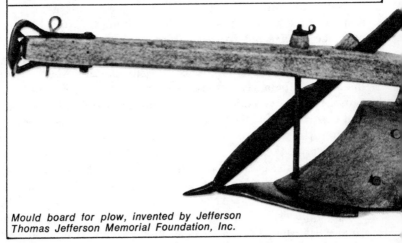

Mould board for plow, invented by Jefferson

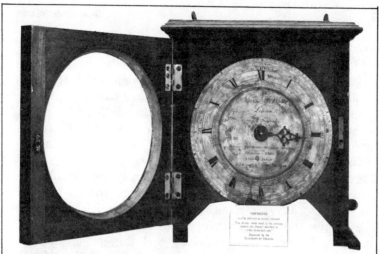

Odometer, used by Jefferson to measure distances
Thomas Jefferson Memorial Foundation, Inc.

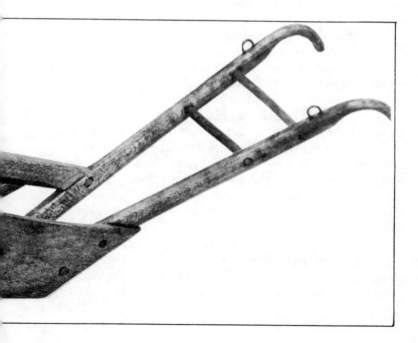

more so than to compare America with the whole world.
Besides, the purpose of the comparison is to try an hypothesis, which makes the size of animals depend on the *heat*
and *moisture* of climate. If, therefore, we take a region so
extensive as to comprehend a sensible distinction of climate,
and so extensive too as that local accidents, or the intercourse of animals on its borders, may not materially affect
the size of those in its interior parts, we shall comply with
those conditions which the hypothesis may reasonably demand. The objection would be the weaker in the present
case, because any intercourse of animals which may take
place on the confines of Europe and Asia, is to the advantage of the former, Asia producing certainly larger animals
than Europe. Let us then take a comparative view of the
quadrupeds of Europe and America, presenting them to the
eye in three different tables, in one of which shall be enumerated those found in both countries; in a second, those
found in one only; in a third, those which have been domesticated in both. To facilitate the comparison, let those of
each table be arranged in graduation according to their
sizes, from the greatest to the smallest, so far as their sizes
can be conjectured. The weights of the large animals shall
be expressed in the English avoirdupois and its decimals;
those of the smaller, in the same ounce and its decimals.
Those which are marked thus *, are actual weights of particular subjects, deemed among the largest of their species.
Those marked thus +, are furnished by judicious persons,
well acquainted with the species, and saying, from conjecture only, what the largest individual they had seen would
probably have weighed. The other weights are taken from
Mssrs. Buffon and D'Aubenton, and are of such subjects as
came casually to their hands for dissection. This circumstance must be remembered where their weights and mine
stand opposed; the latter being stated not to produce a conclusion in favor of the American species, but to justify a
suspension of opinion until we are better informed, and a

suspicion, in the meantime, that there is no uniform difference in favor of either; which is all I pretend.

Weights and Measures
Jefferson to Dr. Robert Patterson,
November 10, 1811

The world of science knows no national boundaries. Jefferson's proposal for an international metric system demonstrates not only his knowledge of the intricate scientific calculations involved but the equally intricate political problem of how "we shall offer this metrical system to the world."

DEAR SIR: Your favor of September 23d came to hand in due time, and I thank you for the nautical almanac it covered for the year 1813. I learn with pleasure that the Philosophical Society has concluded to take into consideration the subject of a fixed standard of measures, weights and coins, and you ask my ideas on it; insulated as my situation is, I am sure I can offer nothing but what will occur to the committee engaged on it, with the advantage on their part of correction by an interchange of sentiments and observations among themselves. I will, however, hazard some general ideas because you desire it, and if a single one be useful, the labor will not be lost.

The subject to be referred to as a standard, whether it be matter or motion, should be fixed by nature, invariable and accessible to all nations, independently of others, and with a convenience not disproportioned to its utility. What subject in nature fulfils best these conditions? What system shall we propose on this, embracing measures, weights and coins? and in what form shall we present it to the world? These are the questions before the committee.

Some other subjects have, at different times, been pro-

posed as standards, but two only have divided the opinions
of men: first, a direct admeasurement of a line on the
earth's surface, or second, a measure derived from its motion on its axis. To measure directly such a portion of the
earth as would furnish as element of measure, which might
be found again with certainty in all future times, would be
too far beyond the competence of our means to be taken
into consideration. I am free, at the same time, to say that
if these were within our power in the most ample degree,
this element would not meet my preference. The admeasurement would of course be of a portion of some great circle of
the earth. If of the equator, the countries over which that
passes, their character and remoteness, render the undertaking arduous, and we may say impracticable for most
nations. If of some meridian, the varying measures of its
degrees from the equator to the pole, require a mean to be
sought, of which some aliquot part may furnish what is
desired. For this purpose the 45th degree has been recurred
to, and such a length of line on both sides of it terminating
at each end in the ocean, as may furnish a satisfactory law
for a deduction of the unmeasured part of the quadrant.
The portion resorted to by the French philosophers, (and
there is no other on the globe under circumstances equally
satisfactory), is the meridian passing through their country
and a portion of Spain, from Dunkirk to Barcelona. The
objection to such an admeasurement as an element of
measure, are the labor, the time, the number of highly-
qualified agents, and the great expense required. All this,
too, is to be repeated whenever any accident shall have
destroyed the standard derived from it, or impaired its
dimensions. This portion of that particular meridian is
accessible of right to no one nation on earth. France, indeed,
availing herself of a moment of peculiar relation between
Spain and herself, has executed such an admeasurement.
But how would it be at this moment, as to either France or
Spain? and how is it at all times as to other nations, in
point either of right or of practice? Must these go through

the same operation, or take their measures from the standard prepared by France? Neither case bears that character of independence which the problem requires, and which neither the equality nor inconvenience of nations can dispense with. How would it now be, were England the deposit of a standard for the world? At war with all the world, the standard would be inaccessible to all other nations. Against this, too, are the inaccuracies of admeasurements over hills and valleys, mountains and waters, inaccuracies often unobserved by the agent himself, and always unknown to the world. The various results of the different measures heretofore attempted, sufficiently prove the inadequacy of human means to make such an admeasurement with the exactness requisite.

Let us now see under what circumstances the pendulum offers itself as an element of measure. The motion of the earth on its axis from noon to noon of a mean solar day, has been divided from time immemorial, and by very general consent, into 86,400 portions of time called seconds. The length of a pendulum vibrating in one of these portions, is determined by the laws of nature, is invariable under the same parallel, and accessible independently to all men. Like a degree of the meridian, indeed, it varies in its length from the equator to the pole, and like it, too, requires to be reduced to a mean. In seeking a mean in the first case, the 45th degree occurs with unrivalled preferences. It is the mid-way of the celestial ark from the equator to the pole. It is a mean between the two extreme degrees of the terrestrial ark, or between any two equi-distant from it, and it is also a mean value of all its degrees. In like manner, when seeking a mean for the pendulum, the same 45th degree offers itself on the same grounds, its increments being governed by the same laws which determine those of the different degrees of the meridian.

In a pendulum loaded with a Bob, some difficulty occurs in finding the centre of oscillation; and consequently the distance between that and the point of suspension. To lessen this, it has been proposed to substitute for the pendulum, a cylindrical rod of small diameter, in which the displacement of the centre of oscillation would be lessened. It has also been proposed to prolong the suspending wire of the pendulum below the Bob, until their centres of oscillation shall coincide. But these propositions not appearing to have received general approbation, we recur to the pendulum, suspended and charged as has been usual. And the rather as the laws which determine the centre of oscillation leave no room for error in finding it, other than that minimum in practice to which all operations are subject in their execution. The other sources of inaccuracy in the length of the pendulum need not be mentioned, because easily guarded against. But the great and decisive superiority of the pendulum, as a standard of measure, is in its accessibility to all men, at all times and in all places. To obtain the second pendulum for 45° it is not necessary to go actually to that latitude. Having ascertained its length in our own parallel, both theory and observation give us a law for ascertaining the difference between that and the pendulum of any other. To make a new measure therefore, or verify an old one, nothing is necessary in any place but a well-regulated time-piece, or a good meridian, and such a knowledge of the subject as is common in all civilized nations.

Those indeed who have preferred the other element, do justice to the certainty, as well as superior facilities of the pendulum, by proposing to recur to one of the length of their standard, and to ascertain its number of vibrations in a day. These being once known, if any accident impair their standard it is to be recovered by means of a pendulum which shall make the requisite number of vibrations in a day. And among the several commissions established by the Academy of Sciences for the execution of the several branches of their work on measures and weights, that respecting the pendulum was assigned to Messrs. Borda, Coulomb & Cassini, the result of whose labors, however, I have not learned.

Let our unit of measures then be a pendulum of such length as in the latitude of 45°, in the level of the ocean, and in a given temperature, shall perform its vibrations, in small and equal arcs, in one second of mean time.

What ratio shall we adopt for the parts and multiples of this unit? The decimal without a doubt. Our arithmetic being founded in a decimal numeration, the same numeration in a system of measures, weights and coins, tallies at once with that. On this question, I believe, there has been no difference of opinion.

In measures of length, then, the pendulem is our unit. It is a little more than one yard, and less than the ell. Its tenth or dime, will not be quite .4 inches. Its hundredth, or cent, not quite .4 of an inch; its thousandth, or mill, not quite .04 of an inch, and so on. The traveller will count his road by a longer measure. 1,000 units, or a kiliad, will not be quite two-thirds of our present mile, and more nearly a thousand paces than that.

For measures of surface, the square unit, equal to about ten square feet, or one-ninth more than a square yard, will be generally convenient. But for those of lands a larger measure will be wanted. A kiliad would be not quite a rood, or quarter of an acre; a myriad not quite 2½ acres.

For measures of capacity, wet and dry,

The cubic Unit = .1 would be about .35 cubic feet, .28 bushels dry, or ⅞ of a ton liquid.

Dime = .1 would be about 3.5 cubic feet, 2.8 bushels, or about ⅞ of a barrel liquid.

Cent = .01 about 50 cubic inches, or ⅞ of a quart.

Mill = .001 .5 of a cubic inch, or ⅔ of a gill

To incorporate into the same system our weights and coins, we must recur to some natural substance, to be found everywhere, and of a composition sufficiently uniform. Water has been considered as the most eligible substance, and rainwater more nearly uniform than any other kind found in nature. That circumstance renders it preferable to distilled water, and its variations in weight may be called insensible.

The cubic unit of this .1 would weigh about 2,165 lbs. or a ton between the long and short.

The Dime =	.1	a little more than 2. kentals
Cent =	.01	a little more than 20 lbs.
Mill =	.001	a little more than 2 lbs.
Decimmil =	.0001	about 3½ oz. avoirdupois
Centimmil =	.00001	a little more than 6 dwt.
Millionth =	.000001	about 15 grains
Centimmillionth =	.0000001	about 1½ grains
Decimmillionth =	.00000001	about .14 of a grain
Billionth =	.000000001	about .014 of a grain

With respect to our coins, the pure silver in a dollar being fixed by law at 347½ grains, and all debts and contracts being bottomed on that value, we can only state the pure silver in the dollar, which would be very nearly 23 millionths.

I have used loose and round numbers (the exact unit being yet undetermined) merely to give a general idea of the measures and weights proposed, when compared with those we now use. And in the names of the subdivisions I have followed the metrology of the ordinance of Congress of 1786, which for their series below unit adopted the Roman numerals. For that above unit the Grecian is convenient, and has been adopted in the new French system.

We now come to our last question, in what form shall we offer this metrical system to the world? In some one which shall be altogether unassuming; which shall not have the appearance of taking the lead among our sister institutions in making a general proposition. So jealous is the spirit of equality in the republic of letters, that the smallest excitement of what would mar our views, however salutary for all. We are in habits of correspondence with some of these institutions, and identity of character and of object, authorize our entering into correspondence with all. Let us then mature our system as far as can be done at present, by ascertaining the length of the second pendulum at 45° by forming two tables, one of which shall give the equivalent of every different denomination of measures, weights and coins in these States, in the unit of that pendelem, its decimals and multiples; and the other stating the equivalent of all the decimal parts and multiples of that pendulum, in the several denominations of measures, weights and coins of our existing system. This done, we might communicate to one or more of these institutions in every civilized country a copy of those tables, stating as our motive, the difficulty we had experienced, and often the impossibility of ascertaining the value of the measures, weights and coins of other countries, expressed in any standard which we possess; that desirous of being relieved from this, and of obtaining information which could be relied on for the purposes of science, as well as of business, we had concluded to ask it from the learned societies of other nations, who are especially qualified to give it with the requisite accuracy; that in making this request we had thought it our duty first to do ourselves, and to offer to others, what we meant to ask from them, by stating the value of our own measures, weights and coins, in some unit of measure already possessed, or easily obtainable, by all nations; that the pendulum vibrating seconds of mean time, presents itself as such an unit; its length being determined by the laws of nature, and easily ascertainable at all times and places; that we have thought that of 45° would be the most unexceptionable, as being a mean of all other parallels, and open to actual trial in both hemispheres. In this, therefore, as an unit, and in its parts and multiples in the decimal ratio, we have expressed, in the tables communicated, the value of all measures, weights and coins used in the United States, and we ask in return from their body as a table of the weights, measures and coins in use within their country, expressed in parts and multiples of the same unit. Having requested the same favor from the learned societies of other nations, our object is, with their assistance, to place within the reach of our fellow citizens at large a perfect knowledge of the measures, weights and coins of the countries with which they have commercial or friendly intercourse; and should the societies of other countries interchange their respective tables, the learned will be in possession of an uniform language in measures, weights and coins, which may with time become useful to other descriptions of their citizens, and even to their governments. This, however, will rest with their pleasure, not presuming, in the present proposition, to extend our views beyond the limits of our own nation. I offer this sketch merely as the outline of the kind of communication which I should hope would excite no jealousy or repugnance.

Peculiar circumstances, however, would require letters of a more special character to the Institute of France, and the Royal Society of England. The magnificent work which France has executed in the admeasurement of so large a portion of the meridian, has a claim to great respect in our reference to it. We should only ask a communication of their metrical system, expressed in equivalent values of the second pendulum of 45° as ascertained by Mssrs. Borda, Coulomb and Cassini, adding, perhaps, the request of an actual rod of the length of that pendulum.

With England, our explanations will be much more delicate. They are the older country, the mother country, more advanced in the arts and sciences, possessing more wealth and leisure for their improvement, and animated by a pride more than laudable. It is their measures, too, which we undertake to ascertain and communicate to themselves. The subject should therefore be opened to them with infinite tenderness and respect, and in some way which might give them due place in its agency. The parallel of 45° being within our latitude and not within theirs, the actual experiments under that would be of course assignable to use. But as a corrective, I would propose that they should ascertain the length of the pendulum vibrating seconds in the city of

London, or at the observatory of Greenwich, while we should do the same in an equi-distant parallel to the south of 45°, suppose in 38° 29'. We might ask of them, too, as they are in possession of the standards of Guildhall, of which we can have but an unauthentic account, to make the actual application of those standards to the pendulum when ascertained. The operation we should undertake under the 45th parallel (about Passamaquoddy), would give us a happy occasion, too, of engaging our sister society of Boston in our views, by referring to them the execution of that part of the work. For that of 38° 29' we should be at a loss. It crosses the tide waters of the Potomac, about Dumfries, and I do not know what our resources there would be unless we borrow them from Washington, where there are competent persons.

Although I have mentioned Philadelphia in these operations, I by no means propose to relinquish the benefit of observations to be made there. Her science and perfection in the arts would be a valuable corrective to the less perfect state of them in the other places of observation. Indeed, it is to be wished that Philadelphia could be made the point of observation south of 45°, and that the Royal Society would undertake the counterpoint on the north, which would be somewhere between the Lizard and Falmouth. The actual pendulums from both of our points of observation, and not merely the measures of them, should be delivered to the Philosophical Society, to be measured under their eye and direction.

As this is really a work of common and equal interest to England and the United States, perhaps it would be still more respectful to make our proposition to her Royal Society in the outset, and to agree with them on a partition of the work. In this case, any commencement of actual experiments on our part should be provisional only, and preparatory to the ultimate results. We might, in the meantime, provisionally also, form a table adapted to the length of the pendulum of 45°, according to the most approved estimates, including those of the French commissioners. This would serve to introduce the subject to the foreign societies, in the way before proposed, reserving to ourselves the charge of communicating to them a more perfect one, when that shall have been completed.

We may even go a step further, and make a general table of the measures, weights and coins of all nations, taking their value hypothetically for the present, from the tables in the commercial dictionary of the encyclopedie methodique, which are very extensive, and have the appearance of being made with great labor and exactness. To these I expect we must in the end recur, as a supplement for the measures which we may fail to obtain from other countries directly. Their reference is to the foot or inch of Paris, as a standard, which we may convert into parts of the second pendulum of 45°.

I have thus, my dear sir, committed to writing my general ideas on this subject, the more freely as they are intended merely as suggestions for consideration. It is not probable they offer anything which would not have occurred to the committee itself. My apology on offering them must be found in your request. My confidence in the committee, of which I take for granted you are one, is too entire to have intruded a single idea but on that ground.

Be assured of my affectionate and high esteem and respect.

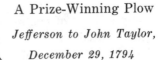

A Prize-Winning Plow

Jefferson to John Taylor,
December 29, 1794

In a day when popular acclaim went to military heroes, Jefferson was honored for the invention of his mould-board by a gold medal and associate membership in the Société d'Agriculture of Paris.

I have imagined and executed a mould-board which may be mathematically demonstrated to be perfect, as far as perfection depends on mathematical principles, and one great circumstance in its favor is that it may be made by the most bungling carpenter, and cannot possibly vary a hair's breadth in its form, by but gross negligence. You have seen the musical instrument called a sticcado. Suppose all its sticks of equal length, hold the fore-end horizontally on the floor to receive the turf which presents itself horizontally, and with the right hand twist the hind-end to the perpendicular, or rather as much beyond the perpendicular as will be necessary to cast over the turf completely. This gives an idea (though not absolutely exact) of my mould-board. It is on the principle of two wedges combined at right angles, the first in the direct line of the furrow to raise the turf gradually, the other across the furrow to turn it over gradually. For both these purposes the wedge is the instrument of the least resistance. I will make a model of the mould-board and lodge it with Colonel Harvie in Richmond for you.

I have just received information that a plough addressed to me has arrived at New York, from England . . . I presume it is the one sent by the Society of the Seine . . . I shall with great pleasure attend to the construction and transmission to the Society of a plough with my mould-board. This is the only part of that useful instrument to which I have paid any particular attention. But knowing how much the perfection of the plough must depend, 1st, on the line of traction; 2d, on the direction of the share; 3d, on the angle of the wing; 4th, on the form of the mould-board; and persuaded that I shall find the three first advantages eminently exemplified in that which the Society sends me, I am anxious to see combined with these a mould-board of my form, in the hope it will still advance the perfection of that machine. But for this I must ask time till I am relieved from the cares which have now a right to all my time, that is to say, till the next Spring. Then giving, in the leisure of retirement, all the time and attention this construction merits and requires,

I will certainly render to the Society the result in a plough
of the best form I shall be able to have executed.

JEFFERSON AND THE AMERICAN INDIN

JEFFERSON AND THE AMERICAN INDIAN

★
★
★

The unity of mankind was a persistent theme in Jeffersonian philosophy. The American Indian seemed an ideal subject for a study of man's origins because he was still living in a "state of nature" and his racial characteristics had not been diluted by mixing with other races.

Jefferson's approach was essentially that of an anthropologist. He concluded that the Indian was related to the peoples of northern Asia, an idea not original with him, but he suggested that these ethnic groups might have originated in America, reversing the accepted pattern of migration from Asia to America.

One reason for this hypothesis was his belief that the wide profusion of language dialects indicated an older civilization. Jefferson, already a master of French, Italian, Greek, and Latin, began to collect data on Indian vocabulary, hoping to find a clue to the problem of racial origin. He had classified over forty different dialects when his notes were destroyed by a fire.

Jefferson was painfully aware of the dilemma of the stone-age man struggling to survive the onslaught of the white man's civilization. When he became President, he recognized that public opinion would be an almost insurmountable obstacle to assimilation of the Indians, which he regarded as the ideal solution. In what was perhaps the most contradictory policy of his career, he urged the Indians to adapt themselves to the white man's civilization, while at the same time he instructed the War Department to create conditions which would force them to sell their land and accept removal to the Trans-Mississippi territory. He justified this seeming hypocrisy on the ground that the alternative would be extermination at the hands of the hordes of land-hungry

frontiersmen. It is perhaps as well that we remember the sympathetic view of the philosopher-scientist rather than the pragmatic
President who had to deal with the realities of an expanding
"empire for liberty."

"Who Is There to Mourn for Logan?"
From Notes on Virginia, Query VI, 1785

. . . Of the Indian of South America I know nothing; for
I would not honor with the appellation of knowledge, what
I derive from the fables published of them. These I believe
to be just as true as the fables of AEsop. This belief is
founded on what I have seen of man, white, red, and black,
and what has been written of him by authors, enlightened
themselves, and writing among an enlightened people. The
Indian of North America being more within our reach, I
can speak of him somewhat from my own knowledge, but
more from the information of others better acquainted with
him, and on whose truth and judgment I can rely. From
these sources I am able to say, in contradiction to this representation, that he is neither more defective in ardor, nor
more impotent with his female, than the white reduced to
the same diet and exercise; that he is brave, when an enterprise depends on bravery; education with him making the
point of honor consist in the destruction of an enemy by
stratagem, and in the preservation of his own person free
from injury; or, perhaps, this is nature, while it is education which teaches us to honor force more than finesse; that
he will defend himself against a host of enemies, always
choosing to be killed, rather than to surrender, though it be
to the whites, who he knows will treat him well; that in
other situations, also, he meets death with more deliberation
and endures tortures with a firmness unknown almost to
religious enthusiasm with us; that he is affectionate to his
children, careful of them, and indulgent in the extreme;

that his affections comprehend his other connections, weakening, as with us, from circle to circle, as they recede from the centre; that his friendships are strong and faithful to the uttermost extremity; that his sensibility is keen, even the warriors weeping most bitterly on the loss of their children, though in general they endeavor to appear superior to human events; that his vivacity and activity of mind is equal to ours in the same situation; hence his eagerness for hunting, and for games of chance. The women are submitted to unjust drudgery. This I believe is the case with every barbarous people. With such, force is law. The stronger sex imposes on the weaker. It is civilization alone which replaces women in the enjoyment of their natural equality. That first teaches us to subdue selfish passions, and to respect those rights in others which we value in ourselves. Were we in equal barbarism, our females would be equal drudges. The man with them is less strong than with us, but their women stronger than ours; and both for the same obvious reason; because our man and their woman is habituated to labor, and formed by it. With both races the sex which is indulged with ease is the least athletic. An Indian man is small in the hand and wrist, for the same reason for which a sailor is large and strong in the arms and shoulders, and a porter in the legs and thighs. They raise fewer children than we do. The cause of this are to be found, not in a difference of nature, but of circumstance. The women very frequently attending the men in their parties of war and of hunting, child-bearing becomes extremely inconvenient to them. It is said, therefore, that they have learned the practice of procuring abortion by the use of some vegetable; and that it even extends to prevent conception for a considerable time after. During these parties they are exposed to numerous hazards, to excessive exertions, to the greatest extremities of hunger. Even at their homes the nation depends for food, through a certain part of every year, on the gleanings of the forest; that is, they experience a famine once in every year. With all animals, if the female be badly fed, or not fed

at all, her young perish; and if both male and female be
reduced to like want, generation becomes less active, less
productive. To the obstacles, then, of want and hazard,
which nature has opposed to the multiplication of wild animals, for the purpose of restraining their numbers within
certain bounds, those of labor and of voluntary abortion are
added with the Indian. No wonder, then, if they multiply
less than we do. Where food is regularly supplied, a single
farm will show more of cattle, than a whole country of forests can of buffaloes. The same Indian women, when married to white traders, who feed them and their children
plentifully and regularly, who exempt them from excessive
drudgery, who keep them stationary and unexposed to accident, produce and raise as many children as the white
women. Instances are known, under these circumstances, of
their rearing a dozen children. An inhuman practice once
prevailed in this country, of making slaves of the Indians.
It is a fact well known to us, that the Indian women so en-
slaved produced and raised as numerous families as either
the whites or blacks among whom they lived. It has been
said that Indians have less hair than the whites, except on
the head. But this is a fact of which fair proof can scarcely
be had. With them it is disgraceful to be hairy on the body.
They say it likens them to hogs. They therefore pluck the
hair as fast as it appears. But the traders who marry their
women, and prevail on them to discontinue this practice,
say, that nature is the same with them as with the whites.
Nor, if the fact be true, is the consequence necessary which
has been drawn from it. Negroes have notoriously less hair
than the whites; yet they are more ardent. But if cold and
moisture be the agents of nature for diminishing the races
of animals, how comes she all at once to suspend their operation as to the physical man of the new world, whom the
Count acknowledges to be "*à peu près de même stature que
l'homme de notre monde*," and to let loose their influence on
his moral faculties? How has this "combination of the elements and other physical causes, so contrary to the enlarge-

ment of animal nature in this new world, these obstacles to the development and formation of great germs." been arrested and suspended, so as to permit the human body to acquire its just dimensions, and by what inconceivable process has their action been directed on his mind alone? To judge of the truth of this, to form a just estimate of their genius and mental powers, more facts are wanting, and great allowance to be made for those circumstances of their situation which call for a display of particular talents only. This done, we shall probably find that they are formed in mind as well as in body, on the same module with the "*Homo sapiens Europaeus.*" The principles of their society forbidding all compulsion, they are to be led to duty and to enterprise by personal influence and persuasion. Hence eloquence in council, bravery and address in war, become the foundations of all consequence with them. To these acquirements all their faculties are directed. Of their bravery and address in war we have multiplied proofs, because we have been the subjects on which they were exercised. Of their eminence in oratory we have fewer examples, because it is displayed chiefly in their own councils. Some, however, we have, of very superior lustre. I may challenge the whole orations of Demosthenes and Cicero, and of any more eminent orator, if Europe has furnished more eminent, to produce a single passage, superior to the speech of Logan, a Mingo chief, to Lord Dunmore, then governor of this State. And as a testimony of their talents in this line, I beg leave to introduce it, first stating the incidents necessary for understanding it.

In the spring of the year 1774, a robbery was committed by some Indians on certain land-adventurers on the river Ohio. The whites in that quarter, according to their custom, undertook to punish this outrage in a summary way. Captain Michael Cresap, and a certain Daniel Greathouse, leading on these parties, surprised, at different times, travelling and hunting parties of the Indians, having their women and children with them, and murdered many. Among these were unfortunately the family of Logan, a chief celebrated in peace and war, and long distinguished as the friend of the whites. This unworthy return provoked his vengeance. He accordingly signalized himself in the war which ensued. In the autumn of the same year a decisive battle was fought at the mouth of the Great Kanhaway, between the collected forces of the Shawanese, Mingoes and Delawares, and a detachment of the Virginia militia. The Indians were defeated and sued for peace. Logan, however, disdained to be seen among the suppliants. But lest the sincerity of a treaty should be disturbed, from which so distinguished a chief absented himself, he sent, by a messenger, the following speech, to be delivered to Lord Dunmore.

"I appeal to any white man to say, if ever he entered Logan's cabin hungry, and he gave him not meat; if ever he came cold and naked, and he clothed him not. During the course of the last long and bloody war Logan remained idle in his cabin, an advocate for peace. Such was my love for the whites, that my countrymen pointed as they passed, and said, 'Logan is the friend of white men.' I had even thought to have lived with you, but for the injuries of one man. Colonel Cresap, the last spring, in cold blood, and unprovoked, murdered all the relations of Logan, not even sparing my women and children. There runs not a drop of my blood in the veins of any living creature. This called on me for revenge. I have sought it: I have killed many: I have fully glutted my vengeance: for my country I rejoice at the beams of peace. But do not harbor a thought that mine is the joy of fear. Logan never felt fear. He will not turn on his heel to save his life. Who is there to mourn for Logan? —Not one."

Before we condemn the Indians of this continent as wanting genius, we must consider that letters have not yet been introduced among them. Were we to compare them in their present state with the Europeans, north of the Alps, when the Roman arms and arts first crossed those mountains, the comparison would be unequal, because, at that time, those parts of Europe were swarming with numbers; because numbers produce emulation, and multiply the chances of improvement, and one improvement begets another. Yet I may safely ask, how many good poets, how many able mathematicians, how many great inventors in arts or sciences, had Europe, north of the Alps, then produced? And it was sixteen centuries after this before a Newton could be formed. I do not mean to deny that there are varieties in the race of man, distinguished by their powers both of body and mind. I believe there are, as I see to be the case in the races of other animals. I only mean to suggest a doubt, whether the bulk and faculties of animals depend on the side of the Atlantic on which their food happens to grow, or which furnishes the elements of which they are compounded? Whether nature has enlisted herself as a Cis or Trans-Atlantic partisan? I am induced to suspect there has been more eloquence than sound reasoning displayed in support of this theory; that it is one of those cases where the judgment has been seduced by a glowing pen; and whilst I render every tribute of honor and esteem to the celebrated zoologist, who has added and is still adding, so many previous things to the treasures of science, I must doubt whether in this instance he has not cherished error also, by lending her for a moment his vivid imagination and bewitching language.

So far the Count de Buffon has carried this new theory of the tendency of nature to belittle her productions on this side the Atlantic. Its application to the race of whites transplanted from Europe, remained for the Abbe Raynal . . . "America has not yet produced one good poet." When we shall have existed as a people as long as the Greeks did before they produced a Homer, the Romans a Virgil, the French a Racine and Voltaire, the English a Shakespeare and Milton, should this reproach be still true, we will inquire from what unfriendly causes it has proceeded, that the other countries of Europe and quarters of the earth shall have not inscribed any name in the roll of poets. But neither has America produced "one able mathematician, one man of genius in a single art or a single science." In war we have produced a Washington, whose memory will be adored while liberty shall have votaries, whose name shall triumph over time, and will in future ages assume its just station among the most celebrated worthies of the world, when that wretched philosophy shall be forgotten which would have arranged him among the degeneracies of nature. In physics we have produced a Franklin, than whom no one of the present age has made more important discoveries, nor has enriched philosophy with more, or more ingenious solutions of the phenomena of nature. We have supposed Mr. Rittenhouse second to no astronomer living; that in genius he must be the first, because he is self-taught. As an artist he has exhibited as great a proof of mechanical genius as the world has ever produced. He has not indeed made a world; but he has by imitation approached nearer its Maker than any man who has lived from the creation to this day. As in philosophy and war, so in government, in oratory, in painting, in the plastic art, we might show that America, though but a child of yesterday, has already given hopeful proofs of genius, as well as of the nobler kinds, which arouse the best feelings of man, which call him into action, which substantiate his freedom, and conduct him to happiness, as of the subordinate, which serve to amuse him only. We therefore suppose, that this reproach is as unjust as it is kind: and that, of the geniuses which adorn the present age, America contributes its full share. For comparing it with those countries where genius is most cultivated, where are the most excellent models for art, and scaffoldings for the attainment of science, as France and England for instance, we calculate thus: The United States contains three millions of inhabitants; France twenty millions; and the British islands ten. We produce a Washington, a Franklin, a Rittenhouse. France then should have half a dozen in each of these lines, and Great Britain half that number, equally eminent. It may be true that France has; we are but just becoming acquainted with her, and our acquaintance so far gives us high ideas of the genius of her inhabitants. It would be injuring too many of them to name particularly a Voltaire, a Buffon, the constellation of Encyclopedists, the Abbe Raynal himself, &c. &c. We, therefore, have reason to believe she can produce her full quota of genius. The present war having so long cut off all communication with Great Britain, we are not able to make a fair estimate of the state of science in that country. The spirit in which she wages war, is the only sample before our eyes, and that does not seem the legitimate offspring either of science or of civilization. The sun of her glory is fast descending to the horizon. Her philosophy has crossed the channel, her freedom the Atlantic, and herself seems passing to that awful dissolution whose issue is not given human foresight to scan.

A Description of the Indian

From Notes on Virginia, Query XI, 1785

Jefferson assumed that there was a single species of man and that a wide range of factors accounted for the variations within the species.

When the first effectual settlement of our colony was made, which was in 1607, the country from the sea-coast to the mountains, and from the Potomac to the most southern waters of James' river, was occupied by upwards of forty different tribes of Indians. Of these the *Powhatans*, the *Mannahoacs*, and *Monacans*, were the most powerful. Those between the seacoast and falls of the rivers, were in amity with one another, and attached to the *Powhatans* as their link of union. Those between the falls of the rivers and the mountains, were divided into two confederacies; the tribes inhabiting the head waters of Potomac and Rappahannock, being attached to the *Mannahoacs*; and those on the upper parts of James' river to the *Monacans*. But the *Monacans* and their friends were in amity with the *Mannahoacs* and their friends, and waged joint and perpetual war against the *Powhatans*. We are told that the *Powhatans*, *Mannahoacs*, and *Monacans*, spoke languages so radically different, that interpreters were necessary when they transacted business. Hence we may conjecture, that this was not the case between all the tribes, and, probably, that each spoke the language of the nation to which it was attached; which we know to have been the case in many particular instances. Very possibly there may have been anciently three different stocks, each of which multiplying in a long course of time, had separated into so many little societies. This practice results from the circumstance of their having never submitted themselves to any laws, any coercive power, any shadow of government. Their only controls are their manners, and that moral sense of right and wrong, which, like the sense of tasting and feeling in every man, makes a part of his nature. An offence against these is punished by contempt, by exclusion from society, or, where the case is serious, as that of murder, by the individuals whom it concerns. Imperfect as this species of coercion may seem, crimes are very rare among them; insomuch that were it made a question, whether no law, as among the savage Americans, or too much law, as among the civilized Europeans, submits man to the greatest evil, one who has seen both conditions of existence would pronounce it to be the last; and that the sheep are happier of themselves, than under care of the wolves. It will be said, that great societies cannot exist without government. The savages, therefore, break them into small ones.

The territories of the *Powhatan* confederacy, south of the Potomac, comprehended about eight thousand square miles, thirty tribes, and two thousand four hundred warriors. Captain Smith tells us, that within sixty miles of Jamestown were five thousand people, of whom one thousand five hundred were warriors. From this we find the proportion of their warriors to their whole inhabitants, was as three to ten. The *Powhatan* confederacy, then, would consist of about eight thousand inhabitants, which was one for every square mile; being about the twentieth part of our present population in the same territory, and the hundredth of that of the British islands.

Besides these were the *Nottoways*, living on Nottoway river, the *Meherrins* and *Tuteloes* on Meherrin river, who were connected with the Indians of Carolina, probably with the Chowanocs.

The preceding table contains a state of these several tribes, according to their confederacies and geographical situation, with their numbers when we first became acquainted with them, where these numbers are known*. The numbers of some of them are again stated as they were in the year 1669, when an attempt was made by assembly to enumerate them. Probably the enumeration is imperfect, and in some measure conjectural, and that a farther search into the records would furnish many more particulars. What would be the melancholy sequel of their history, may, however, be argued from the census of 1669; by which we discover that the tribes therein enumerated were, in the space of sixty-two years, reduced to about one-third of their former numbers. Spirituous liquors, the small-pox, war, and an abridgement of territory to a people who lived principally on the spontaneous productions of nature, had committed terrible havoc among them, which generation, under the obstacles opposed to it among them, was not likely to make good. That the lands of this country were taken from them by conquest, is not so general a truth as is supposed. I find in our historians and records, repeated proofs of purchase, which cover a considerable part of the lower country; and many more would doubtless be found on further search. The upper country, we know, has been acquired altogether by purchases made in the most unexceptional form.

Westward of all these tribes, beyond the mountains, and

---

* The table referred to could not be located.

extending to the great lakes, were the *Maflawomees*, a most powerful confederacy, who harassed unremittingly the *Powhatans*, and *Manahoacs*. These were probably the ancestors of tribes known at present by the name of the *Six Nations*.

Very little can now be discovered of the subsequent history of these tribes severally. The *Chicahominies* removed about the year 1661, to Mattapony river. Their chief, with one from each of the Pamunkies and Mattaponies, attended the treaty of Albany in 1685. This seems to have been the last chapter in their history. They retained, however, their separate name so late as 1705, and were at length blended with the Pamunkies and Mattaponies, and exist at present only under their names. There remain of the *Mattaponies* three or four men only, and have more negro than Indian blood in them. They have lost their language, have reduced themselves, by voluntary sales, to about fifty acres of land, which lie on the river of their own name, and have from time to time, been joining the Pamunkies, from whom they are distant but ten miles. The *Pamunkies* are reduced to about ten or twelve men, tolerably pure from mixture with other colors. The older ones among them preserve their language in a small degree, which are the last vestiges on earth, as far as I know, of the Powhatan language. They have about three hundred acres of very fertile land, on Pamunky river, so encompassed by water that a gate shuts in the whole. Of the *Nottoways*, not a male is left. A few women constitute the remains of that tribe. They are seated on Nottoway river, in Southampton county, on very fertile lands. At a very early period, certain lands were marked out and appropriated to these tribes, and were kept from encroachment by the authority of the laws. They have usually had trustees appointed, whose duty was to watch over their interests, and guard them from insult and injury.

The *Monacans* and their friends, better known latterly by the name of *Tuscaroras*, were probably connected with the Massawomecs, or Five Nations. For though we are told their languages were so different that the intervention of interpreters was necessary between them, yet do we also learn that the Erigas, a nation formerly inhabiting on the Ohio, were of the same original stock with the Five Nations, and that they partook also of the Tuscarora language. Their dialects might, by long separation, have become so unlike as to be unintelligible to one another. We know that in 1712, the Five Nations received the Tuscaroras into their confederacy, and made them the Sixth Nation. They received the Meherrins and Tuteloes also into their protection; and it is most probable, that the remains of many other of the tribes, of whom we find no particular account, retired westwardly in like manner, and were incorporated with one or the other of the western tribes.

I know of no such thing existing as an Indian monument; for I would not honor with that name arrow points, stone hatchets, stone pipes, and half-shapen images. Of labor on the large scale, I think there is no remain as respectable as would be a common ditch for the draining of lands; unless indeed it would be the barrows, of which many are to be found all over this country. These are of different sizes, some of them constructed of earth, and some of loose stones. That they were repositories of the dead, has been obvious to all; but on what particular occasion constructed, was a matter of doubt. Some have thought they covered the bones of those who have fallen in battles fought on the spot of interment. Some ascribed them to the custom, said to prevail among the Indians, of collecting, at certain periods, the bones of all their dead, wheresoever deposited at the time of death. Others again supposed them the general sepulchres for towns, conjectured to have been on or near these grounds; and this opinion was supported by the quality of the lands in which they are found, (those constructed of earth being generally in the softest and most fertile meadow-grounds on river sides,) and by a tradition, said to be handed down from the aboriginal Indians, that, when they settled in a town, the first person who died was placed erect, and earth

put about him, so as to cover and support him; that when
another died, a narrow passage was dug to the first, the second reclined against him, and the cover of earth replaced,
and so on. There being one of these in my neighborhood, I
wished to satisfy myself whether any, and which of these
opinions were just. For this purpose I determined to open
and examine it thoroughly. It was situated on the low
grounds of the Rivanna, about two miles above its principal
fork, and opposite to some hills, on which had been an Indian town. It was of a spheroidical form, of about forty feet
diameter at the base, and had been of about twelve feet alti-
tude, though now reduced by the plough to seven and a half,
having been under cultivation about a dozen years. Before
this it was covered with trees of twelve inch diameter, and
round the base was an excavation of five feet depth and
width, from whence the earth had been taken of which the
hillock was formed. I first dug superficially in several parts
of it, and came to collections of human bones, at different
depths, from six inches to three feet below the surface.
These were lying in the utmost confusion, some vertical,
some oblique, some horizontal, and directed to every point
of the compass, entangled and held together in clusters by
the earth. Bones of the most distant parts were found together, as, for instance, the small bones of the foot in the
hollow of a scull; many sculls would sometimes be in con-
tact, lying on the face, on the side, on the back, top or bottom, so as, on the whole, to give the idea of bones emptied
promiscuously from a bag or basket, and covered over with
earth, without any attention to their order. The bones of
which the greatest numbers remained, were sculls, jaw-
bones, teeth, the bones of the arms, thighs, legs, feet and
hands. A few ribs remained, some vertebrae of the neck and
spine, without their processes, and one instance only of the
bone which serves as a base to the vertebral column. The
sculls were so tender, that they generally fell to pieces on
being touched. The other bones were stronger. There were
some teeth which were judged to be smaller than those of

an adult; a scull, which on a slight view, appeared to be that of an infant, but it fell to pieces on being taken out, so as to prevent satisfactory examination; a rib, and a fragment of the under-jaw of a person about half grown; another rib of an infant; and a part of the jaw of a child, which had not cut its teeth. This last furnishing the most decisive proof of the burial of children here, I was particular in my attention to it. It was part of the right half of the under-jaw. The processes, by which it was attenuated to the temporal bones, were entire, and the bone itself firm to where it had been broken off, which, as nearly as I could judge, was about the place of the eyetooth. Its upper edge, wherein would have been the sockets of the teeth, was perfectly smooth. Measuring it with that of an adult, by placing their hinder processes together, its broken end extended to the penultimate grinder of the adult. This bone was white, all the others of a sand color. The bones of infants being soft, they probably decay sooner, which might be the cause so few were found here. I proceeded then to make a perpendicular cut through the body of the barrow, that I might examine its internal structure. This passed about three feet from its centre, was opened to the former surface of the earth, and was wide enough for a man to walk through and examine its sides. At the bottom, that is, on the level of the circumjacent plain, I found bones; above these a few stones, brought from a cliff a quarter of a mile off; then a large interval of earth, then a stratum of bones, and so on. At one end of the section were four strata of bones plainly distinguishable; at the other, three; the strata in one part not ranging with those in another. The bones nearest the surface were least decayed. No holes were discovered in any of them, as if made with bullets, arrows, or other weapons. I conjectured that in this barrow might have been a thousand skeletons. Everyone will readily seize the circumstances above related, which militate against the opinion, that it covered the bones only of persons fallen in battle; and against the tradition also, which would make it the common sepulchre of a town, in which the bodies were placed upright, and touching each other. Appearances certainly indicate that it has derived both origin and growth from the accustomary collection of bones, and deposition of them together; that the first collection had been deposited on the common surface of the earth, a few stones put over it, and then a covering of earth, that the second had been laid on this, had covered more or less of it in proportion to the number of bones, and was then also covered with earth; and so on. The following are the particular circumstances which give it this aspect. 1. The number of bones. 2. Their confused position. 3. Their being in different strata. 4. The strata in one part having no correspondence with those in another. 5. The different states of decay in these strata, which seem to indicate a difference in the time of inhumation. 6. The existence of infant bones among them.

But on whatever occasion they may have been made, they are of considerable notoriety among the Indians; for a party passing, about thirty years ago, through the part of the country where this barrow is, went through the woods directly to it, without any instructions or inquiry, and having staid about it for some time, with expressions which were construed to be those of sorrow, they returned to the high road, which they had left about half a dozen miles to pay this visit, and pursued their journey. There is another barrow much resembling this, in the low grounds of the south branch of Shenandoah, where it is crossed by the road leading from the Rockfish gap to Staunton. Both of these have, within these dozen years, been cleared of their trees and put under cultivation, are much reduced in their height, and spread in width, by the plough, and will probably disappear in time. There is another on a hill in the Blue Ridge of mountains, a few miles north of Wood's gap, which is made up of small stones thrown together. This has been opened and found to contain human bones, as the others do. There are also many others in other parts of the country.

Great question has arisen from whence came these aboriginals of America? Discoveries, long ago made, were sufficient to show that the passage from Europe to America was always practicable, even to the imperfect navigation of ancient times. In going from Norway to Iceland, from Iceland to Greenland, from Greenland to Labrador, the first traject is the widest; and this having been practised from the earliest times of which we have any account of that part of the earth, it is not difficult to suppose that the subsequent trajects may have been sometimes passed. Again, the late discoveries of Captain Cook, coasting from Kamschatka to California, have proved that if the two continents of Asia and America be separated at all, it is only by a narrow strait. So that from this side also, inhabitants may have passed into America; and the resemblance between the Indians of America and the eastern inhabitants of Asia, would induce us to conjecture, that the former are the descendants of the latter, or the latter of the former; excepting indeed the Esquimaux, who, from the same circumstance of resemblance, and from identity of language must be derived from the Greenlanders, and these probably from some of the northern parts of the old continent. A knowledge of their several languages would be the most certain evidence of their derivation which could be produced. In fact, it is the best proof of the affinity of nations which ever can be referred to. How many ages have elapsed since the English, the Dutch, the Germans, the Swiss, the Norwegians, Danes and Swedes have separated from their common stock? Yet how many more must elapse before the proofs of their common origin, which exist in their several languages, will disappear? It is to be lamented then, very much to be lamented, that we have suffered so many of the Indian tribes already to extinguish, without our having previously collected and deposited in the records of literature, the general rudiments at least of the languages they spoke. Were vocabularies formed of all the languages spoken in North and South America, preserving their appellations of the most common objects in nature, of those which must be present to every nation barbarous or civilized, with the inflections of their nouns and verbs, their principles of regimen and concord, and these deposited in all the public libraries, it would furnish opportunities to those skilled in the languages of the old world to compare them with these, now, or at any future time, and hence to construct the best evidence of the derivation of this part of the human race.

But imperfect as is our knowledge of the tongues spoken in America, it suffices to discover the following remarkable fact: Arranging them under the radical ones to which they may be palpably traced, and doing the same by those of the red men of Asia, there will be found probably twenty in America, for one in Asia, of those radical languages, so called because if they were ever the same they have lost all resemblance to one another. A separation into dialects may be the work of a few ages only, but for two dialects to recede from one another till they have lost all vestiges of their common origin, must require an immense course of time; perhaps not less than many people give to the age of the earth. A greater number of those radical changes of language having taken place among the red men of America, proves them of greater antiquity than those of Asia.

Address to the Shawnee Nation
February 19, 1807

Part of the problem of Indian relations was the differing concepts of land ownership. The Indian idea was a communal one, and the fact that some chiefs had signed treaties did not, from the Indian point of view, bind those who had not signed.

MY CHILDREN, CHIEFS OF THE SHAWANEE NATION:

I have listened to the speeches of the Blackhoof, Blackbeard, and the other head chiefs of the Shawanese, and have considered them well. As all these speeches relate to the public affairs of your nation, I will answer them together.

You express a wish to have your lands laid off separately to your selves, that you may know what is your own, may have a fixed place to live on, of which you may not be deprived after you shall have built on it, and improved it; you would rather that this should be towards Fort Wayne, and to include the three reserves; you ask a strong writing from us, declaring your right, and observe that the writing you had was taken from you by the Delawares.

After the close of our war with the English, we wished to establish peace and friendship with our Indian neighbors also. In order to do this, the first thing necessary was to fix a firm boundary between them and us, that there might be no trespasses across that by either party. Not knowing then what parts on our border belonged to each Indian nation particularly, we thought it safest to get all those in the north to join in one treaty, and to settle a general boundary line between them and us. We did not intermeddle as to the lines dividing them one from another, because this was their concern, not ours. We therefore met the chiefs of the Wyandots, Delawares, Shawanees, Ottawas, Chippewas, Powtewatamies, Miamis, Eel-Rivers, Weeauks, Kickapoos, Piankeshaws, and Kaskaskies, at Greenville, and agreed on a general boundary which was to divide their lands from those of the whites, making only some particular reserves, for the establishment of trade and intercourse with them. This treaty was eleven years ago, as Blackbeard has said. Since that, some of them have thought it for their advantage to sell us portions of their lands, which has changed the boundaries in some parts; but their rights in the residue remain as they were, and must always be settled among themselves. If the Shawanese and Delawares, and their other neighbors, choose to settle the boundaries between their respective tribes, and to have them marked and recorded in our books, we will mark them as they shall agree among themselves, and will give them strong writings declaring the separate right of each. After which, we will protect each tribe in its respective lands, as well as against other tribes who might attempt to take them from them, as against our own people. The writing which you say the Delawares took from you, must have been the copy of the treaty of Greeneville. We will give you another copy to be kept by your nation.

With respect to the reserves, you know they were made for the purpose of establishing convenient stations for trade and intercourse with the tribes within whose boundaries they are. And as circumstances shall render it expedient to make these establishments, it is for your interest, as well as ours, that the possession of these stations should enable us to make them.

You complain that Blue-jacket, and a part of your people at Greeneville, cheat you in the distribution of your annuity, and take more of it than their just share. It will be difficult to remedy this evil while your nation is living in different settlements. We will, however, direct our agent to enquire, and inform us what are your numbers in each of your settlements, and will then divide the annuities between the settlements justly, according to their numbers. And if we can be of any service in bringing you all together into one place, we will willingly assist you for that purpose. Perhaps your visit to the settlement of your people on the Mississippi under the Flute may assist towards gathering them all into one place from which they may never again remove.

You say that you like our mode of living, that you wish to live as we do, to raise a plenty of food for your children, and to bring them up in good principles; that you adopt our mode of living, and ourselves as your brothers. My children, I rejoice to hear this; it is the wisest resolution you have ever formed, to raise corn and domestic animals, by the culture of the earth, and to let your women spin and weave clothes for you all, instead of depending for these on hunting. Be assured that half the labor and hardships you go through to provide your families by hunting, with food and clothing, if employed in a farm would feed and clothe them better. When the white people first came to this land, they were few, and you were many: now we are many, and you few; and why? because, by cultivating the earth, we produce plenty to raise our children, while yours, during a part of every year, suffer for want of food, are forced to eat unwholesome things, are exposed to the weather in your hunting camps, get diseases and die. Hence it is that your numbers lessen.

You ask for instruction in our manner of living, for carpenters and blacksmiths. My children, you shall have them. We will do everything in our power to teach you to take care of your wives and children, that you may multiply and be strong. We are sincerely your friends and brothers, we are as unwilling to see your blood spilt in war, as our own. Therefore, we encourage you to live in peace with all nations, that your women and children may live without danger, and without fear. The greatest honor of a man is in doing good to his fellow men, not in destroying them. We have placed Mr. Kirk among you, who will have other persons under him to teach you how to manage farms, and to make clothes for yourselves; and we expect you will put some of your young people to work with the carpenters and smiths we place among you, that they may learn the trades. In this way only can you have a number of tradesmen sufficient for all your people.

You wish me to name to you the person authorized to speak to you in our name, that you may know whom to believe, and not be deceived by imposters. My children, Governor Harrison is the person we authorize to talk to you in our name. You may depend on his advice, and that it comes from us. He stands between you and us, to convey with truth whatever either of us wishes to say to the other.

My children, I wish you a safe return to your friends and families, that you may retain your resolution of learning to live in our way, that it may give health and comfort to your families, and add members to your nation. In me you will always find a sincere and true friend.

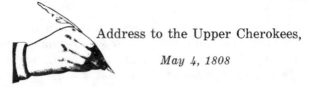

Address to the Upper Cherokees,

May 4, 1808

Contrary to popular tradition, the eastern Indians were both farmers and hunters. The Cherokees confounded the policymakers by settling down on farms and adopting the white man's ways. The Supreme Court in 1830 upheld their treaty rights, but the state of Georgia forced their removal and President Andrew Jackson acquiesced in this defiance of the Court's decision.

MY CHILDREN, CHIEFS OF THE UPPER CHEROKEES:

I am glad to see you at the seat of government, to take you by the hand, and to assure you in person of the friendship of the United States towards all their red children, and of their desire to extend, to them all, their protection of good offices. The journey you have come is a long one, and the object expressed in our conference of the other day is important. I have listened to it with attention, and given it the consideration it deserves. You complain that you do not receive your just proportion of the annuities we pay your nation; that the chiefs of the lower towns take for them more than their share. My children, this distribution is made by the authority of the Cherokee nation, and according to their own rules over which we have no control. We do our duty in delivering the annuities to the head men of the nation, and we pretend to no authority over them, to no right of directing how they are to be distributed. But we will instruct our agent, Colonel Meigs, to exhort the chiefs to do justice to all the parts of their nation in the distribution of these annuities, and pay these annuities in money, which could be more equally divided, if the nation would prefer that, and if we can be assured that the money will not be laid out in strong drink instead of necessaries for your wives and children. We wish to do whatever will best secure your people from suffering for want of clothes or food. It is these wants which bring sickness and death into your families, and prevent you from multiplying as we do. In answer to your question relating to the lands we have purchased from your nation at different times, I inform you that the payments have for the most part been made in money, which has been left, as the annuities are, to the discharge of your debts, and to distribute according to the rules of the nation.

You propose, my children, that your nation shall be divided into two, and that your part, the upper Cherokees, shall be separated from the lower by a fixed boundary, shall be placed under the government of the United States, become citizens thereof, and be ruled by our laws; in fine, to be our brothers instead of our children. My children, I shall rejoice to see the day when the red men, our neighbors, become truly one people with us, enjoying all the rights and privileges we do, and living in peace and plenty as we do, without any one to make them afraid, to injure their persons, or to take their property without being punished for it according to fixed laws. But are you prepared for this? Have you the resolution to leave off hunting for your living, to lay off a farm for each family to itself, to live by industry, the men working that farm with their hands, raising stock, or learning trades as we do, and the women spinning and weaving clothes for their husbands and children? All this is necessary before our laws can suit you or be of any use to you. However, let your people take this matter into consideration. If they think themselves prepared for becoming citizens of the United States, for living in subjection to laws and under their protection as we do, let them consult the lower towns, come with them to an agreement of separation by a fixed boundary, and send to this place a few of the chiefs they have most confidence in, with powers to arrange with us regulations concerning the protection of their persons, punishment of crimes, assigning to each family their separate farms, directing how these shall go to the family as they die one after another, in what manner they shall be governed, and all other particulars necessary for their happiness in their new condition. On our part I will ask the assistance of our great council, the Congress, whose authority is necessary to give validity to these arrangements, and who wish nothing more sincerely than to render your condition secure and happy. Should the principal part of your people determine to adopt this alteration, and a smaller part still choose to continue the hunter's life, it may facilitate the settlement among yourselves to be told that we will give to those leave to go, if they choose it, and settle on our lands beyond the Mississippi, where some Cherokees are already settled, and where game is plenty, and we will take measures for establishing a store there among them, where they may obtain necessaries in exchange for their peltries, and we will still continue to be their friends there as much as here.

My children, carry these words to your people, advise with Colonel Meigs in your proceedings, ask him to inform me from time to time how you go on, and I will further advise you in what may be necessary. Tell your people I take them all by the hand; that I leave them free to do as they choose, and that whatever choice they make, I will still be their friend and father.

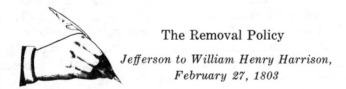

The Removal Policy

Jefferson to William Henry Harrison,
February 27, 1803

The President here delineates the true objectives of the administration's Indian policy.

. . . You will receive herewith an answer to your letter as President of the Convention; and from the Secretary of

War you receive from time to time information and instructions as to our Indian affairs. These communications being for the public records, are restrained always to particular objects and occasions; but this letter being unofficial and private, I may with safety give you a more extensive view of our policy respecting the Indians, that you may better comprehend the parts dealt out to you in detail through the official channel, and observing the system of which they make a part, conduct yourself in unison with it in cases where you are obliged to act without instruction. Our system is to live in perpetual peace with the Indians, to cultivate an affectionate attachment from them, by everything just and liberal which we can do for them within the bounds of reason, and by giving them effectual protection against wrongs from our own people. The decrease of game rendering their subsistence by hunting insufficient, we wish to draw them to agriculture, to spinning and weaving. The latter branches they take up with great readiness, because they fall to the women, who gain by quitting the labors of the field for those which are exercised within doors. When they withdraw themselves to the culture of a small piece of land, they will perceive how useless to them are their extensive forests, and will be willing to pare them off from time to time in exchange for necessaries for their farms and families. To promote this disposition to exchange lands, which they have to spare and we want, for necessaries, which we have to spare and they want, we shall push our trading uses, and be glad to see the good and influential individuals among them run in debt, because we observe that when these debts get beyond what the individuals can pay, they become willing to lop them off by a cession of lands. At our trading houses, too, we mean to sell so low as merely to repay us costs and charges, so as neither to lessen nor enlarge our capital. This is what private traders cannot do, for they must gain; they will consequently retire from the competition, and we shall thus get clear of this pest without giving offence or umbrage to the Indians. In this way our settlements will gradually circumscribe and approach the Indians, and they will in time either incorporate with us as citizens of the United States, or remove beyond the Mississippi. The former is certainly the termination of their history most happy for themselves; but, in the whole course of this, it is essential to cultivate their love. As to their fear, we presume that our strength and their weakness is now so visible that they must see we have only to shut our hand to crush them, and that all our liberalities to them proceed from motives of pure humanity only. Should any tribe be foolhardy enough to take up the hatchet at any time, the seizing the whole country of that tribe, and driving them across the Mississippi, as the only condition of peace, would be an example to others, and a furtherance of our final consolidation.

Combined with these views, and to be prepared against the occupation of Louisiana, by a powerful and enterprising people, it is important that, setting less value on interior extension of purchases from the Indians, we bend our whole views to the purchase and settlement of the country on the Mississippi, from its mouth to its northern regions, that we may be able to present as strong a front on our western as on our eastern border, and plant on the Mississippi itself the means of its own defence. We now own from 31 to the Yazoo, and hope this summer to purchase what belongs to the Choctaws from the Yazoo up to their boundary, supposed to be about opposite the mouth of Acanza. We wish at the same time to begin in your quarter, for which there is at present a favorable opening. The Cahokias extinct, we are entitled to their country by our paramount sovereignty. The Piorias, we understand, have all been driven off from their country, and we might claim it in the same way; but as we understand there is one chief remaining, who would, as the survivor of the tribe, sell the right, it is better to give him such terms as will make him easy for life, and take a conveyance from him. The Kaskaskias being reduced to a few families, I presume we may purchase their whole country for what would place every individual of them at his ease, and be a small price to us,—say by laying off for each family, whenever they would choose it, as much rich land as they could cultivate, adjacent to each other, enclosing the whole in a single fence, and giving them such an annuity in money or goods forever as would place them in happiness; and we might take them also under the protection of the United States. Thus possessed of the rights of these tribes, we should proceed to the settling their boundaries with the Poutewatamies and Kickapoos; claiming all doubtful territory, but paying them a price for the relinquishment of their concurrent claim, and even prevailing on them, if possible, to *cede*, for a price, such of their own unquestioned territory as would give us a convenient northern boundary. Before broaching this, and while we are bargaining with the Kaskaskies, the minds of the Poutewatamies and Kickapoos should be soothed and conciliated by liberalities and sincere assurances of friendship. Perhaps by sending a well-qualified character to stay some time in Decoigne's village, as if on other business, and to sound him and introduce the subject by degrees to his mind and that of the other heads of families, inculcating in the way of conversation, all those considerations which prove the advantages they would receive by a cession on these terms, the object might be more easily and effectually obtained than by abruptly proposing it to them at a formal treaty. Of the means, however, of obtaining what we wish, you will be the best judge; and I have given you this view of the system which we suppose will best promote the interests of the Indians and ourselves, and finally consolidate our whole country to one nation only; that you may be enabled the better to adapt your means to the object, for this purpose we have given you a general commission for treating. The crisis is pressing; whatever can now be obtained must be obtained quickly. The occupation of New Orleans, hourly expected, by the French, is already felt like a light breeze by the Indians. You know the sentiments they entertain of that nation; under the hope of their protection they will immediately stiffen against cessions of lands to us. We had better, therefore, do at once what can now be done.

I must repeat that this letter is to be considered as private and friendly, and is not to control any particular instructions which you may receive through official channel. You will also perceive how sacredly it must be kept within your own breast, and especially how improper to be understood by the Indians. For their interests and their tranquillity it is best they should see only the present age of their history. I pray you to accept assurances of my esteem and high consideration.

JEFFERSON AND THE BLACK AMERICAN

10 ★★★★

There is a tendency these days to dig into the private lives of famous people and to titter and snigger over their use of profanity, their marital quarrels, their sexual scandals, and the many occasions when their deeds did not match their words. Certainly in the past there has been an unfortunate propensity for portraying them as demigods, and certainly it is necessary to understand them as human beings. But before we grind them up, we must recognize that these men and women left their mark on history because they had an instinct and a courage which are denied to most of us. They could recognize those "seasons, in human affairs, of inward and outward revolution . . . when, in truth, *to dare* is the highest wisdom."

During the "second Reconstruction" which brought a revolution in the status of black Americans, it was fashionable to point out the intellectual fraud inherent in the fact that the author of the Declaration of Independence could write that all men are created equal while he himself was an owner of several hundred slaves. In fact, no American statesman of his time gave so much thought and effort to this vexing dilemma. Scientist that he was, Jefferson constantly searched for evidence of the innate equality of the Negro, not only in the biological but the moral sense. His conclusions were always tentative and it is obvious that he frequently rebelled against the rationalism and science of the eighteenth century in order to maintain his equalitarian convictions.

As for political action, Jefferson was responsible for the Virginia law prohibiting the slave trade and he made a tentative effort to introduce a plan for the gradual emancipation of slaves. As a member of the Confederation Congress, he introduced and the Congress enacted a land ordinance for the Northwest Territory which contained a provision excluding slavery, a provision which was retained in the Northwest Ordinance of 1787. As President he induced Congress to end the slave trade in 1808. No American statesman until Abraham Lincoln did as much to mitigate the "peculiar institution." That his achievement was small compared to his other accomplishments does not diminish his effort or his intent.

A Bill Concerning Slaves
1779

This was Jefferson's proposal as a member of the Council of Revisors who were drawing up the statutes for the new state of Virginia.

Be it enacted by the General Assembly, that no persons shall, henceforth, be slaves within this commonwealth, except such as were so on the first day of this present session of Assembly, and the descendants of the females of them.

Negroes and mulattoes which shall hereafter be brought into this commonwealth and kept therein one whole year, together, or so long at different times as shall amount to one year, shall be free. But if they shall not depart the commonwealth within one year thereafter they shall be out of the protection of the laws.

Those which shall come into this commonwealth of their own accord shall be out of the protection of the laws; save only such as being seafaring persons and navigating vessels hither, shall not leave the same while here more than twenty four hours together.

It shall not be lawful for any person to emancipate a slave but by deed executed, proved and recorded as is required by law in the case of a conveyance of goods and chattels, on consideration not deemed valuable in law, or by last will and testament, and with the free consent of such slave, expressed in presence of the court of the county wherein he resides: And if such slave, so emancipated, shall not within one year thereafter, depart the commonwealth, he shall be out of the protection of the laws. All conditions, restrictions and limitations annexed to any act of emancipation shall be void from the time such emancipation is to take place.

If any white woman shall have a child by a negro or mulatto, she and her child shall depart the commonwealth within one year thereafter. If they fail so to do, the woman shall be out of the protection of the laws, and the child shall be bound out by the Aldermen of the county, in like manner as poor orphans are by law directed to be, and within one year after its term of service expired shall depart the commonwealth, or on failure so to do, shall be out of the protection of the laws.

Where any of the persons before described shall be disabled from departing the commonwealth by grievous sickness, the protection of the law shall be continued to him until such disability be removed: And if the county shall in the mean time, incur any expense in taking care of him, as of other county poor, the Aldermen shall be intitled to recover the same from his former master, if he had one, his heirs, executors and administrators.

No negro or mulatto shall be a witness except in pleas of the commonwealth against negroes or mullatoes, or in civil pleas wherein negroes or mulattoes alone shall be parties.

No slave shall go from the tenements of his master, or other person with whom he lives, without a pass, or some letter or token whereby it may appear that he is proceeding by authority from his master, employer, or overseer: If he does, it shall be lawful for any person to apprehend and carry him before a Justice of the Peace, to be by his order punished with stripes, or not, in his discretion.

No slave shall keep any arms whatever, nor pass, unless with written orders from his master or employer, or in his company, with arms from one place to another. Arms in possession of a slave contrary to this prohibition shall be forfeited to him who will seize them.

Riots, routs, unlawful assemblies, trespasses and seditious speeches by a negro or mulatto shall be punished with stripes at the discretion of a Justice of the Peace; and he who will may apprehend and carry him before such Justice.

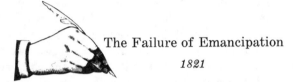

The Failure of Emancipation
1821

The following selection from "The Autobiography" contains Jefferson's account of what happened to his proposals for emancipation.

. . . The bill on the subject of slaves, was a mere digest of the existing laws respecting them, without any intimation of a plan for a future and general emancipation. It was thought better that this should be kept back, and attempted only by way of amendment, whenever the bill should be brought on. The principles of the amendment, however, were agreed on, that is to say, the freedom of all born after a certain day, and deportation at a proper age. But it was found that the public mind would not yet bear the proposition, not will it bear it even at this day. Yet the day is not distant when it must bear and adopt it, or worse will follow. Nothing is more certainly written in the book of fate, than that these people are to be free; nor is it less certain that the two races, equally free, cannot live in the same government. Nature, habit, opinion have drawn indelible lines of distinction between them. It is still in our power to direct the process of emancipation and deportation, peaceably, and in such slow degree, as that the evil will wear off insensibly, and their place be, *pari passu*, filled up by free white laborers. If, on the contrary, it is left to force itself on, human nature must shudder at the prospect held up. We should in vain look for an example in the Spanish deportation or deletion of the Moors. This precedent would fall far short of our case. . . .

Jefferson to M. de Meusnier,
1786

This excerpt is from comments written to M. de Meusnier, author of the *Encyclopedie Politique*, who had asked Jefferson for information to be used for the entry on "Les Etats Unis," dated January 24, 1786.

. . . M. de Meusnier, where he mentions that the slave law has been passed in Virginia, without the clause of emancipation, is pleased to mention, that neither Mr. Wythe, nor Mr. Jefferson was present, to make the proposition they had meditated; from which, people, who do not give themselves the trouble to reflect or inquire, might conclude hastily, that their absence was the cause why the proposition was not made; and, of course, that there were not in the Assembly, persons of virtue and firmness enough to propose the clause for emancipation. This supposition would not be true. There were persons there, who wanted neither the virtue to propose, nor talents to enforce the proposition, had they seen that the disposition of the legislature was ripe for it. These worthy characters would feel themselves wounded, degraded, and discouraged by this idea. Mr. Jefferson would therefore be obliged to M. de Meusnier, to mention it in some such manner as this. "Of the two commissioners, who had concerted the amendatory clause for the gradual emancipation of slaves, Mr. Wythe could not be present, he being a member of the judiciary department, and Mr. Jefferson was absent on the legation to France. But there were not wanting in that Assembly, men of virtue enough to propose, and talents to vindicate this clause. But they saw, that the moment of doing it with success was not yet arrived, and that an unsuccessful effort, as too often happens, would only rivet still closer the chains of bondage, and retard the moment of delivery to this oppressed description of men. What a stupendous, what an incomprehensible machine is man! who can endure toil, famine, stripes, imprisonment, and death itself, in vindication of his own liberty, and, the next moment be deaf to all those motives whose power supported him through his trial, and inflict on his fellow men a bondage, one hour of which is fraught with more misery, than ages of that which he rose in rebellion to oppose. But we must wait, with patience, the workings of an overruling Providence, and hope that that is preparing the deliverance of these, our suffering brethren. When the measure of their tears shall be full, when their groans shall have involved heaven itself in darkness, doubtless, a God of Justice will awaken to their distress, and by diffusing light and liberality among their oppressors, or, at length, by his exterminating thunder, manifest his attention to the things of this world, and that they are not left to the guidance of a blind fatality."

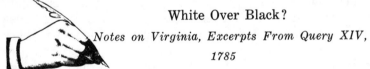

White Over Black?

Notes on Virginia, Excerpts From Query XIV,
1785

This is the fullest exposition that Jefferson made on the subject of black Americans. It reveals not only the prejudices of eighteenth-century Americans but also something of the state of eighteenth-century science.

. . . The bill reported by the revisers does not itself contain this proposition [for emancipation]; but an amendment containing it was prepared, to be offered to the legislature whenever the bill should be taken up, and farther directing, that they should continue with their parents to a certain age, then to be brought up, at the public expense, to

tillage, arts, or sciences, according to their geniuses, till the
females should be eighteen, and the males twenty-one years
of age, when they should be colonized to such place as the
circumstances of the time should render most proper, sending them out with arms, implements of household and of the
handicraft arts, seeds, pairs of the useful domestic animals,
&c., to declare them a free and independent people, and
extend to them our alliance and protection, till they have
acquired strength; and to send vessels at the same time to
other parts of the world for an equal number of white inhabitants; to induce them to migrate hither, proper en-
couragements were to be proposed. It will probably be
asked, Why not retain and incorporate the blacks into the
State, and thus save the expense of supplying by importation of white settlers, the vacancies they will leave? Deep-
rooted prejudices entertained by the whites; ten thousand
recollections, by the blacks, of the injuries they have sustained; new provocations; the real distinctions which nature
has made; and many other circumstances, will divide us
into parties, and produce convulsions, which will never end
but in the extermination of the one or the other race. To
these objections, which are political, may be added others,
which are physical and moral. The first difference which
strikes us is that of color. Whether the black of the negro
resides in the reticular membrane between the skin and
scarf-skin, or in the scarf-skin itself; whether it proceeds
from the color of the blood, the color of the bile, or from
that of some other secretion, the difference is fixed in nature,
and it is as real as if its seat and cause were better known
to us. And is this difference of no importance? Is it not the
foundation of a greater or less share of beauty in the two
races? Are not the fine mixtures of red and white, the expressions of every passion by greater or less suffusions of
color in the one, preferable to that eternal monotony, which
reigns in the countenances, that immovable veil of black
which covers the emotions of the other race? Add to these,
flowing hair, a more elegant symmetry of form, their own

judgment in favor of the whites, declared by their preference of them, as uniformly as is the preference of the Oran-
ootan for the black woman over those of his own species.
The circumstance of superior beauty, is thought worthy
attention in the propagation of our horses, dogs, and other
domestic animals; why not in that of man? Besides those of
color, figure, and hair, there are other physical distinctions
proving a difference of race. They have less hair on the face
and body. They secrete less by the kidneys, and more by the
glands of the skin, which gives them a very strong and disagreeable odor. This greater degree of transpiration, renders them more tolerant of heat, and less so of cold than the
whites. Perhaps, too, a difference of structure in the pul-
minary apparatus, which a late ingenious experimentalist
has discovered to be the principal regulator of animal heat,
may have disabled them from extricating, in the act of
inspiration, so much of that fluid from the outer air, or
obliged them in expiration, to part with more of it. They
seem to require less sleep. A black after hard labor through
the day, will be induced by the slightest amusements to sit
up til midnight, or later, though knowing he must be out
with the first dawn of the morning. They are at least as
brave, and more adventuresome. But this may perhaps proceed from a want of forethought, which prevents their seeing a danger till it be present. When present, they do not go
through it with more coolness or steadiness than the whites.
They are more ardent after their female; but love seems
with them to be more an eager desire, than a tender delicate
mixture of sentiment and sensation. Their griefs are transient. Those numberless afflictions, which render it doubtful
whether heaven has given life to us in mercy or in wrath,
are less felt, and sooner forgotten with them. In general,
their existence appears to participate more of sensation
than reflection. To this must be ascribed their disposition to
sleep when abstracted from their diversions, and unem-
ployed in labor. An animal whose body is at rest, and who
does not reflect, must be disposed to sleep of course. Com-

paring them by their faculties of memory, reason, and imagination, it appears to me that in memory they are equal to the whites; in reason much inferior, as I think one could scarcely be found capable of tracing and comprehending the investigations of Euclid; and that in imagination they are dull, tasteless, and anomalous. It would be unfair to follow them to Africa for this investigation. We will consider them here, on the same stage with the whites, and where the facts are not apocryphal on which a judgment is to be formed. It will be right to make great allowances for the difference of condition, of education, of conversation, of the sphere in which they move. Many millions of them have been brought to, and born in America. Most of them, indeed, have been confined to tillage, to their own homes, and their own society; yet many have been so situated, that they might have availed themselves of the conversation of their masters; many have been brought up to the handicraft arts, and from that circumstance have always been associated with the whites. Some have been liberally educated, and all have lived in countries where the arts and sciences are cultivated to a considerable degree, and all have had before their eyes samples of the best works from abroad. The Indians, with no advantages of this kind will often carve figures on their pipes not destitute of design and merit. They will crayon out an animal, a plant, or a country, so as to prove the existence of a germ in their minds which only wants cultivation. They astonish you with strokes of the most sublime oratory; such as prove their reason and sentiment strong, their imagination glowing and elevated. But never yet could I find that a black had uttered a thought above the level of plain narration; never saw even an elementary trait of painting or sculpture. In music they are more generally gifted than the whites with accurate ears for tune and time, and they have been found capable of imagining a small catch. Whether they will be equal to the composition of a more extensive run of melody, or of complicated harmony, is yet to be proved. Misery is often the parent of the most affect-

ing touches in poetry. Among the blacks is misery enough,
God knows, but no poetry. Love is the peculiar oestrum of
the poet. Their love is ardent, but it kindles the senses only,
not the imagination. Religion, indeed, has produced a
Phyllis Whately; but it could not produce a poet. The com-
positions published under her name are below the dignity
of criticism. The heroes of the Dunciad are to her, as Her-
cules to the author of that poem. Ignatius Sancho has
approached nearer to merit in composition; yet his letters
do more honor to the heart than the head. They breathe the
purest effusions of friendship and general philanthropy, and
show how great a degree of the latter may be compounded
with strong religious zeal. He is often happy in the turn of
his compliments, and his style is easy and familiar, except
when he affects a Shandean fabrication of words. But his
imagination is wild and extravagant, escapes incessantly
from every restraint of reason and taste, and, in the course
of its vagaries, leaves a tract of thought as incoherent and
eccentric, as is the course of a meteor through the sky. His
subjects should often have led him to a process of sober
reasoning; yet we find him always substituting sentiment
for demonstration. Upon the whole, though we admit him to
the first place among those of his own color who have presented themselves to the public judgment, yet when we
compare him with the writers of the race among whom he
lived and particularly with the epistolary class in which he
has taken his own stand, we are compelled to enrol him at
the bottom of the column. This criticism supposes the letters
published under his name to be genuine, and to have received amendment from no other hand; points which would
not be of easy investigation. The improvement of the blacks
in body and mind, in the first instance of their mixture with
the whites, has been observed by everyone, and proves that
their inferiority is not the effect merely of their condition
of life. We know that among the Romans, about the Augus-
tan age especially, the condition of their slaves was much

more deplorable than that of the blacks on the continent of America. The two sexes were confined in separate apartments, because to raise a child cost the master more than to buy one. Cato, for a very restricted indulgence to his slaves in this particular, took from them a certain price. But in this country the slaves multiply as fast as the free inhabitants. Their situation and manners place the commerce between the two sexes almost without restraint. The same Cato, on a principle of economy, always sold his sick and superannuated slaves. He gives it as a standing precept to a master visiting his farm, to sell his old oxen, old wagons, old tools, old and diseased servants, and everything else become useless. . . . The American slaves cannot enumerate this among the injuries and insults they receive. It was the common practice to expose in the island Aesculapius, in the Tyber, diseased slaves whose cure was like to become tedious. The emperor Claudius, by an edict, gave freedom to such of them as should recover, and first declared that if any person chose to kill rather than to expose them, it should not be deemed homicide. The exposing them is a crime of which no instance has existed with us; and were it to be followed by death, it would be punished capitally. We are told of a certain Vedius Pollio, who, in the presence of Augustus, would have given a slave as food to his fish, for having broken a glass. With the Romans, the regular method of taking the evidence of their slaves was under torture. Here it has been thought better never to resort to their evidence. When a master was murdered, all his slaves, in the same house, or within hearing, were condemned to death. Here punishment falls on the guilty only, and as precise proof is required against him as against a freeman. Yet notwithstanding these and other discouraging circumstances among the Romans, their slaves were often their rarest artists. They excelled too in science, insomuch as to be usually employed as tutors to their master's children. Epictetus, Terence, and Phaedrus, were slaves. But they were of the race of whites. It is not their condition then, but nature, which has produced the distinction. Whether further observation will or will not verify the conjecture, that nature has been less bountiful to them in the endowments of the head, I believe that in those of the heart she will be found to have done them justice. That disposition to theft with which they have been branded, must be ascribed to their situation, and not to any depravity of the moral sense. The man in whose favor no laws of property exist, probably feels himself less bound to respect those made in favor of others. When arguing for ourselves, we lay it down as a fundamental, that laws, to be just, must give a reciprocation of right; that, without this, they are mere arbitrary rules of conduct, founded in force, and not in conscience; and it is a problem which I give to the master to solve, whether the religious precepts against the violation of property were not framed for him as well as his slave? And whether the slave may not as justifiably take a little from one who has taken all from him, as he may slay one who would slay him? That a change in the relations in which a man is placed should change his ideas of moral right or wrong, is neither new, nor peculiar to the color of the blacks. Homer tells us it was so two thousand six hundred years ago. . . .

> Jove fix'd it certain, that whatever day
> Makes man a slave, takes half his worth away.

But the slaves of which Homer speaks were whites. Notwithstanding those considerations which must weaken their respect for the laws of property, we find among them numerous instances of the most rigid integrity, and as many as among their better instructed masters, of benevolence, gratitude, and unshaken fidelity. The opinion that they are inferior in the faculties of reason and imagination, must be hazarded with great diffidence. To justify a general conclusion, requires many observations, even where the subject may be submitted to the anatomical knife, to optical glasses, to analysis by fire or by solvents. How much more then where it is a faculty, not a substance, we are examining; where it eludes the research of all the senses; where the conditions of its existence are various and variously combined; where the effects of those which are present or absent bid defiance to calculation; let me add too, as a circumstance of great tenderness, where our conclusion would degrade a whole race of men from the rank in the scale of beings which their Creator may perhaps have given them. To our reproach it must be said that though for a century and a half we have had under our eyes the races of black and of red men, they have never yet been viewed by us as subjects of natural history. I advance it, therefore, as a suspicion only, that the blacks, whether originally a distinct race, or made distinct by time and circumstances, are inferior to the whites in the endowments both of body and mind. It is not against experience to suppose that different species of the same genus, or varieties of the same species, may possess different qualifications. Will not a lover of natural history then, one who views the gradations in all the races of animals with the eye of philosophy, excuse an effort to keep those in the department of man as distinct as nature has formed them? This unfortunate difference of color, and perhaps of faculty, is a powerful obstacle to the emancipation of these people. Many of their advocates, while they wish to vindicate the liberty of human nature, are anxious also to preserve its dignity and beauty. Some of these, embarrassed by the question, "What further is to be done with them?" join themselves in opposition with those who are actuated by sordid avarice only. Among the Romans emancipation required but one effort. The slave, when made free, might mix with, without staining the blood of his master. But with us a second is necessary, unknown to history. When freed, he is to be removed beyond the reach of mixture.

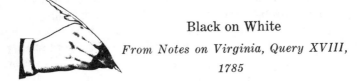

Black on White
From Notes on Virginia, Query XVIII,
1785

Jefferson points out some of the insidious and subtle effects of the "peculiar institution."

It is difficult to determine on the standard by which the manners of a nation may be tried, whether *catholic* or *particular*. It is more difficult for a native to bring to that standard the manners of his own nation, familiarized to him by habit. There must doubtless be an unhappy influence on the manners of our people produced by the existence of slavery among us. The whole commerce between master and slave is a perpetual exercise of the most boisterous passions, the most unremitting despotism on the one part, and degrading submissions on the other. Our children see this, and learn to imitate it; for man is an imitative animal. This quality is the germ of all education in him. From his cradle to his grave he is learning to do what he sees others do. If a parent could find no motive either in his philanthropy or his self-love, for restraining the intemperance of passion towards his slave, it should always be a sufficient one that his child is present. But generally it is not sufficient. The parent storms, the child looks on, catches the lineaments of wrath, puts on the same airs in the circle of smaller slaves, gives a loose to the worse of passions, and thus nursed, educated, and daily exercised in tyranny, cannot but be stamped by it with odious peculiarities. The man must be a prodigy who can retain his manners and morals undepraved by such circumstances. And with what execration should the statesman be loaded, who, permitting one half the citizens thus to trample on the rights of the other, transforms those into despots, and these into enemies, destroys the morals of the one part, and the *amor patriae* of the other. For if a slave can have a country in this world, it must be any other in preference to that in which he is born to live and labor for another; in which he must lock up the faculties of his nature, contribute as far as depends on his individual endeavors to the evanishment of the human race, or entail his own miserable condition on the endless generations proceeding from him. With the morals of the people, their industry also is destroyed. For in a warm climate, no man will labor for himself who can make another labor for him. This is so true, that of the proprietors of slaves a very small proportion indeed are ever seen to labor. And can the liberties of a nation be thought secure when we have removed their only firm basis, a conviction in the minds of the people that these liberties are of the gift of God? That they are not to be violated but with his wrath? Indeed I tremble for my country when I reflect that God is just; that his justice cannot sleep forever; that considering numbers, nature and natural means only, a revolution of the wheel of fortune, an exchange of situation is among possible events; that it may become probable by supernatural interference! The Almighty has no attribute which can take side with us in such a contest. But it is impossible to be temperate and to pursue this subject through the various considerations of policy, of morals, of history natural and civil. We must be contented to hope they will force their way into everybody's mind. I think a change already perceptible, since the origin of the present revolution. The spirit of the master is abating, that of the slave rising from the dust, his condition mollifying, the way I hope preparing, under the auspices of heaven, for a total emancipation, and that this is disposed, in the order of events, to be with the consent of the masters, rather than by their extirpation.

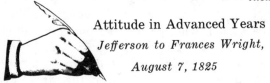

Attitude in Advanced Years
Jefferson to Frances Wright,
August 7, 1825

Even in old age, Jefferson considered the question of emancipation a vital concern.

. . . At the age of eighty-two, with one foot in the grave, and the other uplifted to follow it, I do not permit myself to take part in any new enterprises, even for bettering the condition of man, not even in the great one which is the subject of your letter, and which has been through life that of my greatest anxieties. The march of events has not been such as to render its completion practicable within the limits of time allotted to me; and I leave its accomplishment as the work of another generation. And I am cheered when I see that on which it is devolved, taking it up with so much good will, and such minds engaged in its encouragement. The abolition of the evil is not impossible; it ought never therefore to be despaired of. Every plan should be adopted, every experiment tried, which may do something towards the ultimate object. That which you propose is well worthy of trial. It has succeeded with certain portions of our white brethren, under the care of a Rapp and an Owen; and why may it not succeed with the man of color? An opinion is hazarded by some, but proved by none, that moral urgencies are not sufficient to induce him to labor; that nothing can do this but physical coercion. But this is a problem which the present age alone is prepared to solve by experiment. It would be a solecism to suppose a race of animals created, without sufficient foresight and energy to preserve their own existence. It is disproved, too, by the fact that they exist, and have existed through all the ages of history. We are not sufficiently acquainted with all the nations of Africa, to say that there may not be some in which habits of industry are established, and the arts practised which are necessary to render life comfortable. The experiment now in

progress in St. Domingo, those of Sierra Leone and Cape
Mesurado, are but beginning. Your proposition has its aspects of promise also; and should it not answer fully to
calculations in figures, it may yet, in its developments, lead
to happy results. These, however, I must leave to another
generation. The enterprise of a different, but yet important
character, in which I have embarked too late in life, I find
more than sufficient to occupy the enfeebled energies remaining to me, and to divert them to other objects, would
be a desertion of these. You are young, dear Madam, and
have powers of mind which may do much in exciting others
in this arduous task. I am confident they will be so exerted,
and I pray to Heaven for their success, and that you may be
rewarded with the blessings which such efforts merit.

Epitaph for an African Slave

Shores there are, bless'd shores for us remain,
And favor'd isles with golden fruitage crown'd
Where tufted flow'rets paint the verdant plain,
Where ev'ry breeze shall med'cine every wound.
There the stern tyrant that embitters life,
Shall vainly suppliant, spread his asking hand;
There shall we view the billow's raging strife,
Aid the kind breast, and waft his boat to land.

JEFFERSON AND RELIGION

11 ★ ★ ★

Jefferson's religious views should properly be considered in two categories. One was his attitude toward the religious establishment and the relationship of church and state. On this question he was outspoken and vehement. He believed that freedom of conscience was basic to any system of free government, and he was determined that any connection between the state and all religious denominations should be severed. When the opponents of his bill to establish religious liberty in Virginia offered a compromise which would have levied a tax to support the clergy of all faiths, he and his friend, James Madison, were adamant. Jefferson regarded "the priests" as parasites who subsisted at the taxpayers' expense and seldom performed their pastoral duties or showed much concern for the spiritual well-being of their parishioners.

The other side of Jefferson and religion was his personal religious beliefs. He was vilified as an atheist during his political career and many were convinced that his election to the presidency signified the death of God in America. Yet it is probable that no statesman of his time studied the Bible more closely, and he eventually edited a version of the New Testament gospels that contained what he believed to be a rationally acceptable account of the life of Christ.

He regarded his own religious convictions as a very personal and private matter, and it is only in a few intimate letters that these views are revealed. He was tolerant of other people's beliefs and he was the largest contributor to the Episcopal church in Albemarle because he considered it an important community institution. He regarded himself as a Christian, but it is doubtful that his carefully reasoned and highly individual creed would have been acceptable to many theologians of his day.

Bill For Establishing Religious Freedom,
1779

Jefferson regarded the passage of this bill by the Virginia legislature as one of the bitterest political battles of his career.
When he dictated the inscription for his gravestone, he listed the
bill for religious freedom with the Declaration of Independence
and the founding of the University of Virginia as the only accomplishments he wished to be memorialized.

SECTION I.   Well aware that the opinions and belief of
men depend on their own will, but follow involuntarily the
evidence proposed to their minds; that Almighty God hath
created the mind free, and manifested his supreme will that
free it shall remain by making it altogether insusceptible of
restraint; that all attempts to influence it by temporal punishments, or burthens, or by civil incapacitations, tend only
to beget habits of hypocrisy and meanness, and are a departure from the plan of the holy author of our religion,
who being lord both of body and mind, yet choose not to
propagate it by coercions on either, as was in his Almighty
power to do, but to exalt it by its influence on reason alone;
that the impious presumption of legislature and ruler, civil
as well as ecclesiastical, who, being themselves but fallible
and uninspired men, have assumed dominion over the faith
of others, setting up their own opinions and modes of thinking as the only true and infallible, and as such endeavoring
to impose them on others, hath established and maintained
false religions over the greatest part of the world and
through all time: That to compel a man to furnish contributions of money for the propagation of opinions which he
disbelieves and abhors, is sinful and tyrannical; that even
the forcing him to support this or that teacher of his own
religious persuasion, is depriving him of the comfortable
liberty of giving his contributions to the particular pastor
whose morals he would make his pattern, and whose powers
he feels most persuasive to righteousness; and is withdraw-

ing from the ministry those temporary rewards, which proceeding from a approbation of their personal conduct, are an additional incitement to earnest and unremitting labours for the instruction of mankind; that our civil rights have no dependance on our religious opinions, any more than our opinions in physics or geometry; and therefore the proscribing any citizen as unworthy the public confidence by laying upon him an incapacity of being called to offices of trust or emolument, unless he profess or renounce this or that religious opinion, is depriving him injudiciously of those privileges and advantages to which, in common with his fellow-citizens, he has a natural right; that it tends also to corrupt the principles of that very religion it is meant to encourage, by bribing with a monopoly of worldly honours and emoluments, those who will externally profess and conform to it; that though indeed these are criminals who do not withstand such temptation, yet neither are those innocent who lay the bait in their way; that the opinions of men are not the object of civil government, nor under its jurisdiction; that to suffer the civil magistrate to intrude his powers into the field of opinion and to restrain the profession or propagation of principles on supposition of their ill tendency is a dangerous fallacy, which at once destroys all religious liberty, because he being of course judge of that tendency will make his opinions the rule of judgment, and approve or condemn the sentiments of others only as they shall square with or suffer from his own; that it is time enough for the rightful purposes of civil government for its officers to interfere when principles break out into overt acts against peace and good order; and finally, that truth is great and will prevail if left to herself; that she is the proper and sufficient antagonist to error, and has nothing to fear from the conflict unless by human interposition disarmed of her natural weapons, free argument and debate; errors ceasing to be dangerous when it is permitted freely to contradict them.

SECTION II. We the General Assembly of Virginia do

enact that no man shall be compelled to frequent or support any religious worship, place, or ministry whatsoever, nor shall be enforced, restrained, molested, or burthened in his body or goods, or shall otherwise suffer, on account of his religious opinions or belief; but that all men shall be free to profess, and by argument to maintain, their opinions in matters of religion, and that the same shall in no wise diminish, enlarge, or affect their civil capacities.

SECTION III. And though we well know that this Assembly, elected by the people for their ordinary purposes of legislation only, have no power to restrain the acts of succeeding Assemblies, constituted with powers equal to our own, and that therefore to declare this act to be irrevocable would be of no effect in law; yet we are free to declare, and do declare, that the rights hereby asserted are of the natural rights of mankind, and that if any act shall be hereafter passed to repeal the present or to narrow its operations, such act will be an infringement of natural right.

 Notes On Religion
1776 (?)

Although the date is uncertain, these notes were intended to be used in the debate over separation of church and state in the Virginia Assembly.

Sabellians. Christian heretics. That here is but one person in the Godhead. That the "Word" and the holy spirit are only virtues, emanations or functions of the deity.

Sorcinians. Christian heretics. That the Father is the one only god. That the Word is no more than an expression of the godhead and had not existed from all eternity; that Jesus Christ was god no otherwise than by his superiority above all creatures who were put in subjection to him by the father. That he was not a mediator, but sent to be a pattern of conduct to men. That punishments of hell are not eternal.

Arminians. They think with the Romish church (against the Calvinists) that there is an universal grace given to all men, and that man is always *free* and at liberty to receive or reject grace. That God creates men free, that his justice would not permit him to punish men for crimes they are predestinated to commit. They admit the presence of god, but distinguish between fore-knowing and predestinating. All the fathers before St. Austin were of this opinion. The church of England founded her article of predestination on his authority.

Arians. Christian heretics. They avow there was a time when the Son was not, that he was created in time mutable in nature, and like the angels liable to sin; they deny the three persons in the trinity to be of the same essence. Erasmus and Grotius were Arians.

Apollinarians. Christian heretics. They affirm there was but one nature in Christ, that his body as well as soul was impassive and immortal, and that his birth, death, and resurrection was only in appearance.

Macedonians. Christian heretics. They teach that the Holy ghost was a mere creature, but superior in excellence to the Angels. See Broughton, verbo "Heretics," an enumeration of 48 sects of Christians pronounced Heretics.

Locke's system of Christianity is this: Adam was created happy and immortal; but his happiness was to have been *Earthly* and *Earthly* immortality. By *sin* he lost this—so that he became subject to total death (like that of brutes) to the crosses and unhappiness of this life. At the intercession however of the son of god this sentence was in part remitted. A life conformable to the law was to restore them again to immortality. And moreover to them who *believed* their *faith* was to be counted for righteousness. Nor that faith without works was to save them; St. James, c. 2 says expressly the contrary; and all make the fundamental pillars of Christianity to be faith and *repentance*. So that a reformation of life (included under *repentance*) was essential, and defects in this would be made up by their *faith*;

i.e., their faith should be counted for righteousness. As to that part of mankind who never had the gospel preached to them, they are 1. Jews.—2. Pagans, or Gentiles. The Jews had the law of works revealed to them. By this therefore they were to be saved: and a lively faith in God's promises to send the Messiah would supply small defects. 2. The Gentiles. St. Paul says—Romans 2, 13, "the Gentiles have the law written in their hearts," *i.e.*, the law of nature: to which adding a *faith* in God and his attributes that on their repentance he would pardon them, they also would be justified. This then explains the text "there is no other *name* under heaven by which a man may be saved," *i.e.*, the defects in good works shall not be supplied by a faith in Mahomet Foe [?] or any other except Christ.

The fundamentals of Christianity as found in the gospels are 1. Faith, 2. Repentance. That faith is every [where] explained to be a belief that Jesus was the Messiah who had been promised. Repentance was to be proved sincerely by good works. The advantages accruing to mankind from our Saviour's mission are these.

1. The knowledge of one god only.
2. A clear knowledge of their duty, or system of morality, delivered on such authority as to give it sanction.
3. The outward forms of religious worship wanted to be purged of that farcical pomp and nonsense with which they were loaded.
4. An inducement to a pious life, by revealing clearly a future existence in bliss, and that it was to be the reward of the virtuous.

The Epistles were written to persons *already Christians*. A person might be a Christian then before they were written. Consequently the fundamentals of Christianity were to be found in the preaching of our Saviour, which is related in the gospels. These fundamentals are to be found in the epistles dropped here and there, and promiscuously mixed with other truths. But these other truths are not to be made fundamentals. They serve for edification indeed and explain-

ing to us matters in worship and morality, but being written occasionally it will readily be seen that their explanations are adapted to the notions and customs of the people
they were written to. But yet every sentence in them
(though the writers were inspired) must not be taken up
and made a fundamental, without assent to which a man is
not to be admitted a member of the Christian church here,
or to his kingdom hereafter. The Apostles creed was by
them taken to contain all things necessary to salvation, and
consequently to a communion.

Shaftesbury *Charact*. As the Ancients tolerated vision-
aries and enthusiasts of all kinds so they permitted a free
scope to philosophy as a balance. As the Pythagoreans and
latter Platonists joined with the superstition of their times
the Epicureans and Academicks were allowed all the use of
wit and railery against it. Thus matters were balanced;
reason had play and science flourished. These contrarieties
produced harmony. Superstition and enthusiasm thus let
alone never raged to bloodshed, persecution, &c. But now a
new sort of policy, which considers the future lives and
happiness of men rather than the present, has taught to
distress one another, and raised an antipathy which if temporal interest could ever do now *uniformity* of opinion, a
hopeful project! is looked on as the only remedy against
this evil and is made the very object of government itself.
If magistracy had vouchsafed to interpose thus in other
sciences, we should have as bad logic, mathematics and
philosophy as we have divinity in countries where the law
settles orthodoxy.

Suppose the state should take into head that there should
be an uniformity of countenance. Men would be obligated
to put an artificial bump or swelling here, a patch there
&c., but this would be merely hypocritical, or if the alternative was given of wearing a mask 99/100ths must immediately mask. Would this add to the beauty of nature? Why
otherwise in opinions? In the middle ages of Christianity
opposition to the State opinions was hushed. The conse-

quence was, Christianity became loaded with all the Romish follies. Nothing but free argument, raillery and ridicule will preserve the purity of religion. 2 Cor. I. 24. the apostles declare they had no dominion over the faith.

A heretic is an impugner of fundamentals. What are fundamentals? The protestants will say those doctrines which are clearly and precisely delivered in the holy Scriptures. Dr. Vaterland would say the Trinity. But how far this character of being clearly delivered will suit the doctrine of the trinity I leave others to determine. It is nowhere expressly declared by any of the earliest fathers, and was never affirmed or taught by the Church before the Council of Nice (Chillingas Pref. #18. 33). Iraneaus says "who are the clean? those who go on firmly, believing in the Father and in the Son." The fundamental doctrine or the firmness of the Christian faith in this early age then was to believe in the *Father and Son.* Constantine wrote to Arius and Alexander treating the question "as vain foolish and impertinent as a dispute of words without sense which none could explain nor any comprehend, &c.". . .

Another plea for Episcopal government in Religion in England is its similarity to the political government by a king. No bishop, no king. This then with us is a plea for government by a presbytery which resembles republican government.

The clergy have ever seen this. The bishops were always mere tools of the crown.

The Presbyterian spirit is known to be so congenial with friendly liberty, that the patriots after the restoration finding that the humour of people was running too strongly to exalt the prerogative of the crown promoted the dissenting interest as a check and balance, and thus was produced the Toleration Act.

St. Peter gave the title of *clergy* to all god's people till Pope Higinus and the succeeding prelates took it from them and appropriated it to priests only. I Milt. 230.

Origen, being yet a layman, expounded the scriptures

publickly and was therein defended by Alexander of Jerusalem and Theodotn of Caesarea producing in his behalf divers examples that the privilege of teaching was anciently permitted to laymen. The first Nicene council called in the assistance of many learned lay brethren. ib. 230

Bishops were elected by the hands of the whole church. Ignatius (the most ancient of the extant fathers) writing to the Philadelphians says "that it belongs to them as to the church of god to chuse a bishop." Camden in his description of Scotland says "that over all the world bishops had no certain diocese till pope Dionysius about the year 268 did cut them out, and that the bishops of Scotland extended their function in what place soever they came, indifferently till temp. Malcolm 3. 1070."

Cyprian, epist. 68. says "the people chiefly hath power either of chusing worthy or refusing unworthy bishops the council of Nice contrary to the African churches exorts them to chuse orthodox bishops in the place of the dead." I Milt. 254.

Nicephorus Phocas the Greek emperor Ann. 1000 first enacted that no bishops should be chosen without his will. Ignatius in his epistle to those of Tra [illegible] confesseth that the presbyters are his fellowsellers and fellow henchers and Cyprian in the 6. 4. 52. epistle calls the presbyters, "his compresbyters" yet he was a bishop. A modern bishop to be moulded into a primitive one must be elected by the people, undiocest, unrevenued, unlorded. I. Milt. 255. From the dissensions among sects themselves arises necessarily a right of chusing and necessity of deliberating to which we will conform but if we chuse for ourselves, we must allow others to chuse also, and to reciprocally. This establishes religious liberty.

Why require those things in order to ecclesiastical communion which Christ does not require in order to life eternal? How can that be the church of Christ which excludes such persons from its communion as he will one day receive into the kingdom of heaven.

The arms of a religious society or church are exhortations, admonitions and advice, and ultimately expulsion or excommunication. This last is the utmost limit of power.

How far does the duty of toleration extend?

1. No church is bound by the duty of toleration to retain within her bosom obstinate offenders against her laws.
2. We have no right to prejudice another in his *civil* enjoyments because he is of another church. If any man err from the right way, it is his own misfortune, no injury to thee; nor therefore art thou to punish him in the things of this life because thou supposeth he will be miserable in that which is to come—on the contrary according to the spirit of the gospel, charity, bounty, liberality is due to him.

Each church being free, no one can have jurisdiction over another one, not even when the civil magistrate joins it. It neither acquires the right of the sword by the magistrate's coming to it, nor does it lose the rights of instruction or excommunication by his going from it. It cannot by the accession of any new member acquire jurisdiction over those who do not accede. He brings only himself, having no power to bring others. Suppose for instance two churches, one of Arminians another of Calvinists in Constantinople, has either any right over the other? Will it be said the orthodox one has? Every church is to itself orthodox; to others *erroneous* or heretical.

No man complains of his neighbor for ill management of his affairs, for an error in sowing his land, or marrying his daughter, for consuming his substance in taverns, pulling down building &c. in all these he has his liberty: but if he do not frequent the church, or there conform to ceremonies, there is an immediate uproar.

The care of every man's soul belongs to himself. But what if he neglect the care of it? Well what if he neglect the care of his health or estate, which more nearly relate to the state. Will the magistrate make a law that he shall not be poor or sick? Laws provide against injury from others; but not from ourselves. God himself will not save men against their wills.

If I be marching on with my utmost vigour in that way which according to the sacred geography leads to Jerusalem straight, why am I beaten and ill used by others because my hair is not of the right cut; because I have not been dressed right, because I eat flesh on the road, because I avoid certain by-ways which seem to lead into briars, because among several paths I take that which seems shortest and cleanest, because I avoid travellers less grave and keep company with others who are more sour and austere, or because I follow a guide crowned with a mitre and cloathed in white, yet these are the frivolous things which keep Christians at war.

If the magistrate command me to bring my commodity to a publick store house I bring it because he can indemnify me if he erred and I thereby lose it; but what indemnification can he give one for the kingdom of heaven?

I cannot give up my guidance to the magistrates, because he knows no more of the way to heaven than I do, and is less concerned to direct me right than I am to go right. If the Jews had followed their Kings, among so many, what number would have led them to idolatry? Consider the vicissitudes among the Emperors, Arians, Athana &c. or among our princes. H. 8. E. 6. Mary. Elizabeth. *Locke's* Works 2d vol.

Why persecute for difference in religious opinion?
1. For love to the Person.
2. Because of tendency of these opinions to dis [illegible gap in text].
1. When I see them persecute their nearest connection and acquaintance for gross vices, I shall believe it may proceed from love. Till they do this I appeal to their own consciences if they will examine, wh. they do not find some other principle.
2. Because of tendency. Why not then level persecution at the crimes you fear will be introduced? Burn or hang the adulterer, cheat &c. Or exclude them from offices.

Strange should be so zealous against things which tend to produce immorality and yet so indulgent to the immorality when produced. These moral vices all men acknowledge to be diametrically against Christianity and obstructive of salvation of souls, but the fantastical points for which we generally persecute are often very questionable; as we may be assured by the very different conclusions of people. Our Savior chose not to propagate his religion by temporal punishments or civil incapacitation, if he had, it was in his almighty power. But he chose to extend it by its influence on reason, there by shewing to others how they should proceed.

The commonwealth is "a Society of men constituted for protecting their civil interests."

Civil interests are "life, health, indolency of body, liberty and property." That the magistrate's jurisdictions extends only to civil rights appears from these considerations.

1. The magistrate has no power but what the people gave.

The people have not given him the care of souls because they could not, they could not, because no man has *right* to abandon the care of his salvation to another.

No man has *power* to let another prescribe his faith. Faith is not faith without believing. No man can conform his faith to the dictates of another. The life and essence of religion consists in the internal persuasion or belief of the mind. External forms of worship, when against our belief are hypocrisy and impiety. Rom. 14. 23. "he that doubteth is damned, if he eat, because he eateth not of faith: for whatsoever is not of faith, is sin."

2. If it be said the magistrate may make use of arguments and so draw the heterodox to truth, I answer, every man has a commission to admonish, exhort, convince another of error.

12. [sic] A church is "a voluntary society of men, joining themselves together of their own accord, in order to the public worshipping of god in such a manner as they judge acceptable to him and effectual to the salvation

of their souls." It is *voluntary* because no man is *by nature* bound to any church. The hope of salvation is the cause of his entering into it. If he find anything wrong in it, he should be as free to go out as he was to come in.

13. What is the power of that church. As it is a society it must have some laws for its regulation. Time and place of meeting. Admitting and excluding members &c. Must be regulation but as it was a spontaneous joining of members, it follows that its laws extend to its own members only, not to those of any other voluntary society, for then by the same rule some other voluntary society might usurp power over them.

Christ has said "wheresoever 2 or 3 are gathered together in his name he will be in the midst of them." This is his definition of a society. He does not make it essential that a bishop or presbyter govern them. Without them it suffices for the salvation of souls.

Compulsion in religion is distinguished peculiarly from compulsion in every other thing. I may grow rich by art I am compelled to follow, I may recover health by medicines I am compelled to take against my own judgment, but I cannot be saved by a worship I disbelieve and abhor.

Whatsoever is lawful in the Commonwealth, or permitted to the subject in ordinary way, cannot be forbidden to him for religious uses: and whatsoever is prejudicial to the Commonwealth in their ordinary uses and therefore prohibited by the laws ought not to be permitted to churches in their sacred rites. For instance it is unlawful in the ordinary course of things or in a private house to murder a child. It should not be permitted any sect then to sacrifice children: it is ordinarily lawful (or temporarily lawful) to kill calves or lambs. They may therefore be religiously sacrificed, but if the good of the state required a temporary suspension of killing lambs, as during a siege, sacrifices of them may then be rightfully suspended also. This is the true extent of toleration.

Truth will do well enough if left to shift for herself. She seldom has received much aid from the power of great men to whom she is rarely known and seldom welcome. She has no need of force to procure entrance into the minds of men. Error indeed has often prevailed by the assistance of power or force. Truth is the proper and sufficient antagonist to error. If anything pass in a religious meeting seditiously and contrary to the public peace, let it be punished in the same manner and no otherwise than as if it had happened in a fair or market. These meetings ought not to be sanctuaries for faction and flagitiousness.

Locke denies toleration to those who entertain opinions contrary to those moral rules necessary for the preservation of society; as for instance, that faith is not to be kept with those of another persuasion, that Kings excommunicated forfeit their crowns, that dominion is founded in grace, or that obedience is due to some foreign prince, or who will not own and teach the duty of tolerating all men in matters of religion, or who deny the existence of a god (it was a great thing to go so far—as he himself says of the parliament who framed the act of toleration but where he stopped short we may go on).

He says "neither Pagan nor Mahomedan nor Jew ought to be excluded from the civil rights of the Commonwealth because of his religion." Shall we suffer a Pagan to deal with us and not suffer him to pray to his god? Why have Christians been distinguished above all people who have ever lived, for persecutions? Is it because it is the genius of their religion? No, its genius is the reverse. It is the refusing *toleration* to those of a different opinion which has produced all the bustles and wars on account of religion. It was the misfortune of mankind that during the darker centuries the Christian priests following their ambition and avarice combining with the magistrate to divide the spoils of the people, could establish the notion that schismatics might be ousted of their possessions and destroyed. This notion we have not yet cleared ourselves from. In this case no wonder the oppressed should rebel, and they will continue to rebel and raise disturbance until their civil rights are full restored to them and all partial distinctions, exclusions and incapacitations removed.

An Evaluation of the Merit of the Doctrines of Jesus, in Comparison With Others
Jefferson to Dr. Benjamin Rush,
April 21, 1803

Jefferson discussed this subject with Rush over a four-year period. This syllabus is a summary of some of his conclusions.

In a comparative view of the Ethics of the enlightened nations of antiquity, of the Jews and of Jesus, no notice should be taken of the corruptions of reason among the ancients, to wit, the idolatry and superstition of the vulgar, nor of the corruptions of Christianity by the learned among its professors.

Let a just view be taken of the moral principles inculcated by the most esteemed of the sects of ancient philosophy, or of their individuals; particularly Pythagoras, Socrates, Epicurus, Cicero, Epictetus, Seneca, Antoninus.

I.   Philosophers. 1. Their precepts related chiefly to ourselves, and the government of those passions which, unrestrained, would disturb our tranquility of mind. In this branch of philosophy they were really great. 2. In developing our duties to others, they were short and defective. They embraced, indeed, the circles of kindred and friends, and inculcated patriotism, or the love of our country in the aggregate, as a primary obligation; towards our neighbors and countrymen they taught justice, but scarcely viewed them as within the circle of benevolence. Still less have they inculcated peace, charity, and love to our fellow-men, or embraced with benevolence the whole family of mankind.

II.   Jews. 1.   Their system was Deism; that is, the belief in one only god. But their ideas of him and of his attributes were degrading and injurious.   2. Their Ethics were not only imperfect, but often irreconcilable with the sound dictates of reason and morality, as they respect intercourse with those around us; and repulsive and anti-social, as respecting other nations. They needed reformation, therefore, in an eminent degree.

III.   Jesus.   In this state of things among the Jews, Jesus appeared. His parentage was obscure; his condition poor; his education null; his natural endowments great; his life correct and innocent; he was meek, benevolent, patient, firm, disinterested, and of the sublimest eloquence.

The disadvantages under which his doctrines appear are remarkable.

1.   Like Socrates and Epictetus, he wrote nothing himself.
2.   But he had not, like them, a Xenophon or an Arrian to write for him. I name not Plato, who only used the name of Socrates to cover the whimsies of his own brain. On the contrary, all the learned of his country, entrenched in its power and riches, were opposed to him, lest his labors should undermine their advantages; and the committing to writing of his life and doctrines fell on unlettered and ignorant men; who wrote, too, from memory, and not till long after the transactions had passed.
3.   According to the ordinary fate of those who attempt to enlighten and reform mankind, he fell an early victim to the jealousy and combination of the altar and the throne, at about thirty-three years of age, his reason having not yet attained the maximum of its energy, nor the course of his preaching, which was but of three years at most, presented occasions for developing a complete system of morals.
4.   Hence the doctrines which he really delivered were defective as a whole, and fragments only of what he did

deliver have come to us mutilated, misstated, and often unintelligible.

5. They have been still more disfigured by the corruptions of schismatizing followers, who have found an interest in sophisticating and perverting the simple doctrines he taught, by engrafting on them the mysticisms of a Grecian sophist, frittering them into subleties, and obscuring them with jargon, until they have caused good men to reject the whole in disgust, and to view Jesus himself as an impostor.

Notwithstanding these disadvantages, a system of morals is presented to us, which, if filled up in the style and spirit of the rich fragments he left us, would be the most perfect and sublime that has ever been taught by man.

The question of his being a member of the God-head, or in direct communication with it, claimed for him by some of his followers, and denied by others, is foreign to the present view, which is merely an estimate of the intrinsic merits of his doctrines.

1. He corrected the Deism of the Jews, confirming them in their belief of one only God, and giving them juster notions of his attributes and government.

2. His moral doctrines, relating to kindred and friends, were more pure and perfect than those of the most correct of the philosophers, and greatly more so than those of the Jews; and they went far beyond both in inculcating universal philanthropy not only to kindred and friends, to neighbors and countrymen, but to all mankind, gathering all into one family, under the bonds of love, charity, peace, common wants and common aids. A development of this head will evince the peculiar superiority of the system of Jesus over all others.

3. The precepts of philosophy, and of the Hebrew code, laid hold of actions only. He pushed his scrutinies into the heart of man; erected his tribunal in the region of his thoughts, and purified the waters at the fountain head.

4. He taught, emphatically, the doctrines of a future state, which was either doubted, or disbelieved by the Jews; wielded it with efficacy, as an important incentive, supplementary to the other motives to moral conduct.

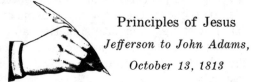

Principles of Jesus

Jefferson to John Adams,

October 13, 1813

After his retirement, Jefferson became reconciled with his old friend, John Adams. The two began a notable exchange of correspondence which lasted for what remained of their lives.

To compare the morals of the Old, with those of the New Testament, would require an attentive study of the former, a search through all its books for its precepts, and through all its history for its practices, and the principles they prove. As commentaries, too, on these the philosophy of the Hebrews must be inquired into, their Mishna, their Gemara, Cabbala, Jezirah, Sohar, Cosri, and their Talmud, must be examined and understood, in order to do them full justice. Brucker [History of Philosophy], it would seem, has gone deeply into these repositories of their ethics, and Enfield his epitomizer, concludes in these words: "Ethics were so little understood among the Jews, that in their whole compilation called the Talmud, there is only one treatise on moral subjects. Their books of morals chiefly consisted in a minute enumeration of duties. From the law of Moses were deduced six hundred and thirteen precepts, which were divided into two classes, affirmative and negative, two hundred and forty-eight in the former, and three hundred and sixty-five in the latter. It may serve to give the reader some idea of the low state of moral philosophy among the Jews in the middle age, to add that of the two hundred and forty-eight affirmative precepts, only three were considered as obligatory upon women, and that in order to obtain salvation, it was judged sufficient to fulfil any one single law in the hour of death; the observance of the rest being deemed necessary, only to increase the felicity of the future life. What a wretched depravity of sentiment and manners must have prevailed, before such corrupt maxims could have obtained credit! It is impossible to collect from these writings a consistent series of moral doctrine." Enfield, B. 4, chap. 3. It was the reformation of this "wretched depravity" of morals which Jesus undertook.

In extracting the pure principles which he taught, we should have to strip off the artificial vestments in which they have been muffled by priests, who have travestied them into various forms, as instruments of riches and power to themselves. We must dismiss the Platonists and Plotinists, the Stagyrites and Gamalielites, the Eclectics, the Gnostics and Scholastics, their essences and emanations, their Logos and Demiurges, AEons and Daemons, male and female, with a long train of &c. &c. &c., or, shall I say at once, of nonsense. We must reduce our volume to the simple evangelists, select, even from them, the very words only of Jesus, paring off the amphiboligisms into which they have been led, by forgetting often, or not understanding, what had fallen from him, by giving their own misconceptions as his dicta, and expressing unintelligibly for others what they had not understood themselves. There will be found remaining the most sublime and benevolent code of morals which has ever been offered to man. I have performed this operation for my own use, by cutting verse by verse out of the printed book, and arranging the matter which is evidently his, and which is as easily distinguishable as diamonds in a dunghill. The result is an octave of forty-six pages, of pure and unsophisticated doctrines, such as were professed and acted on by the *unlettered* Apostles, the Apostolic Fathers, and the Christians of the first century. Their Platonising successors, indeed, in after times, in order to legitimate the corruptions which they had incorporated into the doctrines of Jesus, found it necessary to disavow the primitive Christians, who had taken their principles from the mouth of Jesus himself, of his Apostles, and the Fathers contemporary with them. They excommunicated their followers as heretics, branding them with the opprobrious name of Ebionites or Beggars.

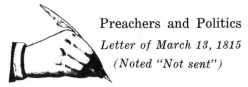

Preachers and Politics
Letter of March 13, 1815
(Noted "Not sent")

Undoubtedly one of the principal reasons for Jefferson's hostility to organized religion was his detestation of what he called "the priesthood."

On one question only I differ from him [Alexander McLeod], and it is that which constitutes the subject of his first discourse, the right of discussing public affairs *in the pulpit*. I add the last words, because I admit the right in *general conversation* and in *writing*; in which last form it has been exercised in the valuable book you have now favored me with.

The mass of human concerns, moral and physical, is so vast, the field of knowledge requisite for man to conduct them to the best advantage is so extensive, that no human being can acquire the whole himself, and much less in that degree necessary for the instruction of others. It has of necessity, then, been distributed into different departments, each of which, singly, may give occupation enough to the whole time and attention of a single individual. Thus we have teachers of Languages, teachers of Mathematics, of Natural Philosophy, of Chemistry, of Medicine, of Law, of History, of Government, &c. Religion, too, is a separate department, and happens to be the only one deemed requisite for all men, however high or low. Collections of men associate together, under the name of congregations, and employ a religious teacher of the particular sect of opinions of which they happen to be, and contribute to make up a stipend as a compensation for the trouble of delivering them, at such periods as they agree on, lessons in the religion they profess. If they want instruction in other sciences or arts, they apply to other instructors; and this is generally the business of early life. But I suppose there is not an instance of a single congregation which has employed their preacher for the mixed purposes of lecturing them *from the pulpit* in Chemistry, in Medicine, in Law, in the science and principles of Government, or in anything but Religion exclusively. Whenever, therefore, preachers, instead of a lesson in religion, put them off with a discourse on the Copernican system, on chemical affinities, on the construction of government, or the characters or conduct of those administering it, it is a breach of contract, depriving their audience of the kind of service for which they are salaried, and giving them, instead of it, what they did not want, or, if wanted, would rather seek from better sources in that particular art or science. In choosing our pastor we look to his religious qualifications, without inquiring into his physical or political dogmas, with which we mean to have nothing to do. I am aware that arguments may be found, which may twist a thread of politics into the cord of religious duties. So may they for every other branch of human art or science. Thus, for example, it is a religious duty to obey the laws of our country; the teacher of religion, therefore, must instruct us in those laws, that we may know how to obey them. It is a religious duty to assist our sick neighbors; the preacher must, therefore, teach us medicine, that we may do it understandingly. It is a religious duty to preserve our own health; our religious teacher, then, must tell us what dishes are wholesome, and give us recipes in cookery, that we may learn how to prepare them. And so, ingenuity, by generalizing more and more, may amalgamate all the branches of science into any one of them, and the physician who is paid to visit the sick, may give a sermon instead of medicine, and the merchant to whom money is sent for a hat, may send a handkerchief instead of it. But not withstanding this possible confusion of all sciences into one, common sense draws lines between them sufficiently distinct for the general purposes of life, and no one is at a loss to understand that a recipe in medicine or cookery, or a demonstration in geometry, is not a lesson in religion. I do not deny that a congregation may, if they please, agree with their preacher that he shall instruct them in Medicine also, or Law, or Politics. Then, lectures in these, from the pulpit, become not only a matter of right, but of duty also. But this must be with the consent of every individual; because the association being voluntary, the mere majority has no right to apply the contributions of the minority to purposes unspecified in the agreement of the congregation. I agree, too, that on all other occasions, the preacher has the right, equally with every other citizen, to express his sentiments, in speaking or writing, on the subjects of Medicine, Law, Politics, &c., his leisure time being his own and his congregation not obliged to listen to his conversation or to read his writings; and no one would have regretted more than myself, had any scruple as to this right withheld from us the valuable discourses which have led to the expression of an opinion as to the true limits of the right. I feel my portion of indebtment to the reverend author for the distinguished learning, the logic and the eloquence with which he has proved that religion, as well as reason, confirms the soundness of those principles on which our government has been founded and its rights asserted.

These are my views on this question. They are in opposition to those of the highly respected and able preacher, and are, therefore, the more doubtingly offered. Difference of opinion leads to inquiry, and inquiry to truth; and that, I am sure, is the ultimate and sincere object of us both. We both value too much the freedom of opinion sanctioned by our constitution, not to cherish its exercise even where in opposition to ourselves.

Unaccustomed to reserve or mystery in the expression of my opinions, I have opened myself frankly on a question suggested by your letter and present. And although I have not the honor of your acquaintance, this mark of attention, and still more the sentiments of esteem so kindly expressed in your letter, are entitled to a confidence that observations not intended for the public will not be ushered to their notice, as has happened to me sometimes. Tranquillity, at my age, is the balm of life. While I know I am safe in the honor and charity of a McLeod, I do not wish to be cast forth to the Marats, the Dantons, and the Robespierres of the priesthood; I mean the Parishes, the Ogdens, and the Gardiners of Massachusetts.

Doctrines of Jesus
Jefferson to Dr. Benjamin Waterhouse,
June 26, 1822

It is obvious that the man who vowed to oppose "every form of tyranny over the mind of man" would be especially offended by religious dogma.

The doctrines of Jesus are simple, and tend all to the happiness of man.
1. That there is one only God, and he all perfect.
2. That there is a future state of rewards and punishments.
3. That to love God with all thy heart and thy neighbor as thyself, is the sum of religion.

These are the great points on which he endeavored to reform the religion of the Jews. But compare with these the demoralizing dogmas of Calvin.
1. That there are three Gods.
2. That good works, or the love of our neighbor, are nothing.
3. That faith is everything, and the more incomprehensible the proposition, the more merit in its faith.
4. That reason in religion is of unlawful use.

5. That God, from the beginning, elected certain individuals to be saved, and certain others to be damned; and that no crimes of the former can damn them; no virtues of the latter save.

Now, which of these is the true and charitable Christian? He who believes and acts on the simple doctrines of Jesus? Or the impious dogmatists, as Athanasius and Calvin? Verily I say these are the false shepherds foretold as to enter not by the door into the sheepfold, but to climb up some other way. They are mere usurpers of the Christian name, teaching a counter-religion made up of the *deliria* of crazy imaginations, as foreign from Christianity as is that of Mahomet. Their blasphemies have driven thinking men into infidelity, who have too hastily rejected the supposed author himself, with the horrors so falsely imputed to him. Had the doctrines of Jesus been preached always as pure as they came from his lips, the whole civilized world would now have been Christian. I rejoice that in this blessed country of free inquiry and belief, which has surrendered its creed and conscience to neither kings nor priests, the genuine doctrine of one only God is reviving, and I trust that there is not a young man now living in the United States who will not die an Unitarian.

But much I fear, that when this great truth shall be reestablished, its votaries will fall into the fatal error of fabricating formulas of creed and confessions of faith, the engines which so soon destroyed the religion of Jesus, and made of Christendom a mere Aceldama; that they will give up morals for mysteries, and Jesus for Plato. How much wiser are the Quakers, who, agreeing in the fundamental doctrines of the gospel, schismatize about no mysteries, and, keeping within the pale of common sense, suffer no speculative differences of opinion, any more than of feature, to impair the love of their brethren. Be this the wisdom of Unitarians, this the holy mantle which shall cover within its charitable circumference all who believe in one God, and who love their neighbor!

A Personal View of Religion
Jefferson to Margaret Bayard Smith,
August 6, 1816

This is one of the very few occasions in which Jefferson expressed his own private and personal feelings.

I recognize the same motives of goodness in the solicitude you express on the rumor supposed to proceed from a letter of mine to Charles Thompson, on the subject of the Christian religion. It is true that in writing to the translator of the Bible and Testament, that subject was mentioned: but equally so that no adherence to any particular mode of Christianity was there expressed; nor any change of opinions suggested. A change from what? The Priests, indeed, have heretofore thought proper to ascribe to me religious, or rather anti-religious sentiments of their own fabric, but such as soothed their resentments against the Act of Virginia for establishing religious freedom. They wish him to be thought atheist, deeist, or devil, who could advocate freedom from their religious dictations, but I have ever thought religion a concern purely between our God and our consciences for which we were accountable to him, and not to the priests. I never told my own religion nor scrutinized that of another. I never attempted to make a convert, nor wish to change another's creed. I have ever judged of the religion of others by their lives; and by this test, my dear Madam, I have been satisfied yours must be an excellent one, to have produced a life of such exemplary virtue and correctness, for it is in our lives and not from our words, that our religion must be read. By the same test the world must judge me.

But this does not satisfy the priesthood, they must have a positive, a declared assent to all their interested absurdities. My opinion is that there would never have been an infidel, if there had never been a priest. The artificial structure they

have built on the purest of all moral systems for the purpose
of deriving from it pence and power revolts those who think
for themselves and who read in that system only what is
really there. These, therefore, they brand with such nick-
names as their enmity chooses gratuitously to impute. I
have left the world in silence, to judge of causes from their
effects: and I am consoled in this course, my dear friend,
when I perceive the candor with which I am judged by your
justice and discernment; and that, notwithstanding the
slander of the Saints, my fellow citizens have thought me
worthy of trust. The imputations of irreligion having spent
their force, they think an imputation of change might now
be turned to account as a bolster for their duperies. I shall
leave them as heretofore to grope on in the dark.

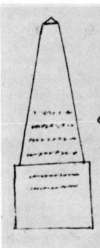

could the dead feel any interest in Monu[ments]
ments or other remembrances of them, when, as
Anacreon says: Ολιγη δε κεισομεσθα
Κονις, οστεων λυθεντων
the following would be to my Manes the most
gratifying.
On the grave
a plain die or cube of 3.f without any
mouldings, surmounted by an Obelisk
of 6.f. height, each of a single stone:
on the faces of the Obelisk the following
inscription, & not a word more

Here was buried
Thomas Jefferson

author of the Declaration of American Independence
of the Statute of Virginia for religious freedom
& Father of the University of Virginia.

because by these, as testimonials that I have lived, I wish most to
be remembered. ~~it is~~ to be of the coarse stone of which
my columns are made, that no one might be tempted
hereafter to destroy it for the value of the materials.
my bust by Ceracchi, with the pedestal and truncated
column on which it stands, might be given to the University
if they would place it in the Dome room of the Rotunda.
on the Die of the Obelisk might be engraved
Born apr. 2. 1743. O.S.
Died ——— ,

Jefferson's rendering of his own tombstone

Thomas Jefferson's tombstone
Thomas Jefferson Memorial Foundation